A *KANSAS CITY STAR* BEST B<
A FINALIST FOR BOOKS FOR A BETTEF
ONE OF *NEWSDAY*'S FAVORITE E

"Lerner, a literary agent who was most _____
Doubleday, assumes the posture of the writer's sympathetic friend, coach and psychotherapist all rolled into one. . . . Lerner candidly draws on her experience working both sides of the fence, as poet and teacher of writing workshops as well as editor and agent. She offers hard-nosed advice on topics often overlooked, such as the dynamics of author/editor and author/agent relations; struggles against the temptation of alcohol and drugs; the testing of book titles for marketability; acrimony over jacket art. . . . The book's real value, however, lies in compelling the ambivalent writer to confront his or her inner dreams, demons and strengths."
—*Publishers Weekly*

"For those who occasionally lose their courage or waver in their inspiration—or for those who simply yearn for someone to talk to during the lonely business of writing—this is an indispensable book. Written with insight, humor, and no small amount of common sense, Betsy Lerner's *The Forest for the Trees* is the best survival kit for writers I know of. Lerner understands every psychological strategy writers have available to them, and knows the brute realities of the publishing world from the inside out."
—Daphne Merkin,
author of *Enchantment*
and *Dreaming of Hitler*

"As an editor Betsy Lerner is a writer's dream come true. The generosity and respect she shows for her authors is unparalleled. She is unnervingly intelligent, authoritative yet gentle in her judgments, has a keen sense of story and an equally keen sense of the myriad difficulties and delusions a writer faces. She is, furthermore, gifted with wit, originality, and just the right degree of wickedness."
—Rosemary Mahoney,
author of *Whoredom in Kimmage*
and *A Likely Story*

continued on the next page . . .

"What writers want is good company and by writing this book, Lerner has given them just that. *The Forest for the Trees* provides excellent companionship for the long distance race confronting every writer. . . . [Lerner's] prose is supple, witty, always informative and frequently moving. . . . This elegant and funny and informative and passionate and moving book is not only a course in the great dance but a fine example of the dance itself. *The Forest for the Trees* will move many tortured writers that much closer to becoming well-published authors." —*The Providence Sunday Journal*

"A fascinating look into the mind of an editor and the publishing world . . . As a writer reading it, I felt an almost guilty thrill, as if I were reading the notes of my therapist." —Lucy Grealy, author of *The Autobiography of a Face*

"Experienced book editor Lerner has done everything right in her desire to offer relevant guidance to writers. . . . This combination memoir and handbook is reading for the soul." —*Booklist*

"I wish this book had been around when I first started writing. It's both inspiring and comforting, a fascinating picture of the writer's mind, as well as real, hard information about publishing, editors, and agents—a must for anyone who hopes to write. Betsy Lerner is that rare entity, someone who has been involved in publishing and writing and who remains empathetic and enthusiastic as well as practical." —Tama Janowitz, author of *A Certain Age*

"Betsy Lerner has three great qualities for an editor: intelligence, sensitivity, and passion. She writes with wit and astounding perceptivity. Writers, take heed!" —Nan Talese, publisher and editorial director, Nan A. Talese/Doubleday

"You couldn't, as an author, have a more savvy editor to guide you unscathed through the slings and arrows of outrageous publishing. Obey her, and all shall be well." —Thomas Cahill, author of *How the Irish Saved Civilization, The Gifts of the Jews,* and *Desire of the Everlasting Hills*

THE
FOREST
FOR THE
TREES

AN EDITOR'S ADVICE TO WRITERS

BETSY LERNER

RIVERHEAD BOOKS, NEW YORK

THE BERKLEY PUBLISHING GROUP
Published by the Penguin Group
Penguin Group (USA) Inc.
375 Hudson Street, New York, New York 10014, USA
Penguin Group (Canada), 90 Eglinton Avenue East, Suite 700, Toronto, Ontario M4P 2Y3, Canada
(a division of Pearson Penguin Canada Inc.)
Penguin Books Ltd., 80 Strand, London WC2R 0RL, England
Penguin Group Ireland, 25 St. Stephen's Green, Dublin 2, Ireland
(a division of Penguin Books Ltd.)
Penguin Group (Australia), 250 Camberwell Road, Camberwell, Victoria 3124, Australia
(a division of Pearson Australia Group Pty. Ltd.)
Penguin Books India Pvt. Ltd., 11 Community Centre, Panchsheel Park, New Delhi—110 017, India
Penguin Books (NZ), cnr Airborne and Rosedale Roads, Albany, Auckland 1310, New Zealand
(a division of Pearson New Zealand Ltd.)
Penguin Books (South Africa) (Pty.) Ltd., 24 Sturdee Avenue, Rosebank, Johannesburg 2196,
South Africa

Penguin Books Ltd., Registered Offices: 80 Strand, London WC2R 0RL, England

The passage from Maxwell E. Perkins's March 30, 1942, letter to Marcia Davenport, is excerpted with permission of Scribner, a Division of Simon & Schuster, from *Editor to Author: The Letters of Maxwell E. Perkins*, edited by John Hall Wheelock. Copyright 1950 by Charles Scribner's Sons. Copyright renewed © 1978 by John Hall Wheelock.

An excerpt from the letter Susan Cheever wrote to the *New Yorker* in response to James Atlas's article "The Fall of Fun" is used with Cheever's permission.

First Riverhead hardcover edition: March 2000
First Riverhead trade paperback edition: April 2001
Riverhead trade paperback ISBN: 1-57322-857-5

The Library of Congress has catalogued the Riverhead hardcover edition as follows:

Lerner, Betsy.
    The forest for the trees: an editor's advice to writers / Betsy Lerner.
        p.   cm.
    Includes bibliographical references.
    ISBN 1-57322-152-X
    I. Authorship.   2. Authors and publishers.   I. Title.
    PN147.L44   2000   99-053355   CIP
    805'.02—dc21

PRINTED IN THE UNITED STATES OF AMERICA

20   19   18   17   16   15   14   13

FOR MY AUTHORS

CONTENTS

I really think that the great difficulty in bringing "The Valley of Decision" into final shape is the old one of not being able to see the forest for the trees. There are such a great number of trees. We must somehow bring the underlying scheme or pattern of the book into emphasis, so that the reader will be able to see the forest in spite of the many trees.

—*Maxwell Perkins, in a letter to Marcia Davenport*
(A. Scott Berg, in his biography Max Perkins: Editor of Genius, *recounts that Davenport had turned in a completely disjointed manuscript of nearly 800,000 words, which she revised over a five-month period, according to the editor's extensive notes. The book went on to sell 600,000 copies.)*

THE
FOREST
FOR THE
TREES

INTRODUCTION

I NEVER DREAMED OF BECOMING AN EDITOR. Like many English majors, I spent much of my time in college reading novels and poetry, never quite fixing my attention on how I might parlay those interests into a job. In the final months of college, I went to the Career Placement Office, only to discover that I should have signed up in my junior year for the ongoing programs and job fairs. When I visited the head of the English Department to explore the possibility of graduate school, he stared at me in disbelief: Applications had been filled out in the fall.

During those frantic months of trying to secure employment, I met with the daughter of one of my mother's friends, an editor at Putnam. I put on my only dress for the interview, a cotton plaid A-line jumper with a rattan belt, and rode my bike to the publisher's offices on Madison Avenue. To calm my nerves before going in, I wolfed down a Häagen-Dazs ice cream cone. In the elevator, I realized the chocolate had stained my jumper. The editor's office was lined with shelves of books, their jackets face out. Most had huge type embossed in silver and gold. I didn't recognize a single title. Her desk was tidy, but the floor was piled high with manuscripts. I could tell that she was rushed, that her mother had put her up to this meeting, and I sat there somewhat lumpen and extremely ill prepared. After some pleasantries, she started the interview proper by asking whether I was interested in hardcover or paperback publishing. I looked nervously back and forth between her and her bookshelves, as if I were still in school and there was a chance that someone else might answer. *Hardcover or paperback?* Was there a difference? I asked.

Thirty résumés and a half-dozen interviews later, I had failed the typing test at every major publishing house in New York that would see me.

I wound up taking the only job I was offered, as a receptionist in the library of a large financial institution. I probably don't have to point out that it paid twice as much as an entry-level publishing position. More important, it required no typing. In a few months' time, I was promoted to corporate file coordinator, which was every bit as Kafkaesque as it sounds. I spent most of my lunch hours endlessly browsing the dusty shelves a few blocks south at the Gotham Book Mart, a tiny shop wedged among the diamond dealers of Forty-seventh Street. I also picked up the monthly Poetry Calendar there, a broadsheet with tiny print that listed readings for the coming weeks, and scanned the bulletin board bursting with notices of all matters literary. It was there I found a small advertisement for a poetry workshop. Enrollment was limited, and six poems had to be submitted for the leader's review by the following Monday. I worked feverishly all weekend, selecting and revising the poems. When I learned, a few weeks later, that I had been accepted, I felt for the first time in a very long while that things just might work out for me.

That workshop, as it turned out, was a pivotal life experience. The teacher, Jorie Graham, then a young woman with only one book to her credit, changed the way I allowed myself to feel about writing. Until then, my writing had been a secret, almost shameful act. But during those Monday-night sessions among fellow poets I felt transformed, listening intently as Graham passionately critiqued our work and described her own fledgling efforts as a writer. I will never forget her exquisite recitation; she would hold the final syllable before a line break for a breath longer than anticipated or rush one line into the next to give it urgency and life. A year later, with a sheaf of twenty full-length poems, I applied to graduate school for an MFA in poetry.

To say that attending graduate school is the end of innocence is not an exaggeration. Once again I was wholly unprepared for what would befall me there or for the characters I would meet along the way. But for all the indignities suffered around the workshop table, one thing was very clear: I discovered that I was good at suggesting changes that could improve a fellow student's poem, whether it meant moving one stanza from the middle to the beginning, deleting a line altogether, or sometimes just changing a title. In my final year I became editor of the literary magazine, and I found that the pieces I liked best, believed had the most merit, were usually those that stirred debate or aroused strong feeling, whether or not we included them in our pages. I didn't know it then, but I was becoming an editor.

When I was granted an internship at Simon & Schuster in my final semester, my publishing career began in earnest. I remember my first day on the job. I had arrived early and was sitting in the reception area when a young woman came flying through, waving a sheet of paper and screaming, "Number six, number six!" The next thing I knew, she and an older woman were grabbing each other's elbows and jumping up and down, still screaming. I later learned that the older woman was the publisher and that one of their books had hit the bestseller list. I wondered if anything would ever make me that excited. One short year later, I caught a glimpse of myself running down that same corridor screaming with glee, an advance bestseller list in hand. A book my boss had been working on for many years, which I had helped in its final production stages, had hit the list. I had found my passion.

❧

When I entered the business, I believed that writers were exalted beings. How else could they capture in a single phrase the emotional truth of a lifetime or render a scene that seemed more lifelike than life? How else could they risk their lives and livelihoods on a string of sentences, baring their souls in a world ever more hostile to artists and art? I was in awe of all writers, even those with less than perfectly realized works.

They had broken through, and somewhere books existed with their names on them. Of course, it didn't take long for those pedestals to crumble.

As an editor, I was both privy to and subjected to every aspect of my authors' lives. And the more I worked with writers, the more I found myself thinking about the characteristics that contributed to any given writer's success or failure. I saw mediocre writers who were brilliant at networking and superb writers who couldn't part with their pages. Some seemed blessed with the confidence of entitlement, others cursed with paralyzing insecurities. I saw their defenses and fears, their hopes and ambitions. Very soon I was able to recognize which writers would hunker down for the long haul, revising their texts over and over, and which felt that simply producing a manuscript should be enough to secure a publishing contract. I also began to understand the cyclical nature of the publishing business, the brutality of the media, and the vagaries of the marketplace. But more than anything else, I grew close to my authors and saw firsthand how they soldiered on in their lonely work.

Before I entered publishing, I believed, like most people, that the life of a writer was to be envied. As one of my heroes, Truman Capote, wrote, "When God hands you a gift, he also hands you a whip." Now I understand that writers are a breed apart, their gifts and their whips inextricably linked. The writer's psychology is by its very nature one of extreme duality. The writer labors in isolation, yet all that intensive, lonely work is in the service of communicating, is an attempt to reach another person. It isn't surprising, then, that many writers are ambivalent, if not altogether neurotic, about bringing their work forward. For in so doing, a writer must face down that which he most fears: rejection. There is no stage of the writing process that doesn't challenge every aspect of a writer's personality. How well writers deal with those challenges can be critical to their survival.

Editors, like shrinks, have a privileged and exclusive view into a writer's psyche, from the ecstasy of acquisition to the agony of the remainder table. Some editors limit their concern to the challenges on the page, but in my experience the challenges on the page and the challenges in the person go hand in hand. While editors are most certainly concerned with matters of style, structure, voice, and flow, they are often faced with extratextual problems—keeping the writer motivated, seeing the bigger picture, finding the patterns and rhythms, subtexts and operating metaphors that may elude an author drowning in research or blocked midstream. In the most productive author-editor relationship, the editor, like a good dance partner who neither leads nor follows but anticipates and trusts, can help the writer find her way back into the work, can cajole another revision, contemplate the deeper themes, or supply the seamless transition, the telling detail.

This is not a book about how to write. There are dozens of excellent books about writing, be it fiction or nonfiction, from the most technical to the most esoteric. Rather, I hope to help you if you can't start or finish a project, or can't figure out what you should be writing. I offer advice to writers whose neuroses seem to get in their way, those who sabotage their efforts, those who have met with some success but are stalled between projects. I promise not to repeat the most common piece of writing advice: Write what you know. As far as I'm concerned, writers have very little choice in what they write (though I do have some advice for those who can't figure out their form). Nor will I Strunk you over the head with rules about style. Instead, I present ideas about how a writer's styles on and off the page work in tandem. Is your neurotic behavior part of your creative process or just . . . neurotic behavior? Do you expose too much in your writing? Or are you protecting yourself or someone else with silence? Are you an effective self-promoter or a self-saboteur? Have you bought into certain myths about the writing life that aren't helping your career?

The second half of the book describes the publishing process from an editor's point of view. I have tried to share my insights into the world of publishing from my days as a naive editorial assistant through my later years as an editor to show what really goes on there. I have some words of advice about the most commonly asked questions: Do I need an agent? Should I multiply submit my book? How long must I wait for an agent or editor to respond? What can I expect of my agent or editor? What happens once the book is accepted for publication? How do writers come up with titles? What if I hate the jacket? Should I hire my own publicist? But I also try to give a feeling of what it's like to sit behind an editor's desk and read hundreds of manuscripts, of how an editor feels when she is either supported or thwarted in her efforts to acquire a project, or when a favorite author's book is universally panned or, worse, ignored. I've tried to provide a picture of the particular pressures editors and authors feel in today's publishing climate, and of what allows them to carry on in the face of so much industry instability.

In the time since I began gathering notes for this book, even more changes have shocked the publishing industry. Some of the biggest conglomerates in the land have merged; on-line bookselling has emerged as a major distribution channel; devices for downloading books on handheld screens are being touted; writers are wooed by on-line magazines with stock options instead of paychecks. And while I've never been accused of being trendy, I also changed careers in a move that has now been identified as a trend: editors becoming agents. While for me there perhaps could be no greater career than that of book editor, I crossed the line for a combination of reasons, personal and professional, including becoming a mother and wanting more freedom to work closely with a wide variety of authors. Though we are sometimes in adversarial positions, editors and agents essentially want the same thing: to see their authors well published and productive. Both experience that particular rush that comes from discovering a manuscript and helping it find its way in the world.

It is my deepest hope that this book will offer helpful advice to beginning writers, but even more that it will inspire the late bloomers, those who have worked in fits and starts over the years but have never just quit or given up the dream completely. This is also a book for people who sometimes believe the worst about themselves when it comes to their writing, who imagine themselves impostors, poseurs, dilettantes, and manqués. It is for people who torture themselves over their writing.

Whenever I attend writers' conferences, I am struck with the overwhelming sense of alienation that many aspiring writers seem to feel with regard to publishing. Many even believe there is a conspiracy of silence inside publishing houses about the way decisions are made, from acquisitions to the allocation of funds. I think it is nearly impossible for an unpublished writer not to suffer from battle fatigue; the disenfranchised are rarely comfortable. But even the most successful writers suffer from bouts of failure of confidence. In an interview in the *Hungry Mind Review,* Don DeLillo best described the predicament: "The writer has lost a great deal of influence, and he is situated now, if anywhere, on the margins of culture. But isn't this where he belongs? How could it be any other way? And in my personal view this is a perfect place to observe what's happening at the dead center of things. . . . The more marginal, perhaps ultimately the more trenchant and observant and finally necessary he'll become."

This book is about what I've seen and what I know. I wrote it to help writers achieve or get closer to their goals. At the very least, I hope that in contemplating your life as a writer you may get some perspective on your work, and in gaining that perspective, see the forest for the trees.

PART I.
WRITING

1.

THE
AMBIVALENT
WRITER

DO YOU HAVE A NEW IDEA ALMOST EVERY day for a writing project? Do you either start them all and don't see them to fruition or think about starting but never actually get going? Are you a short-story writer one day and a novelist the next? A memoirist on Monday and a screenwriter by the weekend? Do you begin sentences in your head while walking to work or picking up the dry cleaning, sentences so crisp and suggestive that they make perfect story or novel openers, only you never manage to write them down? Do you blab about your project to loved ones, coworkers, or strangers before the idea is fully formed, let alone partially executed? Have you ever accidentally left your notes, diary, or disk behind on a train or plane and bemoaned the loss of what certainly had been your best work? Have you ever been diagnosed with any combination of bipolar disorder, alcoholism, or the skin diseases such as eczema or psoriasis? Do you snap at people who ask how your writing is going? *What's it to them?*

Do you fear that you will someday wonder where the years went? How it is that some no-talent you went to high school with is being published everywhere you look? Or some suck-up from graduate school is racking up prizes and being interviewed in the "At Lunch With" column of *The New York Times*, a series you used to enjoy. Now you can't read it at all without thinking back to your classmate and the fawning way he used to schmooze the professors. *God, he was so transparent.*

If you can relate to the above, you certainly have the obsessive qualities—along with the self-aggrandizement and concurrent feelings of worthlessness—that are part of the writer's basic makeup. However, you also have so many conflicting thoughts and feelings about writing and about yourself as a writer you are unable to choose one idea and see it through. You cannot focus. Just as you settle on one idea, another voice pops into your head. Or just as you sit down to write, you suddenly and inexplicably fall asleep. You are what I call the ambivalent writer. You have something to say, something you may feel desperate to express, but you have no idea how to go about it. As a result, you are highly impressionable; everything strikes you but nothing sticks. You are volatile and vulnerable, but the energy it takes to quiet the voices leaves you depressed and listless. Every time you hear an author read, catch a snippet of *Booknotes* on TV, or browse at your local bookstore, you think: *I could do that.* You are both omnipotent and impotent.

The dictionary's definition of ambivalence is the coexistence of opposing attitudes or feelings such as love and hatred toward a person, object, or idea. For most writers, writing *is* a love-hate affair. But for the ambivalent writer who cannot attempt, sustain, or complete a piece of writing, the ambivalence usually shifts back and forth from the writing to the self. The inner monologue drums: *I am great. I am shit. I am great. I am shit.* But the writer with publication credits, good reviews, and literary prizes is not immune to this mantra either; in fact, the only real difference that I have been able to quantify between those who ultimately make their way as writers and those who quit is that the former were able to contain their ambivalence long enough to commit to a single idea and see it through.

I often encounter writers at conferences who tell me that they have a number of ideas they'd like to get working on but can't figure out which is best. They want some advice about which idea they should pursue, and often have some vague notion about what's selling these days. Asking for advice about what you should write is a little like asking for help getting dressed. I can tell you what I think looks good, but you have to wear it. And as every fashion victim knows, very few people look good in everything. Chances are that you have been writing or trying to write in one particular form all your life. There are very few writers who, by switching genres, say from novels to plays, suddenly achieve great results and conclude that they have been working in the wrong mode all along. But in my experience, a writer gravitates toward a certain form or genre because, like a well-made jacket, it suits him.

It is true that some people can write well in more than one genre. Although his plays may be ignored, T. S. Eliot's brilliant literary criticism changed the way we read modern poetry and had the added bonus of reinforcing the importance of his own work in the canon. Today we have our own poet-critics, such as Czeslaw Milosz and Joseph Brodsky, our poet-novelists, such as Denis Johnson and Margaret Atwood, our novelist-critics, such as John Updike and Cynthia Ozick, and novelist-essayists, such as Susan Sontag and Joan Didion. But we are more likely to be suspicious of someone who attempts to write in more than one genre—who cross-dresses, generically speaking. When I was getting an MFA at Columbia University, it was considered anathema, if not altogether taboo, for someone from the poetry side of the program to write a short story or for someone from the fiction side to write a poem. We suspect those who attempt creative work in more than one genre or field of being dilettantes or dabblers. Gone is the idea of the Renaissance man. In a *Paris Review* interview, Gore Vidal, a modern man of letters if ever there was one, addressed the problem of literary ambidexterity: "Writers are the only people who are reviewed by people of their own kind. And their own kind can often be reasonably generous—*if* you stay in your category. I don't. I do many different things rather better than most people do one thing. And envy is the central fact of writing life."

Finding your form is like finding a mate. You really have to search, and you can't compromise—unless you *can* compromise, in which case your misery will be of a different variety. But just as there are probably only one or two people to whom you could commit yourself, there are probably only a few things you can write about, and only one genre, or maybe two, in which you might excel. It's no coincidence that most authors' bodies of work hover over two or three basic themes or take a single basic shape. Think of the novels of Trollope, Austen, Dickens, or Hardy; think of Hemingway, Faulkner, Fitzgerald. They each revisited the same themes, settings, and conflicts over the course of their writing lives. The James Joyces of the world, those who can move from short story to novel to epic, are rare, but then again, few writers master each form the first time out of the gate.

Even though most writers have a limited literary arsenal, readers find infinite pleasure in watching those gestures change and deepen over time. But if you aren't yet sure what your themes are or what category you should be writing in, you need to take a full accounting of all the reading and all the writing you have ever done or wanted to do. If you are one of the many people who dream of writing but have never successfully finished or, perhaps, even started a piece, I suggest you compile a list of everything you've read over the past six months or year and try to determine if there is a pattern or common denominator. If you read only literary novels, that should tell you something. If you've always kept a diary noting the natural world in all its variety, you might want to try writing nature essays.

It never fails to surprise me, in conversations with writers who seek my advice as to what they should write, how many fail to see before their very eyes the hay that might be gold. Instead of honoring the subjects and forms that invade their dreams and diaries, they concoct some ideas about what's selling or what agents and editors are looking for as they try to fit their odd-shaped pegs into someone else's hole. There is nothing more refreshing for an editor than to meet a writer or read a query letter that takes him completely by surprise, that brings him into a world he didn't know existed or awakens him to a notion that had been there all along but that he had never much noticed.

Some of the most striking and successful books in recent history were clearly born of a writer's obsession and complete disregard for what, supposedly, sells. Few editors would have gone for a queer book about a little-known murder in Savannah that took its sweet time describing every other quirk of the city and its inhabitants before addressing the crime. Whatever John Berendt was thinking when he set out to write *Midnight in the Garden of Good and Evil*, it couldn't have been the bestseller list, because almost anyone in the publishing industry would have told him that nobody would care about the story of a gay antiques dealer who languished in jail after shooting a cheap hustler. The book does, however, draw on what most certainly are Berendt's strengths as a reporter, as a travel writer, and as a southerner with a gothic sensibility and taste for the macabre. Clearly, he was born to write this book, and he worked through whatever ambivalence and uncertainty he might have felt within himself or encountered from others.

Most writers have very little choice in what they write about. Think of any writer's body of work, and you will see the thematic pattern incorporating voice, structure, and intent. What is in evidence over and over is a certain set of obsessions, a certain vocabulary, a way of approaching the page. The person who can't focus is not without his own obsessions, vocabulary, and approach. However, either he can't find his form or he can't apply the necessary discipline that ultimately separates the published from the unpublished.

I am similarly struck by the writer who asks whether he should use his material in a novel or a memoir. Sometimes a writer will make the rounds of New York editors with a hot proposal based on a nonfiction article or an on-line column. Half the editors will tell him to recast the work as fiction. The other half will recommend that he expand it as nonfiction or memoir. When I encounter writers caught in this confusing bind of advice, I always ask how they see it. And sometimes the hopeful writer, eager to please, blithely answers that he will write it however I want it. It's at precisely this moment that I feel like hitting the eject button. To me, that's like saying I'll be straight or gay; you tell me, I have no preference. I can understand an editor having a reasonable opinion as to how or why the piece might work better in the marketplace in one form or the other, but asking someone who has essentially written nonfiction all his life to recast his material as a novel strikes me as folly.

Perhaps I am too old-fashioned in my thinking, but it seems to me that two entirely different sets of muscles are used for fiction and nonfiction writing. Being a journalist for ten years does not prepare you to write a novel any more than writing short stories guarantees your success as a narrative nonfiction writer. One can imagine an editor suggesting that John Berendt take his story and turn it into a novel, but chances are the thing would have crashed and burned.

✺

I believe that the writer who can't figure out what form to write in or what to write is stalling for a reason. Perhaps he is dancing around a subject because he is not ready to handle it, psychologically or emotionally. Perhaps he is unable to pursue a project because doing so would upset his world too much, or the people in it. Maybe not writing, maybe being driven crazy by the desire to write and the inability to follow through, is serving some greater goal, keeping some greater fear at bay. Fear of failure is the reason most often cited to explain why so many aspiring writers never realize their dreams. But I think it's that same fear of failure that absolutely invigorates those who do push through—that is, the fear of not being heard.

Certainly, the desire for success and the fear of failure run along a continuum. And the extent to which either motivates or paralyzes a given artist is dependent on a great many factors, including ability, ego, desire, and drive. But it's important to remember that success and failure are only part of the equation. The making of art and the selling of it are two entirely distinct enterprises. Any number of great writers have not received the appreciation all artists crave, just as in every generation any number of so-called hacks garner tremendous commercial if not critical success. In his lifetime Charles Dickens, who published his novels serially, was considered a hack. Emily Dickinson saw only seven of her hundreds of poems published. Jane Austen published under a pseudonym for her entire life. Artists such

as Virginia Woolf, Hart Crane, Sylvia Plath, and John Berryman, who tragically took their lives in midcareer, never knew
the prizes, cultdom, and canonization their work would later
receive. The ambivalent writer is often so preoccupied with
greatness, both desiring it and believing that every sentence
he commits to paper has to last for eternity, that he can't get
started.

Today too little is made of all the writing that doesn't seek
publication, all the letter writing, e-mail sending, recipe copying, and diary keeping—all the writing that minds our lives.
Now there is a great emphasis on turning one's diary into a
published memoir or novel, and any number of books will advise you how to do so. But I believe there is still enormous value
in the piece of writing that goes no farther than the one person
for whom it was intended, that no combination of written words
is more eloquent than those exchanged between lovers or friends,
or along the pale blue lines of private diaries, where people take
communion with themselves.

It's the writer who seeks publication but who cannot finish
even one project who must ask himself whether his stalling is
also a form of self-protection. I can assure you that you will
never finish any piece of writing if you don't understand what
motivates you to write in the first place and if you don't honor
that impulse, whether it's exile or assimilation, redemption or
destruction, revenge or love. "Getting even is one great reason
for writing," said William Gass in a *Paris Review* interview. "I
write because I hate. A lot. Hard. And if someone asks me the
inevitable next dumb question, 'Why do you write the way you

do?' I must answer that I wish to make my hatred acceptable because my hatred is much of me, if not the best part. Writing is a way of making the writer acceptable to the world—every cheap, dumb, nasty thought, every despicable desire, every noble sentiment, every expensive taste."

If Gass is extreme, I assure you he is not alone. Many of the best books are born of anger or pain, of the struggle for self-definition, freedom, and revolution. The best books, like newborns, come into the world screaming their arrival and gasping for breath—will they survive in the harsh light, in the communal air? If you are writing to prove yourself to the world, to quiet the naysayers at last, to make your cold and distant father take notice, I say go for it. If you are writing because no one has faith in you, or because no one sees you for who you are, or because you feel like an impostor, use those feelings. How else could Dostoyevsky have conjured the unnamed protagonist of his novel *Notes from Underground,* whose opening lines have stayed with me from the moment I first encountered them: *I am a sick man. . . . I am an angry man. I am an unattractive man. . . . I'm sensitive and quick to take offense, like a hunchback or dwarf.*

Chances are you want to write because you are a haunted individual, or a bothered individual, because the world does not sit right with you, or you in it. Chances are you have a deep connection to books because at some point you discovered that they were the one truly safe place to discover and explore feelings that are banished from the dinner table, the cocktail party, the golf foursome, the bridge game. Because the writers who mattered to you have dared to say *I am a sick man.* And because within the world of books there is no censure. In discovering books, you became free to explore the full range of human motives, desires, secrets, and lies. All my life, people have scolded me for having an excess of feeling, saying that I was too sensitive—as if one could be in danger from feeling too much instead of too little. But my outsize emotions were well represented in books, even in those that exercised enormous restraint in the telling: in the hearts of my favorite nineteenth-century novelists' highly repressed heroes and heroines there simmered all the feelings no one ever admits to. In the slyly dark and chilling lines of one my favorite British poets, Philip Larkin, I found images that cracked the world open. I am not suggesting a writer let it bleed so much as I am suggesting that he understand his motivation.

The more popular culture and the media fail to present the real pathos of our human struggle, the more opportunity there is for writers who are unafraid to present stories that speak emotional truth, or that make such an intimate connection that briefly we become children again, listening with rapt attention, the satin binding of our blankets pulled up to our chins. At a time when people are encouraged to follow their bliss, to pursue whatever makes them feel good, I suggest you stalk your demons. Embrace them. If you are a writer, especially one who has been unable to make your work count or stick, you must grab your demons by the neck and face them down. And whatever you do, don't censor yourself. There's always time and editors for that.

Inasmuch as writing is a creative process, a certain amount

of experimentation is essential. And as in the discovery process in a trial, you must devote some time to following leads and interrogating suspects before a clear picture is revealed, before your case is as strong as possible. When I studied with Jorie Graham, I learned how to find these connections. At that time I was composing six- to eight-line poems, and I handed in a dozen or so for my private conference. When I arrived, she asked me to sit down and listen to her read a poem. She proceeded to recite a longish poem of around forty lines that sounded extremely familiar, though I couldn't place it. I actually thought it might be T. S. Eliot. As it turned out, and as you have probably guessed, the lines were mine. Jorie had put the fragments together in a way that provided an actual narrative. She supplied a few transitional words, such as "before" and "now" and "later," at the beginning of stanzas. It was a miracle to me, this transformation of my acorns into an oak. I raced home after the conference and combed through my hundreds of fragment poems and put them into thematic if predictable piles: father, mother, body, and so on. I transformed the scraps into full-length works and finally had a few poems that were satisfying, that provided closure—and that got me accepted to graduate school and published in a few literary journals.

If you are struggling with what you should be writing, look at your scraps. Encoded there are the themes and subjects that you should be grappling with as a writer. If you still can't figure it out, whatever you do, I beg you not to look at the bestseller lists. Do not set out to write the next *Angela's Ashes, Liars' Club,* or *Perfect Storm;* a third of the projects publishers see these days make such claims. People who try to figure out what's hot and re-create it are as close to delusional as you can get. In the first place, once a trend is actually identified it is usually too late; your work will be regarded as opportunistic, as jumping on the bandwagon. It is true that when a trend or phenomenon is identified, a handful of books or more in the same genre enter the fray, and sometimes a writer will cash in on a real or imaginary perception about a certain category of book. But I assure you that you will be better served both professionally and personally if you find your inspiration and models within yourself, not on the bestseller list. Many of the unlikely books that made it there, that took the world by surprise, did so because they were original, inspired, and new.

The best teacher I had in graduate school used to annoy people terribly when she wondered aloud why we were all so competitive with one another. After all, she said, it wasn't as if we were all trying to write the same poem. She got that wrong. We all *were* trying to write the same poem. We were trying to write the one that would get into *The New Yorker,* and with rare exception every writer out there is in the same boat. There comes a time when you have to let go of the *New Yorker* fantasy in service of just getting on with it. If you are guilty of sending your first short story or poem off to the magazine, as well as your second and third, in the vain hope of hitting the jackpot, you are not alone. The question is, where do you go from there? How do you stop trying to sound like Raymond Carver and find your own material and voice?

The ambivalent writer can't hear himself think, can't com-

mit to a single vision, can't stop wondering if six other directions aren't the right ones to take. The ambivalent writer confuses
procrastination with research. He can't hear through the static
to find the one true voice. I know a lot of writers who beat
themselves up on a regular basis, either for not writing or for
not writing well enough. And when they are writing well they
make themselves crazy over other things, not least of which is
how they're going to pay the rent, why they don't have health
insurance, whether or not anyone out there will care. In Virginia
Woolf's treatise on women and writing, *A Room of One's Own*,
the author describes the great difficulty of producing a work of
genius: "Generally material circumstances are against it. Dogs
will bark; people will interrupt; money must be made; health
will break down. Further, accentuating all these difficulties and
making them harder to bear is the world's notorious indifference. It does not ask people to write poems and novels and his-
tories; it does not need them. It does not care whether Flaubert
finds the right word or whether Carlyle scrupulously verifies
this or that fact. Naturally, it will not pay for what it does not
want."

Writing demands that you quiet all the voices that would
have you subscribe to Woolf's notion of the world and its "notorious indifference." Writing demands that you keep at bay the
demons insisting that you are not worthy or that your ideas are
idiotic or that your command of the language is insufficient. But
if you feel you need to seek advice as to *what* you should be
writing, you are probably not ready to write. And this is my
advice to you: stop altogether and see how long you can go

without writing. As with sex, some people have extremely low writing drives, while others become irritable and agitated if they can't express themselves every day. "Very young writers who don't know themselves obviously often don't know what they have to say," said Bernard Malamud. "Sometimes by staying with it they write themselves into a fairly rich vein. Some, by the time they find what they're capable of writing about, no longer want to write. Some go through psychoanalysis or a job in a paint factory and begin to write again. One hopes they then have something worth saying. Nothing is guaranteed. Some writers have problems with subject matter not in their first book, which may mine old childhood experience, or an obsession, or fantasy, or the story they've carried in their minds and imagination to this point, but after that—after this first yield—often they run into trouble with their next few books. Especially if the first book is unfortunately a bestseller."

✦

Writing is a calling, and if the call subsides, so be it. It may return in greater force the next time around. Some people say that you have to write all the time to get anywhere and that discipline will ultimately separate the men from the boys. But I assure you, you will never *make* yourself write. When writers say they have no choice, what they mean is: *Everything in the world conspired to make me quit but I kept going.* And most can't tell you why, as Lorrie Moore recently reiterated in a *Publishers Weekly* interview. "I still think you should become a writer only if you have no choice. Writing has to be an obsession—it's only for those who say 'I'm not going to do anything else.'" Or as she began her brilliant story "How to Become a Writer," which by now should be required reading for anyone entering an MFA program, "First, try to be something, anything, else."

If the voices keep calling, if the itch remains, no matter how punishing the work or inhospitable the world, then you must take a long hard look at all the writing you've been attempting to do all your life and commit to it. Don't let publishers tell you that short stories don't sell if you're a short-story writer, don't give up on your memoir just because there seems to be a momentary glut. Where would today's successful African-American writers be if they believed the thinking that dominated publishing, at least until recently, that black writing doesn't sell? Thirty-three publishers rejected *Chicken Soup for the Soul* because parables weren't in vogue. "Seven million copies later," reported *Time* magazine, "the authors are living happily ever after."

I promise you, I am not offering the single most often repeated piece of writing advice, *Write what you know.* Rather, I am suggesting that you find your form. In his book *On Writing and Publishing*, Mark Twain describes attempting to start the story of Joan of Arc six times over twelve years. "There are some books that refuse to be written. They stand their ground year after year and will not be persuaded. It isn't because the book is not there and worth being written—it is only because the right form for the story does not present itself. There is only one right form for a story, and if you fail to find that form the story will not tell itself. You may try a dozen wrong forms but in each case you will not get very far before you discover that you have not found the right one—and that the story will always stop and decline to go any further."

Writing what you know is a given. Writing what you know is unavoidable. All people write what they know, for God's sake. It's the air you breathe. The challenge is finding the structure that shows your stuff off to its best effect. If the world of writing were an opera, would you be a soprano, a tenor, a baritone, or a bass? Is your best work lyric, dramatic, or interpretive? Can you be happy as part of the chorus, or, like an editor, doing the behind-the-scenes work? If the high wire is for you, if the spotlight is for you, if you believe that everyone should pay attention to you and to your work, then you must stay focused. Ambivalence will never get you anywhere, unless, like Spalding Gray, you mine every personal doubt for material and find a form, in his case the monologue, through which the very subject of ambivalence is rehearsed.

Try to remember that the time before you publish is the only time you will ever work in complete freedom. After you're published you will be forced to contend with the shockingly real voices of critics, agents, editors, and fans. You never get to be a virgin after the first time, and more to the point, you never again have the luxury of writing in total obscurity. But like the married person who bemoans the loss of freedom from her single days, the published author who longingly recalls her past obscurity is a little hard to sympathize with. Though you may suffer from loneliness after you're married, it's bad form to complain about it to your single friends.

Writers take note: your struggle to produce a piece of writing of interest and value means nothing to the reader. The reader doesn't care what you went through to produce your work. He only cares if the piece succeeds, if it looks as if it arrived whole. If you aim to succeed with a book that's destined to last, one thing is certain: your work must bear your own stamp. You must be willing to hone your sentences until they are yours alone. You must have a belief in your vision and voice that is nothing short of fierce. In other words, you must turn your ambivalence into something unequivocal.

2.

THE

NATURAL

EVERY NOW AND THEN A WRITER COMES ALONG whom people call "the real thing." Like the character Robert Redford portrays in the movie *The Way We Were*, there is a romantic ideal of some beautiful creature who runs his onionskin paper through the Smith-Corona and produces breathtaking prose. People say he's a natural, a God-given talent. He's got the touch. I am fascinated by the question of whether this person exists or whether it's another great American myth. God knows, we romanticize the idea of the natural and love the thrill of discovering a fresh, new voice. At the same time, we are suspicious of those for whom success comes too easily, believing that people should suffer for their art. But perhaps the most deeply held belief about what is right and good is the notion that we are all created equal. I say take a look around the table at any writers' workshop, or around any playground, for that matter, and you will quickly deduce one thing: equal we are not.

What does this really mean to the struggling writer? How

many writers were praised early on but were never able to sustain or fulfill their promise? And how many others, who seemed plodding and awkward in every way, continued to work without encouragement, determined to make themselves heard? I cannot tell you how many times I have been approached by aspiring writers at conferences who have asked me to tell them whether their pages show promise; whether they have any talent, or if they should give up. They might as well ask me to evaluate my two-year-old's finger painting. The making of art is a mysterious and spiritual process; the dictates of taste and judgments of others are often the least helpful to a developing artist. I was moved by Jodie Foster's acceptance speech for one of her Academy Awards. Foster thanked her mother, who, she said, acted as if every drawing she brought home from school were a Picasso. Who can say when an artist will make a breakthrough?

In an ideal world everyone should be encouraged for any creative effort. I know a writing instructor who is beloved among her students because she is deeply supportive of their work no matter what stage they're at. "It's not as if they're building bombs or hurting people," she says in defense of her approach, "they're just trying to do creative work." It's not that she doesn't know whose work actually shows promise and which students are likely never to write an interesting sentence as long as they live. It's just that she never fails to be astonished by at least one person per semester who seems at the beginning of the class as hopeless as they come and ends the course with a powerful piece of writing. Then, of course, there's Flannery O'Connor's opinion to consider. When asked whether she thought writing programs in universities actually discouraged young writers, she replied, "Not enough of them."

I won't say there is no such thing as a natural talent, but after working with many authors over the years, I can offer a few observations: having natural ability doesn't seem to make writing any easier (and sometimes makes it more difficult); having all the feeling in the world will not ensure the effective communication of feeling on the page; and finally, the degree of one's perseverance is the best predictor of success. It is some combination of ability and ego, desire and discipline, that produces good work. And a writer's success or faltering can usually be traced to some abundance or deficit of those elements. Some of the most gifted writers I've worked with were also the most self-sabotaging. Lack of discipline, desire for fame, and depression often thwart those whose talents appear most fertile, while those who struggle with every line persevere regardless.

A few years ago I had the privilege of editing the work of a professor whose writing had influenced me enormously in college. I was thrilled to have the opportunity to work with her, and was more than a little chagrined when the editorial process didn't flow as easily as I had hoped. With every successive draft, with each step forward, we took the proverbial two back. Finally, we decided to work face to face to see if we could address the problem. Toward the end of a very long work week, as we sat side by side for the first time, I noticed something very peculiar. The writer inverted her letters as she made notes and sometimes wrote the second or third letter of a word before the first.

I sat up in my seat, regarded my hero, and, before thinking

how my words might sound, blurted out almost accusatorially, "You're dyslexic, aren't you?"

She nodded slowly, as if to say yes, now my secret is out.

"How can you be?" I continued in disbelief. "How can you possibly write?"

Now it was dawning on me why we had struggled so much with the text, and I reeled to think of how arduous this work was for her. Yet her desire to communicate through writing far surpassed her impediment. As I sat shaking my head, she resumed her somewhat aristocratic bearing and said, with more than a hint of pride, "I've written five books, haven't I?"

While it may seem disingenuous to encourage a writer who seems to have no native ability, it is also arrogant to think we know how any given career will develop, or what combination of desire and will may result in a work that will have a profound effect on people even if it is never praised for its beautiful prose. The most popular books are often savaged by critics for their writing style, yet these writers are clearly connecting with readers. At the same time, a natural facility with language does not necessarily mean a natural ability to communicate ideas that find currency in the culture.

When I was getting my MFA, it became eminently clear to me that being in the program meant being indoctrinated with very specific ideas about taste. The people who were highly praised and encouraged were those who worked in a particular vein, whose voices most closely approximated those of the writers who were held up as masters. One woman working on a novel based on her own experiences as an undercover cop was told by a professor that solely because of the subject matter he could not possibly read or respond to her book. There was absolutely no room in the program for any kind of genre writing and absolutely no humor. I'll never forget the humiliation I felt when I thought I had finally made a breakthrough in my own writing by allowing my sense of humor into my work. A professor whom I worshipped sniffed at a few of these new poems before he cocked his eyebrow and said, "Well, if you want to be the poetic equivalent of Fran Lebowitz that's fine, but I can't possibly help you."

Asking whether you've got it, whether you should stick with writing or quit, is a little like asking if you should continue living. It's beside the point. No one can give you a reason to live if you don't have the will. For most writers, being unable to write is tantamount to suicide anyway. "For me, writing is like breathing," Pablo Neruda said in a *Paris Review* interview. "I could not live without breathing and I could not live without writing." The world doesn't fully make sense until the writer has secured his version of it on the page. And the act of writing is strangely more lifelike than life. Even when a writer doesn't have a pen in hand or a keyboard beneath his fingers, the sentences are forming, the observations are being gathered, refined, retained, or rejected. The argument with the spouse, daughter, or checkout girl is being calculated and reduced for a later scene. Everything is fodder.

The natural writer is the one who is always writing, if only in his head—sizing up a situation for material, collecting impressions. James Thurber confessed, "I never quite know when

I'm not writing. Sometimes my wife comes up to me at a party and says, 'Dammit, Thurber, stop writing.' She usually catches me in the middle of a paragraph." Martin Amis describes the same sensation, saying, "You develop an extra sense that partly excludes you from experience. When writers experience things, they're not really experiencing them anything like 100 percent. They're always holding back and wondering what the significance is, or wondering how they'd do it on the page."

For most writers, reading is also a very intense experience; they don't read so much as compete. The writer measures himself against every text he encounters, imagining he could do it better or wishing he had thought of it first. The natural writer would almost always rather be reading, writing, or alone, except of course when he needs to come up for air (that is, for subject matter, food, sex, love, attention). He may be a selfish son of a bitch, he may seem to care more about his work than about the people in his life, he may be a social misfit, a freak, or a smooth operator, but every person who does serious time with a keyboard is attempting to translate his version of the world into words so that he might be understood. Indeed, the great paradox of the writer's life is how much time he spends alone trying to connect with other people.

❦

When I meet a new writer, at some point I usually ask if he or she wrote as a child. I have found that the impulse to write, to record one's private feelings, often appears at a very early age; with few exceptions most authors started writing in childhood.

If as a child you gravitated toward books and kept diaries or made up stories, it speaks to an inherent aptitude for language. In an essay entitled "Why Write," John Updike recalls, "When I was thirteen, a magazine came into the house, *The New Yorker* by name, and I loved that magazine so much I concentrated all my wishing into an effort to make myself small and inky and intense enough to be received into its pages. Once there, I imagined, some transfigured mode of being, called a 'writer's life,' would begin for me."

The child writer is an interesting creature. He tends to identify himself as an outsider and to be aware of an inner life at a young age. He usually has an overly developed sense of privacy and at eight or nine years old may already feel that he has something to hide or something to say. Truman Capote said he was nine or ten when it hit him. "I was walking along the road, kicking stones, and I realized that I wanted to be a writer, an artist. How did it happen? That's what I ask myself. My relatives were nothin', dirt-poor farmers. I don't believe in possession, but something took over inside me, some little demon that made me a writer."

John Cheever started telling stories to reward his classmates for completing their math assignments. "The teacher would promise that I would tell a story. I told serials. This was very shrewd of me, because I knew if I didn't finish the story by the end of the period, which was an hour, then everyone would ask to hear the end during the next period." Cheever was seventeen when he sold his first short story to *The New Republic*, twenty-two when *The New Yorker* started to publish his work regularly.

"I wrote stories from the time I was a little girl," recalled Joan Didion, "but I didn't want to be a writer. I wanted to be an actress. I didn't realize then that it's the same impulse. It's make-believe. It's performance." Bernard Malamud explained that "at eight or nine I was writing little stories in school and feeling the glow. To any one of my friends who'd listen I'd recapitulate at tedious length the story of the last movie I'd seen. . . . As a writer I learned from Charlie Chaplin." Woody Allen said that he had only comic books as a kid, but "was always the class writer. I remember very distinctly, I'd buy those little black-and-white notebooks and say 'Today I'll write a mystery story.' I'd go home and write, and invariably they'd come out funny. I certainly couldn't care less if I ever performed again, and don't care much if I ever direct another film, but I would not like to be in a position not to write."

In the essay "Why I Write," George Orwell said, "From a very early age, perhaps the age of five or six, I knew that when I grew up I should be a writer. . . . I was the middle child of three, but there was a gap of five years on either side, and I barely saw my father before I was eight. For this and other reasons I was somewhat lonely, and I soon developed disagreeable mannerisms which made me unpopular throughout my schooldays. I had the lonely child's habit of making up stories and holding conversations with imaginary persons, and I think from the very start my literary ambitions were mixed up with the feeling of being isolated and undervalued. I knew that I had a facility with words and a power of facing unpleasant facts, and I felt that this created a sort of private world in which I could get my own back for my failure in everyday life."

The child writer may be intensely verbal or intensely with-
drawn. One thing is certain: his urge to write things down is
predicated by the need to validate his experience. The child who
makes sense of his world, escapes or remakes it through reading and writing, may never find another home as welcoming. "I
felt trapped within my home and trapped within school," said
Gloria Naylor, "and it was through the pages of books that I
was released into other worlds. I literally read my way from the
A's to the Z's in the children's section of the library. . . . I don't
believe this would have been enough to have created a writer,
although most writers first begin as avid readers. But a writer
needs something else—a conscious connection between the va-
lidity of their personal experience and the page. . . . From the
age of twelve I made the vital connection between inarticulate
feeling and the written word."

Often the child writer is accused of having an overly active
imagination, of being hyperactive or, the converse, of being too
reflective. (You've got to wonder how many of tomorrow's poets and novelists are being medicated with Ritalin and Prozac at
this very moment.) Gore Vidal certainly would have been a can-
didate for medication. By age six, he claims, he was reading
tales from Livy, by seven or eight he was attempting to write
novels, and between the ages of fourteen and nineteen he had
started five novels. The fifth, his first to be published, when he
was twenty-one, was Williwaw. "I never wanted to be a writer. I
mean, that was the last thing I wanted, I expected to be a politi-
cian," wrote Vidal in an anthology called Conversations with American Writers. "Unfortunately—or fortunately, as the case may be—I
was a writer. I simply could not not write. A writer is someone

who writes, that's all. You can't stop it; you can't make yourself do anything else but that."

Most writers start out closeted, as diary or journal keepers. Some elicit encouragement from teachers or find acclaim as students. Robert Stone benefited from an early experience: "I had won a contest when I was in high school. Because my upbringing was in what you'd call a working class context, I had the impression that being a writer was insubstantial and not altogether respectable. But it was basically what I wanted to do, even though I didn't realize it when I was younger. I always wrote. I always had a kind of narrative impulse to try to make sense out of things by telling stories about them, and I guess I also always had a certain facility with language and was also kind of in love with language."

Whether or not they work on the school paper or literary magazine, win prizes, and have intense relationships with the English teacher who holds weekly poetry readings at her apartment, teenage writers generally begin to develop some sense of themselves as writers. Some find role models in published authors. Updike says he revered Thurber from the age of eleven. "I wrote him a fan letter and when I was twelve he sent me a drawing, which I've carried with me, framed, everywhere I've gone since." Some remain in the closet throughout school, while others flaunt their talents, making a display of their aspirations.

College is the usual place where young writers experiment with writerly personas. I fondly recall the English Department's cast of characters: a handful of poseurs after the fashion of Kerouac and Cassady, one self-styled Gertrude Stein who ran a workshop out of her West Village apartment (very cool, given that most of us starving artists were toughing it out in the dorms with full meal plans), a couple of macho-Hemingways, an effete Oscar Wilde, and of course the moody girl poets. When I was in graduate school, two particular poets stood out. One, who fancied himself a young T. S. Eliot, was a diminutive prig who promptly dispensed with his first name in favor of initials, always wore a blazer, and carried a walking stick. The other seemed the absolute reincarnation of Delmore Schwartz. He never turned in a single piece of writing as far as I can recall, but I believe he slept with most of the women in the program.

✹

Those writers who fulfill their early promise, who achieve wide and early acclaim, whose prose seems as effortless as the easy smiles captured in their glossy author photos, these young naturals face the double-edged sword of fame and its discontents. There is nothing we love more than young, juicy writers with their fresh, unimpeachable voices—and every year there is a new crop. At the beginning of a career a writer is all promise, all future, all horizon. There are no disappointing sales tracks, no mixed reviews, no piles of remainders. Though it is impossible not to envy their highly publicized book deals, their gorgeous dust jackets, and their newfound acclaim, I sometimes imagine young novelists as sacrificial lambs lined up for the slaughter. Our appetite for novelty is insatiable, and these days a writer's career, which should take a lifetime to develop and mature, can flicker and burn out as fast as any starlet's. "It's a lot easier to launch a first novel than it is a writer in mid-career," said superagent Lynn Nesbit in a *New York* magazine article called "How to Make a Bestseller." "Everyone likes to discover someone new. Especially when it's a girl."

Though the twenty-three-year-old wunderkind who gets a story in *The New Yorker* or a publishing contract while finishing her MFA is the envy of all her classmates and this season's publishing flavor, it is as likely as not that she will never be heard from again. I sometimes think a wall should be erected at every university writing program with the names of the missing etched into it. Nowhere is the Darwinian struggle for survival more keen than at our nation's creative writing programs, where the whiff of early success can establish or ruin a person for good. Michael Cunningham recalled his experience at the Iowa Writers' Workshop in an interview for *Publishers Weekly:* "I had a streak of luck at Iowa: a story in *Atlantic Monthly* and another in *The Paris Review,* which led me to the entirely false conclusion that if writing wasn't exactly easy, well, it was going to be easy for me. I would just write things and publish them. Boy, was I mistaken."

As it turns out, ten years elapsed between Cunningham's largely forgotten first novel and publication of the book that would establish his career, *A Home at the End of the World.* "I'm fast on my way to being a fifty-year-old who once had a story in the *Paris Review,*" he recalled. "I was working either as a waiter, a bartender, moving around a lot, falling in love a lot and going wherever it took me." In one of publishing's more gratifying stories, Cunningham would receive the Pulitzer Prize ten years after *A Home at the End of the World* was published, for his daring new novel *The Hours,* which beautifully captured the essence of time. But for every Michael Cunningham who struggles over the years, who persists and sacrifices in the face of constant rejection, and who finally receives well-earned recognition, there are countless others who, after early acceptance or success, either fail to continue producing or find their work met with stony silence.

Describing his journey in a *Poets & Writers* profile, Cunningham said, "Marilyn Monroe once said, 'I wasn't the prettiest, I wasn't the most talented. I simply wanted it more than anyone else.' And I sometimes think that I'm just one of the people who comes here every day and does it, even though I don't feel like it, even though it's difficult and I feel stupid and brain-dead and unequal to the task. . . . I have known writers over the years, enormously talented, who are so self-conscious about it, who are so terrified of ever writing a bad sentence, that they can't write anything at all. I think a certain fearlessness in the face of your own ineptitude is a useful tool." It is impossible, perhaps even for Cunningham himself, to know how he persisted during the long dry spells of his career, how he tolerated the feelings of inadequacy. But once a writer is recognized, once he or she is deemed a success, either early or later in a career, we tend to mythologize that success. To call him a natural.

A collective sigh of relief was heard among the more mature writers of America when *The New York Times Book Review* put on its cover three novelists who first published when they were over forty, under the headline "New Guys on the Block." One of

the writers highlighted was Dennis McFarland, who had en-
rolled in the creative writing program at Goddard College after
giving up a music career. There he was mentored by Frank Conroy. "I wrote a story that [he] liked, so I submitted it to *The New
Yorker*. And what proceeded from that was the odd experience
of having my first published story in *The New Yorker* and then
not having them take anything again for the next eight years."
What's worse, to have loved and lost or never to have loved at
all? But without the encouragement of a mentor, or some other
meaningful encouragement, the older a writer gets without seeing his work in print the less likely it is that he will pursue it.

The eighties was a particularly tough time for most writers,
watching the brat pack getting all the press, sharing headlines
with actors, frequenting the hot clubs. I always thought that one
of the few advantages of being a writer was that you didn't have
to go out and dance in front of people or act as if you enjoyed
being in the world. But now you were supposed to score coke
and get your picture in the style sections. Plus book advances
seemed to follow an inverse formula: the younger you were, the
more money you got.

Take heart, late bloomers. Early success can also mean early
obsolescence. Early success can engender a whole host of problems, perhaps most disastrously when the ego becomes so in-
flated that the writer can never quite hear her inner voice again.
Of course, if your first book is universally panned or, worse,
completely overlooked, it's hard to feel sorry for the writer
whose success is a source of anguish.

Sometimes the newcomer arrives when he is older, more

mature, seasoned, his stories stately and considered. Recently we witnessed the debuts of three such late arrivals: Charles Frazier, Thomas Cahill, and Frank McCourt. A novelist, a popular historian, and a memoirist, respectively, the first in his forties, the second in his fifties, and the third in his sixties. The first book of each of these men is prized in its genre and bears none of the usual earmarks of a first effort. Each is inimitable and grew out of what certainly had to be a lifelong preoccupation, if not obsession. So even if you haven't written the great American whatever by forty, don't give up. And if you strike it big, the way *Cold Mountain, How the Irish Saved Civilization,* and *Angela's Ashes* did, you may even have the maturity to handle your success.

⚘

How much or how little "natural" ability anyone has is nearly impossible to gauge. When Emily Dickinson composed the lines that filled the pages she kept in her lonely desk, she could not know that her pure apprehension of the language, her immutable style and breathtaking line breaks would forever change the landscape of American poetry. She would never know that her unpublished meditations on life and love, with their bone-chilling observations about the human heart, would touch readers a century later.

I would like to believe that there are brilliant poems and novels tucked away in drawers and closets across the country. I would like to believe that there exist correspondences as rich and revelatory as those between Vincent van Gogh and his brother Theo, from Rilke to his wife about Cézanne's powerful influence, and between Flannery O'Connor and the woman identified only as "A" in O'Connor's collected letters, *The Habit of Being,* which provides some of the most astute thoughts on morality and truth that one is likely to find anywhere. I would like to believe that there is writing, which may or may not see the light of day, that possesses genius and that the solitary figure behind its manufacture composed her prose because writing is what came naturally. This is what editors live in the hope of—that one day they will somehow uncover and bring to the world a piece of writing that will change the way we understand or perceive the world.

I am dismayed when I visit freshmen and sophomores in college, and the first question they ask when I finish my spiel is whether they need an agent and how they should go about getting one. I am dismayed when they ask me about advances and whether they should get an MFA, when they talk about the various writing programs as if they were clubs or restaurants, hot for a limited time only. Though I was a largely closeted writer during college, and identified myself as an aspiring poet only to a few friends who also wrote, I do not remember our conversations tending toward deals and dollars. We had no idea what an agent was for or that they even existed. Mostly we wanted to know about writers—how they lived, how they wrote, whom they loved. We took the subway up from Washington Square to Books & Co. on Madison Avenue to hear our favorite poets read from their new books. We haunted the Strand and other bookstores looking for early Lowell or O'Hara. We nursed a single cappuccino for hours at Caffè Dante, scribbling in our diaries about how much everything hurt. We wished that the best minds of our generation had been destroyed by madness instead of packing it in and going to law school.

Perhaps it was naiveté that kept us from asking about agents and deals. (This, of course, would change in graduate school.) In college we were still looking for ways of being in the world, of being on the page. And I believe that a certain amount of innocence is as critical to the creative development of an artist as amniotic fluid is to a fetus. There is a necessary gestation period during which a writer should protect his work, because the minute he sends it out, or joins a writing group, or enrolls in an MFA program, he engages the part of himself that is focused on the result more than the work. For some people it's a quickening experience that can heighten their ambition and potentially improve their work. For others it's disastrous.

Most editors will agree that the work of reviewing manuscripts feels like slow death. We keep reading, and although much of what we read is coherent, very little impresses itself on us. We begin to wonder if our senses have been numbed, if we're suffering from burnout, if we will ever again read something that makes our hearts quicken and about which we will say, This guy's the real thing. This one can write.

Most people, even those who wrote as children or showed promise as teens, usually give up shortly after college. Writing, like drugs and recreational sex, becomes an activity associated with youth. Others who persist get graduate writing degrees or live the life of the temp or bartender as they try to support a writing career, only to eventually quit as a career opportunity with benefits presents itself. Many try to write screenplays in the hopes of striking gold; many pursue careers in publishing; some enter the teaching or legal professions. The writing life is torturous, especially if you hope to make a livelihood from it. No matter how glamorous it may appear, even the most successful authors will say that their lives are fraught with peril and insecurity, both financial and emotional.

Some let the dream go gracefully. Others do not go gently, attempting to write over the years, beginning journals only to let them lapse, showing up for a writing workshop only to disappear after the first session. If this describes you, it does not mean that you lack ability, though it may mean that you lack ego. But if you can't give it up, if hearing how impossible the odds are only makes you dig in deeper, it doesn't really matter if you've got natural talent. Your job is to marshal the talent you do have and find people who believe in your vision. What's important, finally, is that you create, and that those creations define for you what matters most, that which cannot be extinguished even in the face of silence, solitude, and rejection.

3.

THE

WICKED

CHILD

THERE IS NO QUESTION THAT THE WRITER most notable for negatively exposing his family, not to mention his entire tribe, is Philip Roth. The twenty-six-year-old writer from Newark, New Jersey, was robustly accused of both anti-Semitism and Jewish self-hatred when his short story "Defender of the Faith" was published in *The New Yorker* in April 1959. Roth is quick to point out in his autobiographical account of his life as a fiction writer, *The Facts*, that the controversy was largely due to context rather than content. "Had I submitted 'Defender of the Faith' to *Commentary* [instead of *The New Yorker*] . . . I suspect that the magazine would have published it and the criticism the story aroused there would have been relatively unspectacular. It's even possible that the ferment inspired a month later by the publication of *Goodbye, Columbus*—the pulpit sermons, the household arguments, the discussions within Jewish organizations gauging my danger . . . might never have reached troublesome proportions had 'Defender of the Faith' been certified as permissible Jewish discourse by appearing in *Commentary*."

Roth is right, of course. How we accept, reject, dismiss, and award our writers has everything to do with how, when, where, and by whom their work is presented. Still, no one, Roth least of all, was quite prepared for the public outcry. He claims that he had no intention of becoming known as a controversial writer. "[I] had no idea that my stories would prove repugnant to ordinary Jews. I had thought myself something of an authority on ordinary Jewish life, with its penchant for self-satire and hyperbolic comedy, and for a long time continued to be as bemused privately as I was unyielding publicly when confronted by Jewish challengers."

Somehow the exposition of Wasp foibles wasn't nearly as threatening to John Cheever or John Updike's people; but then again their audiences weren't desperately trying to assimilate into the American mainstream. As anyone knows who comes from that same middle-class Jewish background as Roth, the great crime was, is, and always will be letting *them* see *us.* That is why whenever a Jew does something really bad, as for example Ivan Boesky did, many Jews feel on a gut level that the whole religion suffers, that his actions are a reflection on all of us, giving people even more reason to be anti-Semitic. But Roth, being the genius that he is, went right for the Jewish jugular and followed his first short-story collection with *Portnoy's Complaint,* the quintessential Jewish novel of our time, which lifted the curtain on Semitic mishegoss: Jews masturbating, Jews wanting to screw shiksas, Jews being Jewy. It was enough to give a person a heart attack.

Let's face it, if in your writing you lift the veil on your family, your community, or even just yourself, someone will take offense. Call it fiction, call it poetry, call it creative nonfiction— if you write what is most pressing, you are revealing thoughts, secrets, wishes, and fantasies that you (and we as readers) would never otherwise confess to. That is part of the power of a book: it is an unspoken invitation into someone else's world, someone else's psyche. Every time a writer takes us backstage and gives us a glimpse of life behind the curtain, whether it's Toni Morrison's Black America, Amy Tan's Chinese America, Sherman Alexie's Native America, Edmund White's gay America, he or she risks being rejected by the tribe—especially if the portrait is in any way critical. But if you dream of having your work stay alive beyond your tenure on earth, if you hope to see it beside the unforgettable voices that are part of our literary diaspora, then you must be fearless in every aspect of your writing, from the syntax to the symbolism.

Renowned editor and author Gordon Lish, in his famous writing class (which combined equal parts psychotherapy, boot camp, Jerry Springer, and Socratic method), used to shock the assembled company by asking whether we were waiting for our parents to die before writing something worth reading. Some students were offended by this suggestion, but I felt it made a great deal of sense. Writers tend to censor themselves for fear of what other people think, especially those at home. Imagine writing a sex scene or describing the inner thoughts of a character who felt that his mother was controlling and suffocating. Now imagine your mother reading it. You can fictionalize, but you can't hide.

Philip Roth has, over the course of his career, constructed an elaborate hall of mirrors through which he refracts the self as character and character as self. Yet the dialogue between the id and ego running through his books provides an uncensored picture of the inner workings of a post–World War II American male. Paradoxically, the more Roth seems to reveal, the greater an enigma he is. One thing, however, is clear: he never dreamed that his work would hurt or embarrass his parents. "My mother was unambiguously proud of my first published stories. She had no idea that there could be anything seriously offensive about them and, when she came upon articles in the Jewish press intimating that I was a traitor, couldn't understand what my detractors were talking about. When she was once in doubt—having been shaken by a derogatory remark she'd overheard at a Hadassah meeting—she asked me if it could possibly be true that I was anti-Semitic, and when I smiled and shook my head no, she was entirely satisfied." But who cares if your mother approves when the whole of Hadassah thinks you're the devil?

Not all writers need enemies, real or imagined, to fuel their imaginations, nor do they necessarily write to expose their loved ones. I have found in my work with writers that those who appear most confident on the page are often those most confident of their parents' belief in them. One author with whom I worked over many years always struck me as blessed in the area of maternal support. She was the youngest of a large and gifted family but she was the first to publish. Her mother had been a writer and reporter for a major newspaper who, in accordance with the dictates of her era, subverted her drive and talents and redirected her energies into raising her family. She dutifully named each child for a deceased member of the family until the birth of this youngest child, for whom she chose a name of her own liking. "I looked at her in the hospital and saw how beautiful she was," the mother told me at the publication of her daughter's third book. "And then I gave her the most beautiful name I knew." When I asked if she always knew her daughter would be a writer, she replied without hesitation, "Oh yes."

It may be that those who are most loved and adored are those buoyed enough to write in the face of the world's indifference. It may be that the bolstered ego is the one resilient enough to live the disquieting writer's life. Many were convinced that Roth had it in for his mother, given the character of Sophie Portnoy, but they didn't understand that he had permission to create her. Reading *The Facts*, one gets the impression that Roth is the ultimate mama's boy, a prince, and that he could paint a portrait of an *uber*-Jewish mother because he was supremely confident of his own mother's love.

✦

For many writers, though, parental approval remains a thwarted but much-desired ideal, if only on an unconscious level. The stamp of approval that publication can represent may feel like that longed-for approbation from a distracted or depressed mother or a cold and distant father. There is no better record of such anguish than that described in Franz Kafka's *Letter to His Father.* This slim volume is the extended lament of a son whose failure to please his impossibly rigid and terrifying father describes the predicament of all writers who are caught between a child's need and a parent's rejection. "When I began to do something you did not like and you threatened me with the prospect of failure, my veneration for your opinion was so great that the failure became inevitable. . . . I lost confidence in my own actions. I was wavering, doubtful. The older I became, the more material there was for you to bring up against me as evidence of my worthlessness. . . . The aversion you naturally and immediately took to my writing was, for once, welcome to me." But Kafka's tone of sharp adolescent retribution quickly changes direction. "Of course it was a delusion; I was not, or, to put it optimistically, was not yet, free. My writing was all about you; all I did there, after all, was to bemoan what I could not bemoan upon your breast. . . . My valuation of myself was much more dependent on you than on anything else, such as some external success." In other words, the creator of *The Metamorphosis*, one of the twentieth century's most enduring parables of alienation, was himself crushed like a bug.

Just as a patient may spend months if not years in therapy protecting his or her parents, explaining that they did the best they could, rather than facing the sharp pain of their rejection or abuse, the writer resists exposing the family. Indeed, the desire to protect one's family is innate. Yet at the same time, the impetus to write often emanates from the need to express painful or shattering experiences. At the age of twelve, Charles Dickens was sent away from his family to work for twelve hours a day at a blacking factory housed in a rat-infested warehouse. When his father was finally released from debtor's prison, he apparently made no attempt to retrieve Charles from the factory; instead, upon collecting a small inheritance, he moved the rest of the family into a house.

Dickens's sense of abandonment is palpable in all his fiction, much of it peopled with orphans and lost boys. In his autobiography Dickens recalled, "The deep remembrance of the sense I had of being utterly neglected and hopeless, of the shame I felt in my position; of the misery it was to my young heart . . . cannot be written. My whole nature was so penetrated with grief and humiliation of such considerations, that even now, famous and caressed and happy, I often forget in my dreams that I have a dear wife and children; even that I am a man; and wander desolately back to that time in my life." In Leonard Shengold's brilliant book on the effects of childhood abuse and deprivation, *Soul Murder*, he posits that "Dickens became determined never again to suffer such helplessness and misery; the trauma fed an intense ambition."

Writers are motivated by many things, but it is often some variation on the Dickens theme, some lethal combination of hurt and desire, that keeps a writer in the ring. How is it that some writers are able to transform the stuff of their lives—its people and circumstances—into their own creations while others tiptoe around their subjects like Lilliputians around the giant Gulliver? One determining factor is entitlement, the feeling that you have the right to say whatever you want about whomever you want and, what's more, that your notions about people and their actions are defensible. Some writers have no qualms about writing nasty portraits of either strangers or loved ones. That's part of the pleasure of reading someone like Paul Theroux, who on the surface appears to be an equal-opportunity misanthrope.

Theroux's recent and much-maligned memoir, *Sir Vidia's Shadow,* which tells the story of his thirty-year friendship with V. S. Naipaul, was written, he explains, after the abrupt and somewhat brutal ending of the relationship by the older writer. Naipaul mysteriously stopped returning calls and faxes from his protégé, and when questioned by Theroux in a chance meeting on a London street, told him, "Take it on the chin and move on." Well, telling a writer to take anything on the chin and move on is a little like asking a boxer not to hit back. Indeed, Theroux's critics felt that the book was little more than a series of sucker punches at Naipaul, an unseemly airing of dirty linen, or as one reviewer wrote, "one long Oedipal screed."

Theroux was accused primarily of using his mentor in a manner unbecoming a writer. There is a clear bias in the culture against those who pull a *Mommie Dearest.* In a *New York Times Book Review* essay, Theroux rejected the critics' label of revisionist and betrayer. "Meditating upon the world and what is most familiar is the preoccupation of writers," he began. "Sometimes that includes re-creating our nearest and dearest, and our secrets. . . . The best writers are the most fanatical; so the truest portrait of a writer can never be a study in virtue." Virtue or vice, there is no writer who does not brush up against the moral predicament of what is fair game, no writer who doesn't consider whether to withhold a telling detail for reasons of taste or simple human kindness. "I think 'taste' is a social concept and not an artistic one," explained John Updike in an interview reprinted in his collection *Hugging the Shore.* "I'm willing to show good taste, if I can, in somebody else's living room, but our reading life is too short for a writer to be in any way polite. Since his words enter into another's brain in silence and intimacy, he should be as honest and explicit as we are with ourselves."

In many ways writers are scared by their ambitious hearts. Just as they are often accused of exposing others, they often fear being exposed themselves, especially to their families. To be a writer, to come out of the closet, is to announce that you are different in some way. Until a writer is established and thus somewhat protected by the veneer of success that publication brings, his life and his struggle to emerge can be fraught with humiliation. Having a mentor, as the young Theroux learned, can be a defining experience and may provide the necessary confidence to release one's ambition. "His friendship was different from anyone else's. . . . He knew more about my writing ambition than I had dared to tell my own family."

Calling attention to yourself, especially within a family dynamic, may involve more scrutiny than a writer can bear. Is there anything worse than being introduced, at a family wedding, for instance, as "our daughter, she's trying to be a writer." Or having some drunken uncle slap you on the back and ask with a loud laugh how the book's coming along? It is the mentor who understands the struggle and the indignities, the mentor who inhabits the life the young writer craves, and the mentor who, in loco parentis, sets the standard. "It gave me great confidence to have his approval," continued Theroux, "but his approval was anything but casual. I was also intensely aware of his intelligence, and did not write a word without wondering what he would say about it." *Sir Vidia's Shadow* strikes me as a welcome cautionary tale for all writers in search of approval, parental or otherwise. The results can be more bittersweet than cathartic. Though Theroux is a wonderful stylist, beneath the veneer of his highly polished prose is a child's firm belief in his own tantrum.

Most writers, like most children, need to tell. The only problem is that much of what they need to tell will provoke the ire of parent-critics, who are determined to tell writer-children what they can and cannot say. Unless you have sufficient ego and feel entitled to tell your story, you will be stymied in your effort to create. You think you can't write, but the truth is you can't tell. Writing is nothing if not breaking the silence. The problem is, no one likes a snitch. On top of this, contemporary critics would have us believe that we are in an age of unparal-leled navel-gazing. On the contrary, there is far greater cultural censure in taking one's pain seriously. As Alice Miller notes in her book *Banished Knowledge*, "Not to take one's own suffering seriously, to make light of it or even laugh at it, is considered good manners in our culture. This attitude is even called a virtue, and many people are proud of their lack of sensitivity toward their own fate and above all their own childhood." ·

Interestingly, for all the familial anxiety attendant on the publication of a first book, I am always struck when I find that the dedication page is devoted to the author's parents. Indeed, some of the most damning books about childhood or family life are thus dedicated. William Golding dedicated his parable of childhood cannibalization, *Lord of the Flies*, to "my mother and my father." Pat Conroy's unforgettable first novel, *The Great Santini*, about the abuse a young boy suffers at the hands of his brutal military father, "is dedicated with love and thanks to Frances 'Peggy' Conroy, the grandest of mothers and teachers, and to Colonel Donald Conroy, U.S.M.C. Ret., the grandest of fathers and Marine aviators." Dorothy Allison dedicated her first novel, *Bastard out of Carolina*, a horrific story about the abuse of a young girl and her mother's failure to protect her, to her deceased mother: "For Mama. Ruth Gibson Allison 1935–1990." Even J. D. Salinger dedicated his masterpiece, *The Catcher in the Rye*, to his mother.

Of course, parental approval isn't the most important thing in the world. One hopes that by the time a person reaches maturity, peer approval, mate approval, and more important, self-approval pick up where your parents leave off. But you don't have to be a Freudian to recognize the impact of parental influence. Our house is our world, and within its walls we find safety and comfort or coldness and danger or, more likely, something in between. We are praised and scolded according to a great many criteria, and we piece together our own little fictions of how and why we are the way we are.

If when you were a child stories took you far away, if characters from books kept you company as you peered out a rainy window and tried to discern that great mystery of how other people live, then you know that books are the most important things in life. If you were drawn to books and in turn to writ-

ing, chances are you found the world wanting. You knew that
a record had to be kept, or the world or you would disappear.
People are motivated to write for a variety of reasons, but it's
the child writer who has figured out, early on, that writing is
about saving your soul.

❦

Where, after all, does the drama of the gifted child begin but at
her own dinner table? The material we continue to grapple
with all our lives has more to do with that kid than any grown
writer wants to admit. That's where you were told in any number of spoken and unspoken ways that you were good enough,
or not good enough, or too good to be true. That's where you
got the message that you would either go very far or amount to
nothing. That's where you first encountered acceptance, rejection, approbation, or opprobrium. The messages you received
may have enabled you to raise your hand in class, read your
story aloud; something told you that people cared about what
you had to say. Or perhaps you went underground because you
had been told that your ideas were shameful or dangerous. Or
that you were suspect.

Just as one child takes the message of his glorious future and
goes very far, another is paralyzed by the expectation. Likewise,
the child who is consistently disparaged may make something
of himself, just to show the bastard who called him worthless.
Or he may set out on a course of self-destruction, believing himself as unworthy as the adult who crippled his small soul. But
more than any emotional Molotov cocktail of abuse and depri-

vation, or any showers of love and support, I sometimes think, what distinguishes the person who goes on to become a serious writer is his or her tolerance or love of solitude.

Nothing in our culture applauds the desire to be alone. Being alone, in fact, is the great crime. From the time we are little, parents tend to worry if we spend too much time by ourselves. In school, there is probably nothing worse than being branded as a loner. The culture is suspicious of people who want to be alone. It's okay if you turn out to be Thomas Pynchon, but not so okay if you wind up on national news as the Unabomber, being led away from a small shack in the woods.

I can't think of a riskier business than writing. Not only because so few succeed in conventional terms, with publication and some payment, but because it almost certainly requires banishment. First, there is the literal act of removing oneself, of choosing solitude. Then there is the psychological separation, holding oneself apart. And finally, the potential rejection of friends and family, critics and publishers. You don't have to be Philip Roth to incite the tribe. Far less incendiary portraits will forever taint your relations with loved ones. But you cannot censor yourself; successful writing never comes about through half-measures. For most people the first book is about the family, if only metaphorically, and it must be conquered as surely as the walls at Jericho.

I now think that I was drawn to poetry during my high school years because it must have seemed to my young mind that I could hide my feelings, if not the truth itself, behind the language of metaphor and simile. To me, poems were like great collages that could be assembled so as to keep some people out. Images were locks to which only extremely perceptive readers had the key. Finally, a teacher in graduate school called me out. My poems were a series of opaque images connected by bad grammar, she said during a private conference in one of the airless rooms at Columbia's Dodge Hall. Then she placed her thin blue pencil on the table, looked me directly in the eyes, and asked if I was intentionally trying to confuse people, or did my obfuscation have some aesthetic design? At that moment I wished for two things: an oxygen mask to eject from some invisible overhead compartment, and an adult to place it over my ashen face.

I wasn't at the point in my writing life where I believed I had control over my intention. If someone had asked why I wrote, I would have said, *I just write.* I also would have claimed, *I can't help what I write.* As hard as I worked at my revisions and line breaks, I was working equally hard to keep meaning at bay. I was terrified for anyone—most of all myself—to discover what my dark heart harbored. You see, I was a good child. And I was heavily invested in being a good, achieving daughter. So you can imagine how terrifying it was when I first took my teacher's advice and finally stopped writing incomprehensible poems and wrote some pieces that even my parents could understand.

It would be overly simplistic and false to blame fear of exposure as the single reason I quit writing and became an editor. I think I quit writing poems for a variety of reasons, some of which I still struggle with. I do know that when I began my life as an editorial assistant after graduate school I found it far easier to work on other people's writing and I liked my job; after all, it provided plenty of vicarious writing experiences. As I got promoted through the editorial ranks, I found a great deal of the work rewarding and validating, such as good reviews for my authors, and their appreciation of my contribution. My closeness to authors and their work satisfied much of my own creative drive. As I reflect, it strikes me as no accident that as an editor I have been drawn to writers who go out on an emotional ledge. And that as I work with them, I am not unaware of my nose pressed up to the glass, in awe of their gifts as well as their fearlessness.

Conversely, when I read a relatively well-written manuscript that makes no particular impression (which would describe most of the manuscripts editors evaluate), I can't help thinking, *Good child*. Here is yet another well-behaved manuscript that will be seen but not heard. Usually, somewhere in the first fifty pages is a clue as to what the story is really about. But in order to honor the story, in order to tell the truth (and I don't mean what happened in "real life" in any conventional sense, but the emotional truth), to raise what is only hinted at, the writer would have had to risk his place at the table, which is often too threatening. Unless you are the child who stormed your parents' bedroom, unless your role in life is whistleblower, it's damn hard to blow the house down when it's the only one you've got. Whether out of hurt, jealousy, shame, or a sense of violation, most family members will not be happy with your work whether you've written them in or, as in a will, written them out.

❧

One of the most public and wholesale rejections of a writer occurred in 1975, when *Esquire* published "La Côte Basque," an early chapter from Truman Capote's novel-in-progress *Answered Prayers*. Capote's women friends from New York's café society were horrified by the exposure of their secrets and promptly banished him from their inner circle. According to his editor, Joe Fox, at Random House, "Virtually every friend he had in this world ostracized him for telling thinly disguised tales out of school, and many of them never spoke to him again." Their little writer friend, the elfin troublemaker, had taken things just a little too far. Capote crossed a line he claimed he hadn't known existed, though he confessed to a certain amount of delicious anticipation before the piece ran, and he agreed to be photographed for the magazine's cover with a fedora wickedly tilted atop his head while he pared his fingernails with a very long blade.

In George Plimpton's oral history of Capote, John Barry Ryan, who worked with the writer on John Huston's film *Beat the Devil*, was bemused by the reaction. "The people who after 'befriending' Truman, accepting this asp onto their bosoms, were surprised that the snake bit!" he recounted. "Snakes bite! Truman certainly signed no Official Secrets Act. Everybody who was exposed to him in the period I'm familiar with knew if you told Truman something, it was the equivalent of telling forty other people. You would no more ask Truman to treat something as if for his ears only than you would throw bread upon the water and expect it to come back!" But as Liz Smith pointed out in her *New York* magazine article, detailing the public outrage in response to the story, "It is one thing to tell the nastiest story to all your fifty best friends; it's another to set it down in cold Century Expanded type." Capote committed the literary equivalent of premeditated murder: in cold type.

The reaction of Capote's New York City peers wasn't entirely unlike the response of a group of Dubliners more than fifty years earlier when a chronicle of Irish life with a cast of hundreds was published in a novel that was beginning to make some waves. According to Richard Ellman's biography, James Joyce waited in vain for the commendation of his fellow Dubliners when he published his masterpiece, *Ulysses.* Instead, "a tremor went through quite of few of his countrymen, who feared the part he might have assigned to them. 'Are you in it?' or 'Am I in it?' they asked the few people known to have copies."

Every writer uses the people in his life—for what other experience does he or she have? For every Dubliner who was scandalized by the publication of *Ulysses* and every East Side socialite who was shocked by Capote's "La Côte Basque," there are probably as many people who felt hurt that they were not included. After all, while it may smart to read something written with a caustic pen about you, it must also smart to be deemed unworthy of comment. And there is always someone who imagines himself in a writer's book, who thinks he is the basis for a character, when nothing was farther from the writer's mind. Joan Didion explains that her first novel, *Run River,* wasn't autobiographical except that it took place in Sacramento. "A lot of people there seemed to think that I had somehow maligned them and their families, but it was just a made-up story. The central incident came from a little one-inch story in *The New York Times* about a trial in the Carolinas."

If you are going to be honest and write about all the untidy emotions, the outsize desires, the hideous envy, and disturbing fantasies that make us human, how can you not offend your loved ones, your neighbors and community? If you are a mother and you write a book about a mother who kills her child, how will people look at you? *What will they think?* If you confess to something far less heinous, such as enjoying being spanked, as Daphne Merkin did in *The New Yorker*, your morals will still be scrutinized by those who think such behavior is unbecoming to a mother. Henry Miller can enjoy a good spanking; an Upper East Side mom has some explaining to do. How can a writer have his main character, say Rabbit in *Rabbit at Rest*, sleep with his daughter-in-law and not at least arouse the suspicions of his loved ones? I'm not suggesting that anyone in Updike's family thinks he's guilty of such a transgression, but if I were his son or daughter-in-law I might feel a little uncomfortable at the next Thanksgiving dinner.

Writers want to believe that their readers are sophisticated enough to understand that writing and life are two different things, especially when it comes to fiction. And that once a writer creates a scene, a character, or a snippet of dialogue, describes a room, a scent, an inflection of voice, she leaves reality behind. Edith Wharton describes this frustration in her autobiography, *A Backward Glance*. "All novelists who describe what is called 'society life' are pursued by the exasperating accusation of putting flesh-and-blood people into their books. Anyone gifted with the least creative faculty knows the absurdity of such a charge. 'Real people' transported into a work of the imagination would instantly cease to be real; only those born of the creator's brain can give the least illusion of reality. . . . Nothing can be more trying to the creative writer than to have a clumsy finger point at one of the beings born in that mysterious other-world of invention, with the playful accusation: 'Of course we all recognize your aunt Eliza!'"

Though the writer's aim is to convey truth, it certainly isn't to tell the truth per se. There is simply nothing worse than a novice writer who cries out in his own defense, when a scene is criticized for not seeming real, that "it really happened that way." No, no, no. Everything you put on the page is a deliberate manipulation of what happened, written to keep the reader entertained, moved, sympathetic, horrified, scared, whatever. You are never writing what *really* happened. Instead, you are choosing words, building images, creating a rhythm, sense, and structure through which to move your characters and unfold your story. You are making a thousand minuscule choices that you hope will add up in such a way that your readers believe what they're reading is real. And this is why, when the writer is successful, the best fiction reads like nonfiction and the best nonfiction like a novel.

It was Capote who first blatantly and brilliantly combined the two categories with his "nonfiction novel" *In Cold Blood*. The effect was dazzling, and the book forever changed the face of contemporary nonfiction. Perhaps the acclaim so emboldened him that when he set out to write *Answered Prayers*, which he planned as the contemporary equivalent of Proust's *Remembrance of Things Past*, he couldn't imagine that his efforts would be spurned. Like Edith Wharton, he expected some sophistication on the part of his refined society friends and was astonished by their nearly universal abandonment. "What did they expect?" he was quoted as saying. "I'm a writer, I use everything. Did all those people think I was just there to entertain them?" The desperation of his question supplies its own answer.

Though more than a few theories exist about the balance of this uncompleted novel, Capote's editor postulates that he never committed another word to the page. Increasing alcoholism and addiction were partially responsible for his inability to continue as a writer. But it also seems painfully true that Capote's great talent, which opened every door of his life and secured the love of those whose attention he craved, had finally and irrevocably slammed shut. "The problem was," said John Knowles, "he had no stature socially speaking. He had no family. He was only an ornament. There was nothing for him to fall back on. You could drop Truman overnight because you weren't going to alienate anybody. Truman was just all by himself out there."

Which is how most writers feel at the end of the day—especially if they've gone out on a limb. Even if you have position or family or people depending on you, the truth is that everyone is provincial at heart. Everyone defends his or her cave and clan. If you attack with humor you'll be given more leeway, but not much. But writing isn't about attacking, defending, or proving once and for all that these people are bad, phony, corrupt, or evil. Great writing is meant to crush us, entertain and move us, return us to ourselves with some greater understanding of the world and its workings.

✦

You must give yourself permission to tell. Most important, give up the vain hope that people will like your work. People like vanilla ice cream. Hope that they love your work or hate it. That they find it exquisite or revolting. I think Cocteau had the right idea when he said, "Listen carefully to first criticisms made of your work. Note just what it is about your work that the critics don't like and cultivate it. That's the only part of your work that's individual and worth keeping." Throw off the shackles of approval, of wanting to be liked. The minute you capitulate to changing even a single adjective to please someone else, or choose one adjective over another to protect a person's feelings, you pull the plug on your own respirator.

Philip Roth admits that the attacks on him and his work at the beginning of his career were absolutely decisive in his growth and success a writer. As he tells it in *The Facts*, after a particularly ugly public ordeal during which he was attacked by nearly all sides at a symposium called "The Crisis of Conscience in Minority Writers of Fiction," held at Yeshiva University, Roth swore over a pastrami sandwich at the Stage Delicatessen never to "write about Jews again." "I couldn't see then," Roth writes, "fresh from the event, that the most bruising public exchange of my life constituted not the end of my imagination's involvement with the Jews, let alone an excommunication, but the real beginning of my thralldom. . . . The Yeshiva battle, instead of putting me off Jewish fictional subjects for good, demonstrated as nothing had before the full force of aggressive rage that made the issue of Jewish self-definitions inflammatory. . . . How could I conclude otherwise when I was told that every word I wrote was a disgrace, potentially endangering every Jew?"

Unlike Capote, who was deeply dependent on the love and positive attention of his friends, Roth was fueled by the disdain his work exacted. Or rather, realizing he had touched a live wire, he proceeded to aim for the socket with his future books. As painful as any negative attention might be—symposiums gone wrong, scathing reviews, rejection by your entire people, nasty remarks at your mother's Hadassah meeting, a tell-all memoir by your ex that exposes your cruelty—it is only temporal. As Roth figured out early on, if your book causes a commotion, even the negative kind, you will have made a platform for yourself, something very few writers attain, and from there you will have something to live up to or something to live down. "My humiliation before the Yeshiva belligerents—indeed, the angry Jewish resistance that I aroused virtually from the start—was the luckiest break I could have had," Roth writes. "I was branded."

Many aspiring writers have gathered their marbles and gone home for far less cause. It takes a supreme talent and fierce self-belief to write in the face of so much acrimony. If you are a good child, you must stop trying to please or protect others with your work or, worse, your silence. And if you are a wicked child, you must transform your ambition into something more universal than the particulars of your own circumstance. If you can do that, you will have the last word.

4.

THE
SELF-PROMOTER

IN AN AGE WHEN FAME IS TANTAMOUNT TO godliness, perhaps the only modesty left is false modesty. We don't denigrate an investment banker for making lots of money, or a prosecutor for a ruthless closing statement. Bald ambition in other professions is far more acceptable than in the arts—we still like our poets starving and our novelists tucked away in garrets, not running for office. Indeed, it was shocking to see Tama Janowitz in the first of a series of advertisements that Apple Computer ran showing what "real" people had stored on their Powerbooks. What kind of writer would make herself the object of such blatant commercialism? One who wants to extend her fame—or perhaps one who simply needs a new computer. If it's okay for athletes to endorse sportswear, why shouldn't Katie Roiphe hoist a spanking new Coach bag? Or John Irving? Lillian Hellman draped herself in mink, the Blackglama ad copy above her head asking the question every writer contemplates, whether he admits it or not: What becomes a legend most?

The contemporary frenzy of literary self-promotion is not without historical precedent. The man considered America's most important poet took it upon himself, just weeks before his thirty-sixth birthday, to self-publish one of the most ecstatic works of literature in the American canon. Imagine how the young Whitman must have felt when, just two months after publication, he opened a letter welcoming him unequivocally into the fold. "I am not blind to the worth of the wonderful gift of *Leaves of Grass*. I find it the most extraordinary piece of wit & wisdom that America has yet contributed," wrote Emerson upon receiving a copy. "I greet you at the beginning of a great career."

The letter was the literary equivalent of the Red Sea parting, providing passage to the promised land. What writer doesn't dream of such a reception? But after the publication of a few less-welcoming notices in various newspapers, the letter mysteriously found its way into the *New York Tribune* without Emerson's permission or knowledge. According to Whitman biographer Justin Kaplan, the editor of the *Tribune* may have persuaded the poet to release the letter, but once the encomium was released, "he fell on it like a hawk." Whitman sent copies of the *Tribune* clipping to Longfellow and other celebrities, arranged to have the letter printed in *Life Illustrated*, and circulated it widely to editors and critics in the form of a small broadside that he had printed up. And then, as if that weren't enough, he had Emerson's words (or blurb, in today's parlance) stamped in gold on the spine of the second edition of his book. "Torn out of context, gaudily displayed, this Ali Baba formula appeared to be an endorsement of the new poems Emerson could not possibly have seen," reports Kaplan. "And further compounding what a Boston paper had called 'the grossest violation of literary comity and courtesy that ever passed under our notice.'"

When you gaze at pictures of Walt Whitman, with his long white beard and searing eyes, when you consider the exuberant life force coursing through his poems, it's a little unsettling to imagine him salivating over his endorsement, tirelessly printing broadsides to distribute, and sucking up to celebrity writers of the day—unless you've spent any real time with poets. Poets have always been scene stealers; their flair for drama and their outsized lives are the stuff of legend. Poets, like their poems, are good at making strong impressions. In a *New Yorker* article entitled "Big Poetry," Stephen Schiff describes Pulitzer Prize–winning poet Jorie Graham as a queenlike figure parading through her fiefdom, "swathed in black from head to foot, with enough bracelets and necklaces and rings to herniate a belly dancer. . . . She wears [them] to plant tulips at dawn." Another Pulitzer Prize winner, Richard Howard, always donned a sequined tie and would delicately lift a monocle, hanging from a long gold chain, to his eye before reciting a poem to our class. I fondly remember sitting cross-legged at the back of a packed auditorium at New York University, unable to see Allen Ginsberg except when he leapt up from behind the lectern to emphasize his words, his bald head springing up like some insane jack-in-the-box. And everyone's favorite eccentric, Marianne Moore, was as famous for her cape and tricorn hat—like a Buñuel priest crossed with Miss Clavel—as for her line breaks.

Perhaps poets have to push that much harder because the world is generally indifferent to their work. Though we share a collective fantasy about the mysterious creation of art and poetry, more often than not those artists whom we do hear from are those most unabashed in staking their claim. In sharp contrast to the gold-stamped self-proclamation of Whitman's arrival, Emily Dickinson's first halting lines to Thomas Wentworth Higginson reveal how one's approach to one's work influences its reception. "Mr. Higginson, Are you too deeply occupied to say if my Verse is alive?" begins her delicate gambit to the *Atlantic Monthly* editor whose "Letter to a Young Contributor" caught her attention. Scholars and readers alike still wonder how a writer of her genius and intensity could have been satisfied without the consummation of publication.

"The Mind is so near itself—it cannot see, distinctly—and I have none to ask—" she continued in that first missive to Higginson, acute with trepidation, confessing that particular vertigo all writers experience as they peer down at their own work and feel dizzyingly insecure. "I enclose my name—asking you, if you please—Sir—to tell me what is true. That you will not betray me— it is needless to ask—since Honor is its own pawn—" It is almost as if in that first letter Dickinson foretold Higginson's eventual betrayal; she died leaving more than two thousand unpublished poems.

When I was making my first, shy forays into the world of literary magazines with my sheaf of poems, I would regularly attend poetry readings. I was always amazed at the young poets who pressed their manuscripts into the hands of famous poets after their readings. *The chutzpah. The nerve.* My friends and I would remain in our seats, collectively outraged at the sheer au-dacity, not to mention the hubris. After all, how could an es-tablished writer, upon completing his reading, his own words still ringing in his ears, possibly be interested in having some young writer's manuscript foisted upon him? What was he ex-pected to *do* with it? Long after my friends and I had stopped condemning those strident young writers, I still found myself obsessed with their actions. I continued to wonder what combi-nation of ingredients propelled a writer to seek an audience outside herself and what mixture relegated her work to the drawer. We will never know what enabled Walt Whitman to promote his work with the fervor of Don King. Nor will we know what series of rejections, internal or external, kept Dick-inson from pursuing publication beyond the censorious Hig-ginson. Though most writers live somewhere between Whitman's narcissism and Dickinson's dysphoria, I suspect that most writ-ers dream of their own fame—whether or not they act on it.

⚜

Do the act of creating and the desire for fame run along the same continuum? Are there brilliant writers out there who never attempt to get their work published? How ironic or sad or tragic is it that one of the greatest living writers has not published for over thirty years? His silence repudiates all who enter the fray and hangs like a pall over writers, critics, and publishers alike. (Every time a publisher compares a first novel to *Catcher in the Rye*, he should go directly to jail or be

fined $200.) In her memoir of her nine-month-long relationship
with J. D. Salinger, Joyce Maynard tells us that she finally
worked up the courage to ask the great writer the blaring question at the center of his silence: Was he still writing? "He responds that he writes every day. Always has. As our friendship
develops, he speaks about his writing just in passing, as if that
goes without saying, and occasionally he will speak of having
had one of those weeks where most of the pages end up in the
trash."

Eventually Maynard broaches the second half of the question, asking Salinger why he doesn't publish anymore. "'Publication is a messy business,' he tells me. 'You'll see what I mean
one day. All those loutish cocktail party–going opinion-givers,
so ready to pass judgment. Bad enough when they do that to a
writer. But when they start in on your characters—and they
do—it's murder.'" But of all the advice Salinger gives the teenager,
his most poignant message has to do with freedom, the freedom
of the artist to work with impunity. "Some day," he tells Maynard, "there will be a story you want to tell for no better reason than because it matters to you more than any other. You'll
stop looking over your shoulder to make sure you're keeping
everybody happy, and you'll simply write what's real and true.
Honest writing always makes people nervous, and they'll think
of all kinds of ways to make your life hell. One day a long time
from now you'll cease to care anymore whom you please or
what anybody has to say about you. That's when you'll finally
produce the work you're capable of."

In publishing her memoir, it might be said, Maynard finally

took Salinger's advice and threw off the shackles of approval, his most of all. But she was roundly criticized for *using* Salinger, for exposing the writer who most avidly protects his privacy for her own fame. Maynard was included in a list of writers whom John Updike labeled "Judas biographers" because she exploited an experience with a more famous writer. No stranger to this kind of attack, Maynard has withstood the enmity of her peers since she first gazed out from the cover of *The New York Times Magazine* at the age of nineteen with her enormous eyes and be-mused smile and a man's watch slipping around her thin wrist. "Maynard is no longer as famous as she once was," reported a *New York Times* feature on the writer, "but ask anyone of roughly her age who grew up in this country, and he will not only know who she is—but chances are he will react to her name with startling venom. Perhaps to them it seems like only yes-terday that, as teen-agers, they picked up that issue of *The New York Times Magazine* with Maynard on the cover and wondered, *Why isn't that me?*"

It is my educated guess that every time a writer gets a big advance, a big feature story, or a big movie deal, or climbs onto the bestseller list, other writers wonder, *Why isn't that me?* And we often conclude that the person at the center of attention somehow manipulated circumstances. "Oh, you know, he's a total self-promoter," we sneer when an up-and-coming writer aligns himself with a powerful editor or agent. No matter how a person arrives, at some point he is seen as complicit in his ad-mission to the inner circle. What we fail to remember is that being a writer includes the implicit hope of becoming known.

How comfortable or uncomfortable a writer is with that exposure may be the decisive factor in whether or not he is heard
from.

I once acquired a book by a young writer whose proposal,
unbeknownst to me, had been making the rounds of the publishing houses, all of which had turned it down. I thought the
proposal was ragged and unorganized, but the emotion and humor came through in a way that touched me. The writer arrived for a meeting on a drizzly March day, her head and upper
body wrapped in a monklike shawl, her long eyelashes dark-
ened by the rain. When she let her shawl drop over the back
of her chair, I saw that her hair was matted down around her
face, and I distinctly remember thinking that she was like a
small kitten just in from the rain. We talked about her memoir
and what she hoped to accomplish with it, and I knew even before she left the meeting that I wanted to work with her; she
was warm and funny and smart. And I had the feeling she
would write a book I wished I could have read when I was
her age.

No sooner did I sign the book up for a modest advance than
my phone started ringing off the hook. "Do you have any idea
who you just signed?" one reporter friend beseeched. "You
know what she's done, don't you?" I acted as if I knew perfectly
well, not wanting to seem the dupe of the century, and called
her agent posthaste. What I discovered was that this kitten had
been a bad little cat; allegations of professional misconduct had
attached themselves to her like lint. "She's a nightmare, I just
hope you know that, a total networker," another editor chimed

in, though he also said he had wanted to acquire the book but couldn't get his company to agree. Her sin, I later discovered, had been in landing a much-coveted job at a very young age with a highly regarded publication. But perhaps her even greater transgression as a writer was that in mining her life for material she used her pen as if it were a needle in her arm.

Just as we are suspicious of the gold digger's love for her ninety-year-old husband, we view the writer who courts fame with suspicion, as if being serious about your work and being determined to see it disseminated were at cross-purposes. After all, how could a ruthless self-promoter or blatant fame-seeker possibly produce a work of importance? The moment you find the spotlight, or it finds you, people will project motivation and intent that may or may not apply to you. "The degree of derision Maynard inspires is astonishing," said Jonathan Yardley of *The Washington Post*. Another writer, a Yale classmate of Maynard's, said, "She has hacked her way through three decades wrapped in a delusion torn from an Oliver Sacks casebook: The Woman Who Mistook Herself for Someone Interesting." It is unclear which sin is greater: writing about oneself or achieving early success. From the audacious act of publishing her first memoir, *Looking Back*, at nineteen, to dropping out of Yale and offering herself up to the great one, to writing about the details of her domestic life in a vastly popular column, working nonstop to keep her three children diapered, fed, and well cared for, Maynard has excavated her life for material.

Does any writer do otherwise? It is easy to say that Joyce Maynard only wants attention, but I would venture to guess that she hopes people will actually like what she writes. It's also easy to attack Maynard because she is a woman, and domestic life and female concerns are considered negligible. You can call her a Judas writer because it is still taboo, or at least bad form, to expose the sins of the fathers. (We all prefer to imagine the solitary genius of J. D. Salinger rather than contemplate his undercooked lamb-burgers and propensity for young girls.) And as with Capote, it's easy to lambaste Maynard because she has no influence to speak of beyond headline fodder; she doesn't control any powerful institutions. But the real reason it is so easy to attack her is that she leaves herself wide open.

※

Even after many years as an editor working with first-time authors, watching them emerge into the spotlight, and observing how that process affects their egos, I find that my feelings waffle between admiration and disgust for those who bask in the glow of their own glory and those who cannot come to terms with their desire for greatness. I've always believed that one has to want in order to get, but when the want becomes all-consuming, or at least more consuming than the work itself, the process is perverted—for better or worse. We editors encounter on a daily basis the many faces of ambition and its guises—including humility. I used to believe that an inverse relationship existed between self-esteem and greatness, that the writers who thought they were really great usually fell quite short of their own high estimation. And those who had a healthy dose of insecurity about their work usually produced the most accomplished prose. But it isn't always so. Sometimes the most self-satisfied and arrogant are truly brilliant. Which is why we keep letting them back for another dizzyingly explosive round of their punches.

Norman Mailer, the writer best known for literally punching out critics and making headlines (though his body of work actually towers over his publicity stunts), collected and annotated all of his assorted writings at the ripe old age of thirty-six, producing a single volume unabashedly titled *Advertisements for Myself*. The jacket featured a head shot that more closely resembled an actor's, with the author sporting a sea captain's cap jauntily tilted toward the back of his head, a stray curl insouciantly jutting onto his forehead. His bedroom eyes are trained somewhere in the middle distance, and his pretty lips are just slightly ajar. The occasion for this collection, according to the author, was "that I am imprisoned with a perception which will settle for nothing less than making a revolution in the consciousness of our time. Whether rightly or wrongly, it is then obvious that I would go so far as to think it is my present and future work which will have the deepest influence of any work being done by an American novelist in these years. I could be wrong, and if I am, then I'm the fool who will pay the bill, but I think we can all agree that it would cheat this collection of its true interest to present myself as more modest than I am." God forbid.

The whole question of ego and writers is extremely tricky, but there is simply nothing more suspect than the self-satisfied writer. We are threatened when a writer bursts on the scene and proclaims his own greatness, as novelist Dale Peck recently did in a much-publicized change of publisher. "I do think I'm one of the best writers around, and I want to be recognized for that," he was quoted as saying in *The New York Observer*. On the one hand, I admire Peck. Good for him for being able to say "I'm the greatest." But his pronouncement also reeks of self-satisfaction, and we like to imagine that our writers are suffering on behalf of their art. No one challenged this notion with greater austerity than Robert Frost, who spoke to the issue of personal risk in a *Paris Review* interview. "So many talk, I wonder how falsely, about what it cost them, what agony it is to write."

No matter how great a person is, in America we still prefer to have greatness conferred by others. The writer who proclaims his greatness, who carries his acceptance speech around in his breast pocket, we tend to think of as a jerk. We like at least a dollop of self-doubt with our greatness. Woody Allen has built an entire persona out of the creation of his highly neurotic characters. No matter how many times he explains that his films aren't autobiographical, as he recently did of *Deconstructing Harry*, we are most comfortable believing that the neurotic, obsessed man at the center of the picture is the filmmaker himself.

Allen said, "People confuse the details of Harry's life with my life, when I'm nothing like Harry. I don't drink to excess or take pills, like Harry. I've never had the nerve or craziness to kidnap my son, like Harry. I've never experienced writer's block. I've never used the lives of my friends in fiction, like Harry. I've done twenty-seven films, and never once has anyone complained." It's impossible for us to believe that the character we have come to know in his films is not the real Woody Allen, so well drawn and hilariously familiar are his symptoms of contemporary neurosis. It's easier to believe that Woody Allen is self-doubting, self-deprecating, and self-obsessed than to see him as a self-assured artist who works in a methodical, single-minded fashion; we like to believe there's some madness or magic in creating. Describing his regimen, Allen makes his work sound as interesting and dangerous as punching a clock. "To make a film every year is not such a big deal. It doesn't take that long to write a script. I write every day. I'm very disciplined. I enjoy it. . . . I have a perfectly sedate life. I wake up, do my treadmill, have breakfast, then I write and practice the clarinet and take a walk and come back and write again and turn on the basketball game or go out with friends. I do it seven days a week. I could never be productive if I didn't have a very regular life."

As ordinary as Allen makes his day job out to be, and perhaps the routine's the result of doing it for as long as he has, most writers nurse the idea that their struggles are unique. "You wouldn't be an artist if you didn't feel somewhere in your heart that you're better than everybody else and you're going to blow them away. . . . It takes a fanaticism and a dedication and a single-mindedness," confesses T. Coraghessan Boyle. (Beware of all writers who substitute initials for their given names—big ambitions are hiding behind those little old initials.)

Behind every writer who looks his editor in the eye and says, "I just want your honest opinion, even if you hate it," "Don't feel you need to look at it right away," "I don't want superstardom," "I don't care if it's not a bestseller," "I'll be happy no matter what happens," there lurks a megalomaniac in the making. There isn't a writer who gets an editor to consider his work or, better yet, a real live publishing contract from a press, who doesn't fantasize that his work might take the world by storm. Let's face it, no one sits down to write something that will be a colossal failure. No one even sits down to write something that will be a modest success. The question is, how much do you let your fantasies circumscribe your work, and how much do they fuel your ambition?

*

The writer's personality and his personality on the page are not necessarily identical, but often there is a resemblance, not unlike that between an owner and his dog. A writer's work emanates from his personality, ego, sensitivities, and blind spots, his projections and unconscious wishes. All these contribute to what we eventually call style. Not everyone can arrive at a party like Oscar Wilde and command the room; most writers are more inwardly focused. But even for those whose personal style attracts attention, the proof is always, finally, on the page.

"I don't think that style is consciously arrived at," said Truman Capote, "any more than one arrives at the color of one's eyes. After all, your style *is* you. At the end the personality of a writer has so much to do with the work The personality has to be humanly there. Personality is a debased word, I know, but it's what I mean," said this writer with personality in abundance. "The writer's individual humanity, his word or gesture toward the world, has to appear almost like a character that makes contact with the reader. If the personality is vague or confused or merely literary, *ça ne va pas.*"

In my experience, the writers who have just the right combination of conviction and fear are the ones to watch for. Exceptions of supreme arrogance aside, even the most celebrated writers are plagued by self-doubt and suffer enormous bouts of failure of confidence. Susan Sontag, in a *New York Times Magazine* feature, confessed to having felt deep insecurity when she began writing *The Volcano Lover.* "When I started the novel, it seemed like climbing Mount Everest," she wrote. "And I said to my psychiatrist, 'I'm afraid I'm not adequate.'" In an interview in *Conversations with American Writers* ten years earlier, she presaged those same insecurities: "I am profoundly uncertain about how to write. I know what I love or what I like, because it's a direct, passionate response. But when I write I'm very uncertain whether it's good enough. That is, of course, the writer's agony."

Even the most successful authors suffer from poseur complexes. In an introduction to Natalie Goldberg's *Writing Down the Bones,* Judith Guest, author of *Ordinary People,* confessed the following feeling after the publication of her runaway bestseller: "Years later I was still telling myself that I wasn't really a writer, but a trickster—and a very lucky trickster at that. I had written a first novel and it had achieved phenomenal success. I had stumbled upon the secret path and uncovered the rules and had been rewarded with much praise. Unfortunately, all of this was proving to be of very little use to me in the writing of the next novel. How could I have forgotten everything so quickly?"

Pulitzer Prize winner Carol Shields became confident about her calling only in middle age. "There was a time," she was quoted as saying, "when I shrugged off my writing in embarrassment." Often the best writers are mortified by their work and fear that it's only a matter of time before others see through them. (*Will this be the day when everyone finds out I can't write?* the Pulitzer Prize–winning poet thinks to himself as he mounts the stage to collect his prize.) For every Mailer or Whitman writing his own ad copy, there are countless writers who can barely look themselves in the eye.

Sometimes a writer appears to be exercising false modesty when he turns in some pages to his editor and expounds on their terribleness, or accepts a prize claiming that he does not deserve it. But for the straight-A student who sits down to take a test while moaning to his classmates that he will most certainly fail, it doesn't matter how many straight A's he's scored; the internal pressure to perform yet again can be paralyzing. And when writers cry wolf, the reason has nothing to do with how well the work seems to be going or how well their previous work was received. No sooner do they complete a new piece of writing than the wolf is at the door.

I was taken aback when a novelist with five books to her credit confessed that between projects she always falls into a deep malaise, during which she is utterly convinced that she will never write again, that she is absolutely lost and has no confidence that she will be able to figure out how to write again. But surely, I suggested to her, the success of your previous books bolsters you to some extent. She was resolute in her an-

swer; it was as if Rumpelstiltskin had produced her manuscripts as far as she was concerned. I could hear in her weary,
watery voice that she was being truthful, though this image didn't
wash—it contradicted the one I had concocted of her based on
her press. She had been the envy of many of my classmates
when her stories started appearing in *The New Yorker* and her
book became a cause célèbre. When I asked what she did when
she was between books, how she dealt with her fear, she
matter-of-factly replied, "I cry to my mom."

⚜

Wanting to be read, wanting the recognition, whether it's
Jacqueline Susann–style, all glitz and limos, or sweeping the
grand slam of literary events, is not a crime. What seems crim-
inal to me is imitating the latest trend in a calculated attempt to
receive recognition. No matter how much you think you deserve attention, no matter how low you're willing to stoop to
get it, the work will prevail or fail on its own merits at the end
of the day. You may think that Bret Easton Ellis was lucky
when Simon & Schuster refused to publish his novel, thus
turning *American Psycho* into a *cause terrible*. But no one could
envy the attention Salman Rushdie received when the Ayatol-
lah's *fatwa* for *The Satanic Verses* catapulted the writer to international fame. These wag-the-dog scenarios were too outrageous
to have been dreamed up by even the most cynical publicist. I
don't think you can blame a writer for becoming famous as a
result of coming under attack. All the same, consider to what
extent the attack was invited. When a writer blasphemes Islam

or chops up hundreds of young women in the pages of his book, he can't pretend that he didn't lob the first grenade. Which is worse anyway: to write an incendiary book that sputters out like a wet match (as many do) or to watch your kerosene-doused pages start a forest fire?

All writers are like bomb-throwers, whether they attack with dense academic prose or jazzy riffs of stream-of-consciousness writing. Every writer wants his words to inflame the hearts and minds of his readers. Every writer attempts to reach across that great abyss, also known as the space between people, with his words. And whether it's Easton Ellis–style, by mutilating hundreds of unsuspecting yuppies, or by denouncing a world religion, or by doing something quieter, more domestic, the writer hopes to leave an indelible impression. Thus, when a "quiet" writer like Elizabeth Bishop, or a "domestic" writer like Carol Shields, or an intellectually sensuous poet like Jorie Graham takes home the Pulitzer, it celebrates the kind of flash that doesn't blind but, on the contrary, illuminates.

Whether you write the way Vermeer paints, or explode on the canvas like Jackson Pollock, you must make your own impression; whether you prance down the hall in a cape, run for mayor, pose nude for your book jacket, schmooze every influential writer in the land, hit every club and literary haunt, or just stay home. You will invite as much comment and attention over the long term as the material warrants and the world deigns to bestow. A world, I don't need to add, that is desperately vying for our entertainment dollars in the form of radio listenership, Neilsen ratings, movie grosses, Internet hits, and the like. Which explains why some writers, especially young writers, in their desire to be heard, try to make a big noise.

You must dazzle your readers if you want to keep them, but they may be just as dazzled by a description of a lonely cloud as by a mushroom cloud. When you venture forth with your work, remember that reputations are built on very little and are lost on even less. How does a writer negotiate a capricious world that would just as soon destroy him as praise him? Mailer, who is clearly going to go out kicking and screaming, reveals the high cost and anguish involved in continuing to produce: "If I am going to go on saying what my anger tells me it is true to say, I must get better at overriding the indifference which comes from the snobs, arbiters, managers and conforming maniacs who manipulate most of the world of letters. . . . There may have been too many fights for me . . . too much brain-blasting rage at the minuscule frustrations of a most loathsome literary world, necrophilic to the core—they murder their writers, and then decorate their graves."

Mailer's sentiments may seem exaggerated, but the sad truth is that all too often the world seizes on a writer's work in death as they never did in life. There is nothing like death to seal your literary fate; thankfully this method is too extreme for even the most ambitious. Still, the list of writers who have died by their own hand is sadly long. Jonathan Swift's epigraph in John Kennedy Toole's posthumously published novel, *A Confederacy of Dunces*, highlights the powerful myth surrounding the misunderstood artist: "When a true genius appears in the world, you may know him by this sign, that the dunces are in confederacy against him." Toole's tragic suicide at the age of thirty-two and his mother's valiant efforts to secure publication are part of the book's lore. Perhaps because *Confederacy of Dunces* was published during my own somewhat tortured college years, the story of its posthumous success obsessed me and my small circle of friends. We endlessly debated whether the book would have garnered the same attention had the author been alive. The unspoken question loomed large: Which demons drove him to write? And which to die?

In some respects, it is even sadder when a writer outlives her fame. "There are writers who die to the world long before they are dead," wrote Brendan Gill in his introduction to *The Portable Dorothy Parker*. "And if this is sometimes by choice, more often it is a fate imposed on them by others and not easily dealt with. A writer enjoys a vogue, and, the vogue having passed, either he consents to endure the obscurity into which he has been thrust or he struggles against it in vain, with a bitterness that tends to increase as his powers diminish." Parker's acerbic wit and famous circle of friends are the stuff of legend. We always imagine her as poised with a bourbon, a cigarette snug in its lacquer holder, and a mordant quip. Surely she would go out in a blaze of glory or slip away under a sea of booze and pills. As Gill points out, "So large a portion of her verses was the seductiveness of a neat, brisk doing away with herself, many people were astonished to read of her death, in 1967, from natural causes, as an old lady of seventy-three. . . . She had indeed taken an unconscionably long time to leave a world of which she had always claimed to hold a low opinion."

A recent skirmish that involved some of our literary lions struck me as the last roars of a few good men attempting to se' cure their place among the immortals. When Tom Wolfe's *A Man in Full,* his first novel to appear in ten years, plopped its massive self down in the number-one spot on the bestseller list, it seemed as if every major author over sixty lined up, like boys at a dunking booth, to knock him down. Norman Mailer, John Updike, and Harold Bloom felt it incumbent on them to take a shot at Wolfe in our most influential papers, claiming his work mere entertainment. Good, yes, but not *literature.* "Why are all these old men rising off their pallets to condemn my book?" asked Wolfe in a *Newsweek* interview. "Because my book has cast a very big shadow, and people like Mailer and Updike find themselves in the dark. And what do you do when you find yourself in the dark? You whistle. They're whistling in the dark." Naturally, this is Wolfe's tune, but the contretemps in and of itself attests to the need of writers, no matter their stature, to secure and promote their own literature.

Only Vladimir Nabokov, whose novel *Lolita,* a literary bombshell if there ever was one, seems to have been completely uninterested in his fame. "I think like a genius, I write like a distinguished author, and I speak like a child," he proclaimed in the opening gesture of his collected interviews and pieces, *Strong Opinions.* "I pride myself on being a person with no public ap' peal. . . . I have never belonged to any club or group. No creed or school has had any influence on me whatsoever. . . . I am not interested in groups, movements, schools of writing, and so forth. . . . I don't fish, cook, dance, endorse books, sign books, co-sign declarations, eat oysters, get drunk, go to church, go to analysts, or take part in demonstrations." And when asked what he thought of contemporary novels, he responded with the supreme confidence of an artist working high above the din: "They seem to be all by one and the same writer—who is not even the shadow of my shadow."

Whether you throw a long shadow or hide within its dark fold, never leaving home but through the tapping out of your own Morse code, as Emily Dickinson did through the long winters of her life, or run for mayor, punch out people twice your size, and stab your wife, as Norman Mailer did while producing some of his generation's most influential prose, you will ultimately live or die by your line.

5.

THE

NEUROTIC

WRITERS LOVE TO WORRY. BY THEIR VERY nature they are neurotic. And they tend to exhibit the gamut of phobic behaviors from nervous tics and insomnia to full-fledged paranoia and delusional episodes. Some pick their skin, some pull out their hair or, in more extreme cases, cut, burn, or scar themselves. Many suffer from allergies, asthma, skin eruptions, rashes. John Updike wrote the equivalent of a love letter to his psoriasis, nearly crediting it as the impetus for his literary career: "What was my creativity, my relentless need to produce, but a parody of my skin's embarrassing overproduction? Was not my thick literary skin, which shrugged off rejection slips and patronizing reviews by the sheaf, a superior version of my poor vulnerable own, and my shamelessness on the page a distraction from my real shame, my skin. . . . Dualism, indeed, such as existed between my skin and myself, instinctively struck me as the very engine of the human."

Some writers are hypochondriacal in the extreme, a condi-

tion that may be an extension of their already vivid imaginations or a bid for help and attention. "I often get very tense working," said novelist and critic William Gass. "So I often have to
get up and wander around the house. It's very bad on my stomach. . . . My ulcer flourishes and I have to chew a lot of pills.
When my work is going well, I am usually sort of sick." For
others, writing is the only way to alleviate what ails them.
"When I'm writing I find it's the only time that I feel completely self-possessed, even when the writing itself is not going too
well," remarked William Styron. "It's fine therapy for people
who are perpetually scared of nameless threats as I am most of
the time—for jittery people. Besides, I've discovered that when
I'm not writing I'm prone to developing certain nervous tics,
and hypochondria."

In addition to physical symptoms, people who write tend to
develop a set of ritualized behaviors with regard to their work.
These habits dictate when, where, and under what circumstances
they feel able to produce. There are early birds and night owls.
Some need a bright café to compose. Others must steal away to
a secluded spot or the equivalent of a safe house where no one
knows their identity. Most require solitude. "The person who
writes books must always be enveloped by a separation from
others," writes Marguerite Duras. "It is the solitude of the author, of writing. To begin with, one must ask oneself what the
silence surrounding one is—with practically every step one
takes in a house, at every moment of the day, in every kind of
light, whether light from outside or from lamps lit in daylight.
This real, corporeal solitude becomes the inviolable silence of

writing." Many, such as Styron, require some combination of solitude and community. "I think it would be hard for me on a South Sea island or in the Maine woods. I like company and entertainment, people around. The actual process of writing, though, demands complete, noiseless privacy, without even music; a baby howling two blocks away will drive me nuts."

I have also found that many writers have a nearly demagogic worship of their writing accouterments. "My schedule is flexible," replied Nabokov in response to a question regarding his work habits, "but I am rather particular about my instruments: lined Bristol cards and well-sharpened, not too hard, pencils capped with erasers." "I write my first version in longhand," explained Capote. "Then I do a complete revision, also in longhand. . . . Then I type a third draft on yellow paper, a very special certain kind of yellow paper." In his *New Yorker* article "Wasn't She Great," Michael Korda described the habits of his diva author Jacqueline Susann. "Jackie wrote on pink paper, and she had apparently not yet discovered the 'Shift' key on her typewriter (a pink IBM Selectric): she wrote everything in capital letters, like a long telegram, and added revisions in a large, forceful circular hand, with what looked like a blunt eyebrow pencil." Hemingway was said to sharpen twenty pencils before he started work. For other writers, the drill is less involved: "First coffee," said Gore Vidal. "Then a bowel movement. Then the muse joins me."

If you become successful as a writer, these ritualistic behaviors will become known as your "process." The paper you write on, the time of day you compose—these details will actually seem interesting to some segment of your reading public as well as to a few graduate students as they labor to unravel the mystery of your genius. Then all the quirks of character become part of what makes you tick. Suddenly it seems significant that you can write your first draft only on a moving vehicle, or that you like to lie in an open coffin, as Dame Edith Sitwell reputedly did, before beginning your day's work.

Should you fail to achieve success, all these behaviors look only like excuses or sick behavior. Every time you put a provision on the conditions under which you can work—I have to write in the morning; I can write only when alone; I need a composition notebook of lined paper exactly like those I used when I studied in France; I can't possibly write if I have a girlfriend/boyfriend; or I can write only if I'm going out with someone—you fail to grasp the essential truth of all great writing: it brooks no provisions. "One must be pitiless about this matter of 'mood,'" said Joyce Carol Oates. "In a sense, the writing will create the mood. If art is, as I believe it to be, a genuinely transcendental function—a means by which we rise out of limited, parochial states of mind—then it should not matter very much what states of mind we are in."

If you are meant to write, if you are ready to write, if what you must do is write, then all you really need is paper and pencil. The daughter of a famous writer asked her father, upon beginning her college career, if she could have a computer. He replied, "If a pencil was good enough for Charles Dickens, it's good enough for you." Once you fully contemplate the fact that Tolstoy revised *War and Peace* over five drafts without the aid of a typewriter, or that every other writer before the advent of computers managed to scratch his quill into parchment or hammer away at his typewriter without the benefit of this month's Microsoft upgrade, you have to admit that your project really does not require a new Powerbook. Yet when the writing demon seizes a person who can't actually commit anything to paper, he will look to almost any voodoo to find the words. Writers everywhere have purchased expensive technology, rented rooms, left loved ones, exiled themselves to grass huts, or worse without bringing a single project to fruition. The problem is, none of this is writing. It's stalling. And the more you indulge any neurotic notions about a set of necessary conditions that will enable you to write, the colder the trail will get.

✷

The definition of phobia is a persistent, abnormal, or irrational fear of a specific thing that compels one to avoid the feared stimulus. The problem for many writers is that writing itself is the feared stimulus. I've heard good excuses in my day, as all editors have, as to why a manuscript will be late. Just once I'd like to hear a writer tell the truth about why he can't deliver. Just once I'd like to hear someone say: no words. The reason no one says it is because when there are no words, nothing will save you: not a laptop with a gazillion gigawatts, not a sabbatical, not even a room of your own. When the words don't come, you could have all of Versailles to yourself and it wouldn't make a damn bit of difference. When the words don't come, the bell is striking midnight and you are Cinderella, or worse, Jack

Nicholson in *The Shining,* typing the same line over and over again: *All work and no play makes Jack a dull boy.* (Interestingly, in his more recent role as a writer in *As Good As It Gets,* Nicholson's character is a best-selling author, rich and prolific, yet riddled with so many neurotic tics and ritualized behaviors that he can barely cross the street.) It is no wonder that writers lie about why the manuscript is late. And for many writers, the possibility of not producing is always one keystroke away.

Sometimes a writer is thrown off his game when he lands a book contract; after years of producing with no hope of publication on the horizon, the long-sought contract paralyzes him. If a writer has a success with her first book, sometimes a second never follows. And when a writer works out of a deeply autobiographical vein, we worry if the well will go dry. The challenge to continue producing in the face of both creative blocks and what can amount to paralyzing fear is a little-discussed fact of writing life. Most writers appear neurotic; the truth is, we don't know the half of it.

This explains, in part, why so many writers develop phobias, rituals, and superstitions. What's useful about neurotic behaviors is that they can give a shapeless day structure. If you must use yellow paper, if you must drink a double espresso before starting, if you can only write for three hours every morning, then at least you have a plan. Developing a successful formula for getting pages written can make a crucial difference. When I studied with the late playwright Charles Ludlam, who founded the Ridiculous Theatrical Company, he said, and I've heard many others echo this strategy, that he always stopped writing in the middle of a scene, even when the work was going well. He couldn't understand those who bemoaned the terror of the blank page when they could arrange to face one with a few sentences. Plus, he added, if you quit while the going's good, you're more inclined to rush back the next day. If all else failed, the Master of Drag recommended we try slipping into an evening gown and wig to see if that would get the writing juices flowing.

Imagine the anxiety level of a job that requires you start all over from square one every day that you work. But that's the writer's situation. Every day you are starting from scratch, even when you're in the middle of a project. Will the muse, as Milton beseeched her, bring your roots rain? Remember, too, that the writer's uncertainty about the quality of his work is another reason to develop an arsenal of neuroses. Unlike the mathematician, who knows when he's solved a problem, or the scientist with his burden of proof, or the lawyer who tries his case before a jury, the solitary writer works in a vacuum, where it's easy to lose all perspective. Judging one's own writing is like looking in a mirror. What you tell yourself about what you see in the reflection has far more to do with how you feel about yourself than with how you actually look.

✦

Do writers develop phobias or are they phobics to begin with? An impossible chicken-and-egg dialectic. The great reclusive writers of our day provide cause for much speculation. Are they painfully shy, or do they hold their readers, the media, and critics in contempt? Do they even read their press? Gnash their teeth? Curse the reviewers? Are they stutterers like the great British poet and novelist Philip Larkin or our American eminence John Updike, who, in "Getting the Words Out," defended his broken speech as avidly as his broken skin: "As with my psoriasis, the affliction is perhaps not entirely unfortunate. It makes me think twice about going on stage and appearing in classrooms and at conferences—all that socially approved yet spiritually corrupting public talking that writers of even modest note are asked to do. Being obliging by nature and anxious for social approval, I would never say no if I weren't afraid of stuttering."

I believe that writers develop phobias, or Updikean defenses, for protection, to create a wall between themselves and other people. Such a wall allows them to enter the supremely narcissistic world of the page—the place where they are the happy masters of the sandbox. Whether a writer never leaves home, like Jane Austen, or is as peripatetic as Mark Twain, antisocial behavior is essential. An absolute solipsism takes over as the writer becomes more alive inside his work than in the real world. For many, the work would never come into existence unless its primacy were indisputable. What looks like neurosis and eccentric behavior may provide the crucial barricade that enables the writer to work when everything in life conspires to distract him or co-opt his energies.

"When I was writing in the house, everything wrote," said Marguerite Duras. "Writing was everywhere. And sometimes when I saw friends, I hardly recognized them. Several years were spent like that, difficult ones for me, yes, this might have lasted for ten years. And even when close friends came to see me, that, too, was horrible. My friends knew nothing about me: they meant well and came out of kindness, believing they would do me good. And strangest of all is that I thought nothing of it. This is what makes writing wild. One returns to a savage state from before life itself."

Whoever you are, whatever your bizarre behaviors, I say cultivate them; push the envelope. Becoming a writer never won anybody any popularity contests anyway. And most writers couldn't win one if they tried. Most have a lumpy writer's body and an uninspired wardrobe and talk too much. Many writers can't help but focus on their work, often steering the conversation to their most recent article or book. There's nothing worse than being cornered by a writer at a party and listening to him drone on, with every other sentence beginning *As I say in my book.*

I've come to look at neurotic behavior as a necessary component of a writer's arsenal, the necessary defenses to screen out the rest of the world so that the ballet inside his head can begin to take shape. Yet just as he needs to block out distraction in order to work, he also needs to let a certain amount filter through. The writer tries desperately to control this flow as he wrestles with sentences on the one hand and the requirements of social life on the other. Inevitably, there are eruptions of mood, of manner, of dermis. The writer struggles to satisfy himself and also meet the minimum requirements most spouses and families expect. He loves his cage and hates his cage. "I am in chains," cried Kafka to his beloved. "Don't touch my chains."

What are we to make of writers who claim that nothing makes them as miserable as writing, and then swear never to be

happier than when they are in the throes of a book? "The professional writers who dread writing, as many do, are usually
those whose critical sense is not only strong but unsleeping, so
that it won't allow them to do even a first draft at top speed,"
explained Malcolm Cowley in his introduction to a volume of
Paris Review interviews. "They are in most cases the 'bleeders'
who write one sentence at a time and can't write it until the
sentence before has been revised." When William Styron, one
of the bleeders, according to Cowley, was asked if he enjoyed
writing, he replied, "I certainly don't. I get a fine warm feeling
when I'm doing well, but that pleasure is pretty much negated
by the pain of getting started each day. Let's face it, writing is
hell." For Hemingway, the pain and pleasure seemed more erot-
ically joined. "I don't [suffer] at all," he wrote. [I] suffer like a
bastard when [I] don't write, or just before, and feel empty and
fucked out afterwards. But [I] never feel as good as while writing." And in *A Moveable Feast*, Hemingway again draws a paral-
lel between the act of writing and lovemaking. "After writing a
story I was always empty and both sad and happy, as though I
had made love."

Analogies between sex and writing are unavoidable. "In the
beginning, when you first start out trying to write fiction, the
whole endeavor's about fun. You don't expect anybody else to
read it. You're writing almost wholly to get yourself off," writes
David Foster Wallace in the anthology *Why I Write*. "Then, if
you have good luck and people seem to like what you do, and
you actually start to get paid for it . . . then things start to get
complicated and confusing, not to mention scary. . . . You're no

longer writing just to get yourself off, which—since any kind of masturbation is lonely and hollow—is probably good. But what replaces the onanistic motive. . . . Onanism gives way to attempted seduction, as a motive."

Connecting with another human being, whether between the sheets of your book or the bedsheets, involves some kind of seduction. Just as it is said that no one really knows what goes on inside a marriage, so it might also be said that no one really knows what happens between an author and a reader. This much is true: Wooing a reader involves a certain amount of courtship, though one of the great mistakes a writer can make is to behave like the literary equivalent of a suitor who comes on too strong. In his excitement, he lets fly all his passion in the first few moments or exposes more than the reader really needs or wants to know. Too often, the neurotic writer who still hasn't learned to trust his own voice rushes to spill the beans, when they might have been better left to stew.

Often a subtle gesture or the withholding of information creates the greatest tension or intrigue. Think of the novelist Kazuo Ishiguro and his superb portrait of frustrated love and repression in *The Remains of the Day*. He creates an extraordinary moment when the young Miss Kenton happens upon Mr. Stevens, the senior butler with whom she is falling in love, reading a cheap romance in the pantry. The butler fiercely guards against her discovering the contents of the book, but Miss Kenton keeps advancing. "Then she was standing before me, and suddenly the atmosphere underwent a peculiar change—almost as though the two of us had been suddenly thrust on to some other plane of being altogether. I am afraid it is not easy to describe clearly what I mean here." The reader yearns for him to throw the silly book down and take Miss Kenton in his arms. But true to his character, the butler, though briefly stirred from his perfectly controlled world, promptly returns to his asexual asceticism after chiding and dismissing his charge. The chaste scene, with its few carefully chosen words, contains more passion than most fully furnished sex scenes.

❦

If there's anything writers are more neurotic about than writing, it's money. Only a fortunate few can actually make a living from writing, and the struggle to support a career that offers no guarantees, no benefits, and no security makes most writers more than a little anxious. Always there is the hope of "hitting the jackpot," having one's work met with praise as well as an audience of some amplitude. When asked how he felt about becoming wealthy by his account of having been poor, Frank McCourt, in a *New York Times Magazine* feature on the "new gilded age," responded, "Because I profited from a book about poverty, irony is my constant companion." When asked if his financial success had a downside, McCourt was characteristically amusing. "There is no downside. Money allows you to whine to your heart's content, and to be as happy or miserable as you choose. If your friends don't want to listen to your complaints, cast them aside! There are plenty of people who, for a large fee, will listen to the whines of the wealthy."

Writer Matthew Klam, the author of the *Times* article, volubly complained that while his friends are Lear-jetting about, the most he'd ever made was $21,000 in a year when he sold some short stories and a book proposal he still hadn't finished. He complained that his lowly financial status is embarrassing, especially when he talks to a good friend who's about to purchase a yacht. "Some days, to ease the undercurrent of tension when we talk," writes Klam, "he pretends to envy me. 'You write because you have no choice, Klam,' he says. 'It's your calling, so stop complaining. Your whole day could be spent in a bathrobe.'"

Many people think that writers, successful or not, actually do spend their entire lives in pajamas. There is a disbelief in our culture that writing, or the creation of any art, is actually work. One of my writers was seeing a therapist with the stated goal of, among other things, taking herself more seriously as a writer, though she already had two critically acclaimed books to her credit. Still, on more than one occasion the therapist felt no compunction in asking the writer to change the time of her appointment. When the writer protested, the therapist explained that since the writer didn't have a "job," moving her appointment shouldn't be a problem. On top of that, the therapist wanted her to come in during the morning (my author's best writing hours) when, the therapist explained, most people were at work; she saved the after-five sessions for the gainfully employed.

The world does not owe writers a living. Still, some writers insist that writing for anything other than money is foolish. Samuel Johnson was one of the earliest defenders of this notion, saying, "No man but a blockhead ever wrote, except for money."

Dorothy Parker, when asked the source of her impetus to write, after roundly dismissing her childhood as inspiration, replied with characteristic brevity, "Need of money, dear." Capote, at the very beginning of his career, insisted on the importance of getting paid. "I never write—indeed, I am physically incapable of writing—anything that I don't think I will be paid for." Few writers start earning money right out of the gate, as Capote did, and most struggle for years before their efforts receive any compensation. But if money is what a writer is after, as opposed to, say, publication, why wouldn't he pursue a career on Wall Street or in some other lucrative profession? Show me a blockhead who says he writes for money and I'll show you a big fat liar.

When Joyce Maynard was accused of writing her Salinger memoir to make money, she voiced a fair opinion. "It troubles me that people speak about writing for money as ugly and distasteful. During the first flurry of criticism for this book, all kinds of people said, 'Oh, she's doing it for the money.' And I thought, Well of course I get paid! Imagine someone suggesting that a doctor shouldn't get paid." But later, in what I think is a more deeply truthful reflection, Maynard also confessed that "no amount of money" could have persuaded her to write this story at any other stage of her life. "And it wouldn't be something I'd get into now if I didn't feel it was the right thing to do." As far as I can tell, people write for exactly two reasons: (1) They are compelled to, and (2) they want to be loved.

Maynard must have known that writing about Jerry Salinger would invite derision. Yet she clearly hoped that people would be interested in her story and empathize with her, no matter how naive that hope now seems. No amount of money can compensate for a writer's lifetime of sacrifices—sacrifices that no one has asked him to make and that few truly appreciate. As a culture we are interested only in success, and by that measure the successful artist's suffering is negated when he wins either monetary or critical acclaim. While the writer whose work fails to find any currency is utterly dismissed. It's a no-win situation. Working in the face of so little understanding must be debilitating, though I fondly recall some remarks Tracy Kidder shared at a sales conference. He described the difficulty of hanging out at an old-age home as he gathered the material for his book *Old Friends*. After describing how depressing the experience could be at times, and how it forced him to grapple with his own mortality, Kidder smirked and looked out at his devoted sales force with his characteristic twinkle. "I'm not gonna bullshit you guys," he said. "I also go fishing every day. How bad can it be?"

Still, I believe that some writers find it easier, or a better coping mechanism, to say that they have chosen a certain topic because it will pay than to acknowledge the personal cost and sacrifice of writing. In a letter to his patron during a crisis of faith, Chekhov confided, "There are moments when I positively lose heart. For whom and for what do I write? . . . Does the public need me or not? I cannot make it out. Write for money? But I never have money, and from the habit of it I am almost indifferent to it. For the sake of money I work poorly." You can't help but wonder if Chekhov wasn't trying a little reverse psychology on his patron, just as Hemingway, echoing the same idea a century later, confessed to Maxwell Perkins in a letter

that he didn't "think there is any question about artistic integri-
ties. It has always been much more exciting to write than to be
paid for it and if I can keep on writing we may eventually all
make some money."

I've heard more than a few writers, upon receiving their
first book contract, exclaim that they would have done the
work for free, so thrilled are they to finally land a publisher.
Short-story writer Nathan Englander, in a *New York Times* interview, said he would have been just as happy to get a complete
set of the Modern Library from his publisher than the highly
publicized advance he received; he was just thrilled to be published by Knopf. Now he tells them! Though Englander might
be a blockhead for saying so, I believe that most writers are motivated by the same love of books.

If there were some way to ensure that doing good work or
working hard would guarantee some kind of financial return,
the way investing in a money market fund does, the writer motivated by money could type his copy into the ATM machine
and wait for his cash. Likewise, any publisher motivated solely
by profit would do better to liquidate his assets and invest his
money in long-term bonds. Though publishers look bigger and
badder with every passing day, it's still a nickel-and-dime business, as one of my first mentors said when I stared in numb
shock at my first profit-and-loss sheet and contemplated how
little profit every book actually generated. If you want money,
invest in stocks. It's that simple. For the working writer there
are simply no reliable dividends. And in a world where self-
worth is measured by one's portfolio, it's awfully hard to keep
singing for your supper.

When writers hear about huge advances for seemingly ludicrous projects or see books they deem unworthy rise on the bestseller lists, they begin to wonder if there isn't some master plot that has been set in motion for the express purpose of driving them mad. A writer's self-worth is tied up in a great many things, but money has the distinction of being the most tangible item in a sea of intangibles. I was taken by a comment Stephen King made in a 1991 *Publishers Weekly* interview. Here was a writer whose body of work at that time included more than 89 million copies of his twenty-seven books in print saying, "I'd like to win the National Book Award, the Pulitzer Prize, the Nobel Prize, I'd like to have someone write a *New York Times Book Review* piece that says, 'Hey, wait a minute, guys, we made a mistake—this guy is one of the great writers of the twentieth century.' But it's not going to happen, for two reasons. One is I'm not the greatest writer of the twentieth century, and other is that once you sell a certain number of books, the people who think about 'literature' stop thinking about you and assume that any writer who is popular across a wide spectrum has nothing to say. The unspoken postulate is that intelligence is rare. It's clear in the critical stance; I hear it in the voice of people from the literary journals where somebody will start by saying, 'I don't read Stephen King,' and they are really saying, 'I don't lower myself.'"

Ask a writer whether he'd rather sell a lot of copies or win the National Book Award, and you will better understand his particular motivations. A rational person wouldn't hesitate to answer the question: understanding that more sales means a wider readership and more money, he would pick copies sold.

But most writers want prestige as much as they want money. I don't think that King would give up a single one of his millions of followers for any prize, though the exclusion of his genre by the literary establishment clearly chafes. Writers should want money; writers deserve money. And I salute any writer who feels he is fairly compensated. But I will never believe that writers are motivated by money—at least not at the outset of their careers. Writers want love, and they hope that through their work, they will be recognized as special. And that is why most writers are so crazy. When a writer gives his editor the pages of his manuscript, he is, in essence, handing over his heart on a plate. And until he gets a response, his entire sense of himself is in limbo. It's like waiting for the results of a biopsy.

❧

As an editor, I was known for having particularly neurotic authors, people who needed what we refer to in the business as lots of handholding. Every editor becomes a de facto therapist, whether or not he engages in the therapeutic as well as the editorial process. His author presents a set of symptoms as clearly as a patient visiting a doctor. Editors have to figure out how to get pages out of those who can't let go. We have to reassure those who can't stop revising (often making the book worse). We have authors who call every day, more than once a day, and those who never call. Those who tell you they want one thing while their agent tells you they want another. Some writers constantly bait their editor for information about other authors. Most lie or exaggerate about how little of our time and attention they need, how much of the editing they accepted, how grateful they are for our efforts. There are myriad ways an author's insecurities may manifest, whether in oversolicitousness or downright abuse. And editors, in turn, respond abusively or solicitously, depending on what the author's behavior provokes in us.

I felt privileged to witness the innermost anxiety of my writers, vicariously living the author's life through those whose books I helped bring into the world. I was fascinated by the way they coped during the nerve-racking months approaching publication. Writers crave and fear exposure in different measures, and how well they deal with becoming public can be a predictor of future success. I was also emboldened by the strength of those whose convictions were tested when their work provoked strong reactions. I was never more proud than when one author held her ground during a heated debate about her book following a reading. At one point a belligerent man stood up with a raised fist and declared that not only was her book a disgrace but that she had wasted her Ivy League education to boot. She told him he didn't have to buy or read her book if he didn't want to, and as far as she was concerned, he could write his own damn book.

When an editor works with an author, she cannot help seeing into the medicine cabinet of his soul. All the terrible emotions, the desire for vindication, the paranoia, and the projection are bottled in there, along with all the excesses of envy, desire for revenge, all the hypochondriacal responses, rituals, and defenses, and the twin obsessions with sex and money. In other words, the stuff of great books. Of course, without craft, no amount of personal eccentricity, no depth of human strangeness will make your work good. You must channel your neurosis in the service of prolonging and improving your writing life. Otherwise, just as surely as the phobic becomes paralyzed in the face of his terror, you will turn writing into your enemy; it, too, in a final paranoid twist, will seem to be out to get you.

Nothing is more vexing for an editor than trying to help a writer who has become too neurotic to write. Scared and defensive, riddled with rationales and justifications, provisions and excuses, he can no longer get back to that place where writing is like a balm. But when the writer faces it all down and delivers something on the page that strikes the heart as true, all is forgiven.

6.

TOUCHING

FIRE

THE ONLY PLACE YOU'RE LIKELY TO FIND more alcoholics than an AA meeting is a writing program. While I was in graduate school, a group of so-called cowboy poets were famous for going out every night and getting drunk, which invariably led to brawling or other crazy behavior, which they would then boast about in the writing lounge the next day, swigging down the tarlike coffee that must certainly be a staple of every writing department lounge. They would get tight and loosen a tooth or two. They would carouse and cheat on their girlfriends back home, wherever that was. They cavalierly rolled their spiral notebooks (no fabric-covered journals for these cowboys) into the back pockets of their jeans as they swaggered into class, always late and always needing to borrow something: a pen, a lighter, an aspirin. They were young guys, getting off on their youth, their muscular poems, their own sense of reverie, as if they had personally discovered language. They took leaks wherever they liked, marking the city and their haunts like a pack of dogs. The booze helped them bond; it lit them up and fueled the nocturnal adventures they later wrote about. Everyone in the program naturally resented them: they were arrogant; they were good-looking. They played their parts so well, it seemed as if central casting had sent us those big drinking poets.

Central casting also sent our writing workshop a few garden-variety drunks, whose drinking led to melancholia rather than carousing and whose poems tended toward the self-pitying. We had one stone-cold junkie, one Valium zombie, a handful of students taking antidepressants (this was before Prozac, a medication that has undoubtedly changed the face of writing programs across the country), a manic-depressive or two, and one wreck who might have walked out of a Cindy Sherman photograph. Every time this woman needed a lipstick or something else from her bag, she made an enormous show of emptying its contents onto the conference table, spilling vials of pills along with keys and combs and pens and papers. Then she would make a frantic show of collecting the contents, stretching her body across the table to retrieve the runaway vials. Of course, we resented her, too. *Such a display! Such carrying on!*

I realize only now that in her own incoherent way she was asking for help. While we romanticize alcoholism and drug addiction in fiction and poetry, the reality is that we flee from those who can't hold their liquor, from those whose instability threatens to capsize our own wobbly ships. Alcoholic and other addictive behaviors keep people away. I had been editing for enough years to know better than to acquire a project from a writer only a year in recovery from his addiction. But I loved his proposal and hoped that the contract would give him a cushion. Though he remained clean, he failed to change any behavior beyond giving up the actual drugs. He would disappear for months at a time, take weeks to return my call, and then promise more pages than even Rumpelstiltskin might have been able to spin from the raw material of his life. I'd beg him to set a realistic goal, such as twenty pages by the end of the month, but he would promise to churn out seventy-five pages in two weeks. We'd go back and forth on this, with him insisting that he needed the pressure to produce. "I'm not just a heroin addict," he'd say with a laugh. "I'm a pressure junkie, too."

I'd assure him that I would be happy with any number of pages he could produce, but I needed some evidence of progress to keep granting him extensions on the project. He'd always sympathize with my position, even joke about my rotten luck for getting him as an author. We'd end the call with some jokes and a mini–pep talk, and I'd hang up the phone all but certain that I'd never see a page. And sadly, I never did. Even after we had been through this drill more than a few times, I would grow frantic when my phone calls to him went unreturned. I would call his agent, and we would both leave worried messages, hoping against hope that he wasn't using drugs again, spiraling into oblivion. Eventually he would call. No, he hadn't been using, only avoiding the project with the fervor with which he once scored drugs. Apologies and guilty self-recriminations would inevitably ensue, an extension would be granted. Finally I realized that I had become part of a new addictive cycle through which this writer replayed his life's central drama: the story of the boy who was worse than everyone else, the story of a boy beyond help. After three years we canceled the contract. It was the only project I ever lost.

Some might argue that the addict renders those who would help him impotent, caught in the powerful grip of his addiction. After the commercial failure of *The Great Gatsby*, F. Scott Fitzgerald's deterioration escalated and his hard drinking began to alienate those closest to him, including his lifelong agent, Harold Ober. After Ober refused to bail Fitzgerald out for the umpteenth time, Fitzgerald broke off business relations. His life from that point on reads like a catalogue of binges, self-recriminations, delusions of productive work and new ideas, periods of being on and off the wagon. The syndrome became so predictable, according to A. Scott Berg in his biography of Maxwell Perkins, that when Fitzgerald secluded himself in a North Carolina hotel to dry out, the loyal editor anticipated the eventual fallout. "He knew Fitzgerald would need the support of all the friends that he could get, but Scott was hard put to find them just then. That year, almost simultaneously, three of his friendships with Perkins's writers deteriorated."

Can you imagine Ernest Hemingway, Thomas Wolfe, and Ring Lardner doing an intervention for their old friend? The sad truth is that alcoholism and addiction have always wrecked lives, and nothing is more painful than watching a brilliant young writer turn into a pathetic drunk or addict, making excuses for months or even years to cover for a lack of productivity, showing up hours late for every appointment, eyes dilated into huge saucers, finally turning in pages so frantic or sloppy in their composition that an editor despairs of being able to make anything out of them.

Drinking or drugging is always a flight response, whether it's from fame, critical attack, rejection, or most commonly, being unable to produce. When an excess of desire and ambition is met with frustration, when all the longing in the world doesn't materialize in a coherent sequence of pages, the vulnerable writer may reach for his favorite poison. I have watched writers lose years to alcohol abuse and then blame the drinking on their inability to write. The writing life is fraught with situations that would drive even the most temperate person to drink. How writers deal with the disappointments and disturbances is as various as the people writing. Pearl Kazin Bell remarked that "Dylan Thomas knew when he was in his mid-thirties that he was never going to write the kind of poetry he had written during the war, that it would just be a bad imitation of things he had done before. I think that's one of the reasons he went on drinking—to be done with it."

✦

From de Quincey's opium eaters to John Cheever's dissolute diaries, history shows that writers and artists have more than their share of addictions. What is unclear is whether they or the culture is more responsible for exaggerating and elevating those excesses to dramatic and, in some cases, romantic-seeming proportions. The reality is that every time someone acts out, loses control, winds up in Silver Hill or, worse, dies by his own hand, some little part of us either condemns such behavior or breathes a sigh of relief. *There but for the grace of God go I.* As a culture, we are as drawn to the Dionysian part of our being as we are wary of it. Self-destruction has a mythical hold on our collective unconscious. The tension is forever fueled by the conflict between our puritanical heritage and our desire for inalienable freedom.

Dramatic drug and alcohol abuse by writers has been overshadowed in the last twenty to thirty years by pyrotechnical drug and alcohol abuse by rock stars, Hollywood actors, and political wives. The glossy magazines are more eager to cover the rehab comings and goings, or slipping and sliding, of Robert Downey, Jr., than to follow the hot new poet at the Iowa Writers' Workshop. Today's writer, unless he dies with a needle in his arm or inside a hotel room littered with bottles, is simply of no interest to the paparazzi. Plus, many of today's writers, mercifully, have sobered up.

As Denis Johnson wrote in "Now," the most widely quoted poem from his first collection, *The Incognito Lounge,* which was circulated widely at AA meetings during the 1980s because it represented a new voice for the newly sober, "Darkness, my name is Denis Johnson / and I am almost ready to / confess." The lines fairly echoed the cadence of the standard AA greeting: *Hello, my name is X, and I am an alcoholic.* Finally, here was a writer chasing down his demons instead of the other way around.

In the last few years we have seen William Burroughs's masterpiece, *Junky,* morph into Linda Yablonsky's *The Story of Junk.* Pete Hamill, the nineties version of a hard-drinking reporter, sobers up and writes a memoir about it in *A Drinking Life*. Another memoir about giving up the sauce, *Drinking: A Love Story*, pops onto the bestseller list. James Atlas writes a piece lamenting that the good old days of wine and roses are history: "The drunken dinner party, the makeout session in a bathroom at Nell's, the joint inhaled in a taxi full of revelers careering through SoHo at dawn—these are ancient history by now, exotica recorded in some yellowed Jay McInerney novel that's gathering dust on the shelf." While aware of his romanticizing, Atlas laments the cultural shift, both economic and political, that no longer celebrates the daring, outsider status of the artist. "Writers and artists wrecked their health, destroyed their marriages, and died young so that the rest of America could enjoy art from a safe distance. The sacrifice had to be made. It was their job. Surely this was the lesson of Hemingway blowing his brains out, of Jackson Pollock wrapping his car around a tree. They died that art might live."

It's hard not to get wistful reading about the various debaucheries chronicled in Atlas's article, the hungover Robert Lowell chain-smoking in the basement of Quincy House, the young, drunken Mailer "brandishing a bottle of whisky" in Sanders Theatre, Hemingway downing daiquiris in Key West. It's easy to imagine that Pollock foretold his chrome-exploding death in every painting he detonated on canvas. But these are not the good old days. These are the days of twelve-step programs, when alcoholism is understood as a disease, not a side effect or an occupational hazard of being a tortured artist. James Atlas might also lament the days when *The New Yorker* didn't run letters to the editor, since he was roundly scolded by Susan Cheever the week after his article ran. "I was amazed to read James Atlas's romantic evocation of the fun we used to have in the New York Literary World. As someone who was a child at those parties where Literary Greats stumbled around lecherously in an opaque cloud of cigarette smoke, I can testify that for those involved—certainly for many wives and most children—that scene was anything but fun. A tragedy of the generation that came before ours was that many of this country's wonderful writers were also alcoholics. Every drunk—whether or not he can write—leaves a trail of destruction, desolation, confusion, and sadness which goes on for generations. It's certainly true that my father's novels and stories are redolent with romantic images of the perfect martini and the ideal adultery, but those stories are *fiction*—images created by a man who never found either."

Indeed. Cheever's journals mark each tortured juncture along the way of his alcoholic dissolution. From the earliest entries to the last, one sees a man struggling with a drinking problem in all its Sisyphean heartbreak. In a 1952 entry Cheever describes the cycle in a moment of total clarity: "When the beginnings of self-destruction enter the heart it seems no bigger than a grain of sand. . . . But when you try to trace back the way you came into this abyss all you find is a grain of sand." By the end of the decade, he is completely resigned, though still somewhat cavalier about his problem. "I am a solitary drunkard. . . . At four or half past four or sometimes five I stir up a Martini, thinking that a great many men who can't write as well as I can already have set themselves down at bar stools." Just a year later Cheever confesses to the toll drinking is taking on his life. "In the morning I am deeply depressed, my insides barely function, my kidney is painful, my hands shake, and walking down Madison Avenue I am in fear of death. . . . I would very easily destroy myself. It is ten o'clock now and I am thinking of a noontime snort."

In charting the ever-diminishing hour from which he is able to successfully abstain from drinking, Cheever remains painfully aware of his losing battle. "Now Thursday morning," he writes in 1967. "Twenty minutes to eleven. I am in the throes of a grueling booze fight. . . . There is really nothing to do but sit here and sweat it out. I can write myself a letter. Dear Myself, I am having a terrible time with booze. Ride it out."

By 1972, Cheever confesses that the "cruel addiction" has accelerated to the point where it starts sometimes before daybreak. "On waking, I want a drink. . . . Now I can think of nothing but the taste of whiskey. . . . At about half past nine my hands begin to shake so that I can't hold a paper or type correctly." Later that same year Cheever finally, mercifully, takes his first faltering steps toward getting help. "After planning to visit A.A. for twenty years," he writes, "I finally make it."

✦

As we learn more about addiction, genetics, and brain chemistry, it seems likely that those who are prone to self-medication may also have a physiological quirk that contributes to the increased craving. It may be merely a genetic glitch that makes one person more susceptible to the addictive powers of drink than another. Whether an artistic temperament is a feature of that same genetic complexity remains to be seen. But even if the link proves dubious, the writers who most publicly drowned their sorrows—Poe, Coleridge, Lowell, Berryman, Sexton, and Thomas—provide enough lore to keep alive the notion that the artistic temperament is inextricably linked to self-medicating behaviors.

Being a writer or wanting to write is to live in a perpetual state of anxiety, where the chances of failing far outweigh the rate of success. It's a constant free fall, especially between projects, for the celebrated and the unknown alike. "Everything is will and the great obstacle is fear," said Gordon Lish in an interview about writing. "It comes down in every instance to this dualism between what one wants and what one may be afraid to have." When the fear becomes overwhelming, when the anxiety nearly takes you out, it may seem that only a gin and tonic can take the terrible edge off. Hard-drinking poets, misunderstood artists, and junkie novelists will go to any length to quell the panic that builds inside them as they contemplate actually writing something or mounting a stage. According to Diane Wood Middlebrook, Anne Sexton needed to drink before every public appearance and had developed a "set of rituals" to get her through her reading tours. "Arriving in any hotel room, she followed an inviolable procedure, going directly to the bathroom to turn on the shower full blast and hang her performance clothes in the steam, then to the ice machine for supplies to chill the first of many glasses of vodka tipped from the stash in her suitcase. Juiced, she was manic, an absolute necessity for performing."

Writers have always used drugs and drink to disinhibit themselves. In the beginning, the intoxicating effects of alcohol and drugs can prove prodigious. But once the tail is wagging the dog, the effects are generally deleterious. "God is your type-writer," a priest once told Sexton, during what appeared to be a spiritual crisis when she could no longer connect the words to her vision, but as her biographer wrote: "Alcohol was now Sexton's chief, self-prescribed medication, taken morning, noon, and night." When a writer crosses the line, when the addiction is all-consuming, even the redemptive powers of art are ren-dered mute. The typewriter is mute. "Alcohol helped generate the curves of feeling on which her poetry lifted its wings," con-tinues Middlebrook, "but it dropped her too, into depression, remorse, sleeplessness, paranoia—the normal host of furies that pursue alcoholics. . . . She had the drunk's fluency but not the artist's cunning."

✦

The only literary affliction more romanticized than addiction is mental illness. The connection between artistic temperament and manic-depressive illness has been extensively described in Kay Redfield Jamison's book *Touched with Fire*. In reviewing the most recent research available, Jamison concludes that com-pared with the general public, writers and artists exhibit a vastly disproportionate rate of manic-depressive or depressive illness. However, and this is the part that is all too often overlooked, "not all (not even most) writers and artists suffer from major mood disorders." It's just that manic bursts of artistic creation make for better copy. Mania is nothing if not intoxicating. And when it is joined with creative energy and vision and inspiration, the results can be dazzling. More often than not, however, the mania is attached to darker forces, and at the very height of an artist's performance there may come the killing hand.

We confer greatness only posthumously upon those who suffer from mental illness. In life, unless you have your disease under control, it will be a source of speculative talk for most people, if not of downright derision. No matter what you do or what you produce, rumors about your so-called condition will follow you, and your behavior, opinions, and work will be scrutinized for signs of your illness. I will never forget an editorial meeting I attended in London a number of years ago. A famous older editor began the meeting by announcing that he wanted to publish the British edition of William Styron's book *Darkness Visible*, about the writer's nervous breakdown. He became increasingly voluble during the meeting, insisting on the importance of the book. The newly installed and rather arrogant young editor-in-chief shot down the acquisition with the classic "too American." At this, the older editor started pounding the table with his fists, searching our stunned faces for commiseration. Then he turned to me, waved the slim volume in my face, and said, "You're American, tell him why it's a bestseller." I was stunned into silence, though I knew the publishing history of the book quite well. First serialized in Tina

Brown's *Vanity Fair*, it had been the talk of New York. The older editor gave me a look I will never forget, the look of a betrayed man. Then he sent the book flying down the center of the conference table in a gesture of surrender and disgust and marched out of the meeting. The editor sitting next to me leaned over and conspiratorially whispered, "He's mad, you know." I later learned that in fact he did suffer from manic-depressive illness.

If you suffer from manic depression, your work and behavior will be judged accordingly. Is your excessive output the result of your mania? Are you brilliant or just theatrical? Are you truly suffering or self-indulgent? No one will say, if your book is years late in coming, Give him as much time as he needs, he's a mad genius. No one sits in an auditorium for hours after a reading is supposed to begin waiting for the mad-genius writer to show up. People don't tolerate the erratic behavior that usually accompanies mood swings—at least not for long. Sure, if they were expecting Virginia Woolf, Lord Byron, or Vincent van Gogh to give a talk, they'd probably wait around. After the fact, after genius is recognized, everyone wants to get up close. But if you had known van Gogh during his lifetime and had seen him in his final months, you probably would have dismissed him as crazy. Most of the world did, especially the people of Arles, who petitioned that van Gogh should remain in confinement following his ear-cutting episode.

We are likewise fascinated, after the fact, by suicide. A person contemplating suicide is not inherently interesting; in fact, his self-absorption can be repelling. Just as colleagues will distance themselves from a person about to lose his job, we tend to distance ourselves from the drowning man lest we get dragged under. It's only after you're gone that the flowers and tributes pour in. Sylvia Plath made so many attempts that her loved ones were probably sick of her. Just keeping up with her mood swings must have been as toxic as inhaling secondhand smoke. Even the briefest sampling of the poet's diary is dizzying in its bipolarity:

> *Tuesday, February 10:* How clear and cleansed and happy I feel.
> *Thursday, February 20:* I myself am the vessel of tragic experience.
> *Tuesday afternoon, March 11:* Oh how my own life shines, beckons . . .
> *Thursday morning, April 17:* I feel as I were rising from a grave, gathering my moldy, worm-riddled limbs in a final effort.

The person bouncing between the poles of mania and depression and/or obsessed with destroying himself is noxious, and most people are worn thin by the constant dependency and the broken promises of a brighter future. The person aloft in manic flight is so utterly self-involved and delusional that his very state of acceleration precludes communion. He is Icarus-like in his quest, which is certain to end in flames. The reason we romanticize these artists is that on some level they make us feel safe. The person touched with fire becomes the container for all of our own suicidal tendencies, the excess emotions that frighten and weaken us. The person who crosses the line stands for our collective self-destructive impulses and maybe, for just a little while, sates the savage god.

Depression, on the other hand, with none of the high-octane creative output, the hypersexuality, the brain computing faster than a superconductor, is a pure drag. The wool-blanketed brain of the depressive fights for a clarity that is just beyond reach. For a person whose emotional oxygen supply grows weaker by the day, there is nothing worse than morning, than springtime, than signs of life. Someone in the throes of clinical depression slowly but surely stops functioning. Very few artists manage to create anything at all during depressive episodes. Mania only makes you think you are great; it does not ensure greatness. And depression only makes you feel worthless; it does not confer worthlessness. It's hard enough to know if your writing is any good without the distorted valuations produced by mood swings.

Still, the evidence we have from writers themselves—whether it's high-flown couplets by Shelley and Byron espousing the genius of madness or the stripped-down confessions of Plath and Lowell—testifies to the depth of intensity that we associate with madness. Art born of illness isn't better because of the illness, though the subject of illness itself can be tantalizing. If the artist takes his mental state as his subject, and if a striking body of work is produced in a manic frenzy, as van Gogh's final paintings apparently were, or as Plath, who wrote her final poems at two a day in the last months of her life, it tends to leave an indelible mark.

It's not surprising when a writer, in the youthful desire to create an artistic persona, gravitates toward the seductive edge described in the work of these artists. But as Kay Redfield Jamison rightly points out, "Most of the controversy surrounding the 'mad genius' debate versus 'healthy artist' debate, however, arises from confusion about what is actually meant by 'madness,' as well as from a fundamental lack of understanding about the nature of manic depressive illness." It's one thing to have intense feelings and indulge one's moods; it's quite another to be catatonic or delusional. I don't think anyone has better summed up the terrible waste that results from manic depression than Robert Lowell in a conversation with his publisher, Robert Giroux, after starting the then newly available drug lithium carbonate, which apparently was extremely effective for the poet. "It's terrible, Bob," he said, "to think that all I've suffered, and all the suffering I've caused, might have arisen from the lack of a little salt in my brain."

Mental illness is still stigmatized and stigmatizing. Whether you live out your insanity undiagnosed and untreated or struggle to find adequate therapy and medications, the path to treatment is rocky and hellish, filled with sycophants and doctors who are more serious mental cases than their patients; medications, if they are useful at all, tend to become less effective over time, and no one really knows anything about doses, side effects, or long-term use. You are never home free.

Still, it's nearly impossible not to romanticize Lowell's illness, his breakdowns, his circle of friends, including Pound, Eliot, Tate, Bishop, Berryman, Jarrell, and Thomas. It's hard not to romanticize his brief encounter at Boston University with the young student Sylvia Plath. Then there were his marriages to three beautiful women writers—Jean Stafford, Elizabeth Hardwick, and Caroline Blackwood—and his supposedly voracious

sexual appetite, which led to the nickname Cal, short for Calig-
ula. And there are the poems, the brilliant formal stanzas of
his youth, the so-called confessional or breakthrough poems of
his middle years and the final poems, rendered in Lowell's
exquisite language stripped down to the core. Take any writer
who has likewise suffered—Blake, Keats, Lowry, Sexton—and
extract only the dramatic highs and the exquisite works of art
left in the wake of the daily disasters, and you will imagine a life
of thrilling artistic genius. When Ted Hughes published what
would be his final collection of poems, about his life with Plath,
it became the rare and anomalous book of poems to appear on
the bestseller list. After so much silence and so many years, a
substantial audience still yearned to spend another moment with
our beloved Sylvia, as if doing so could somehow save her.

✻

I can usually tell within seconds whether one of my writers is
flying high or sinking into depression. The voice gives it all
away: the breathlessness and giddiness of the manic; the monotone or quavering delivery of the depressed. When writers disappear and fail to deliver pages, depression is usually the
reason, and there is very little an editor can do or say to convince them that it will lift, that they will write again. Likewise,
when writers work at a fever pitch, driven by mania or massive
quantities of stimulants, they tend to think they've produced
their best work ever and can become belligerent or hostile when
informed otherwise.

While more than a few of my authors have been in treatment at one time or another, only once did I receive a call from an author's psychiatrist. The doctor told me that my publisher and I were putting undue pressure on this writer, that she needed more time to finish her book, and that touring would probably kill her. I had begged the writer dozens of times over the months during which we were supposed to get the book into production to call it quits and take a much-needed rest. I cited other great writers who suffered breakdowns along the way and to whom we gave extensions in light of health concerns. Long before her shrink came on the scene, I had made my own diagnosis.

But the writer begged and pleaded to keep the publication date. She swore she would get it all done. She said *not* getting the book done would kill her, and I went along with her. She began working around the clock, then took up residence in our offices, where I'd find her collapsed most mornings, a new sheaf of pages spun out on my chair, sometimes brilliant, sometimes incomprehensible. The office she inhabited began to look like an art installation at the Whitney, every surface covered with books, pages, articles, empty cartons of Chinese food, Styrofoam cups, brown bags leaking sugar packets from the endless cups of tea she consumed. The room resembled the inside of her head. And when she occasionally dozed off, my coworkers would peer in and whisper. No one knew what to do with her, and I was losing perspective on the book as well. Certainly what kept me going was my belief in her brilliance and her high-octane prose, which had an energizing effect on me that few other writers could approximate. But I had never been between such a rock and a hard place professionally, and I no longer knew what course of action would prove helpful or harmful. Near collapse myself, I confessed to our deputy publisher that I feared she would never stop revising. He offered to talk with her and impose a final deadline. Then he invoked those two words we all remember well from high school as we raced to finish a test we felt certain we'd fail: *Pencils down.*

In the end she forged ahead and we went forward with the book's publication. I still sometimes wonder if we made the right decision, though I will always be deeply proud of the book. My author was hardly the first to fall apart while producing some of the best writing of her career. Even after what we went through, it's hard not to romanticize that terrifying chapter in her life, and in retrospect I can't help feeling that the frenzy and drama were as much a part of the method as the madness. She convinced me that going forward saved her. Had she been wrong, I would never have forgiven myself.

These questions of art versus life always put me in mind of that high school game we used to play where we pondered what we'd do if the Louvre was burning. You can make only one trip; what do you save? The child stuck inside, or the Mona Lisa? Some, unable to accept the rules, argued for saving both. Some would save the art. For me, there was never any choice. I would save the child.

For writers whose problems are less extreme, I recommend swimming or running; for some, doing laps is lifesaving. I recommend volunteer work: *Get outside yourself!* Or maybe giving up smoking wasn't such a great idea after all. And yes, I recommend therapy. "Many artists and writers believe that turmoil, suffering, and extremes in emotional experience are integral not only to the condition of human suffering but to their abilities as artists," writes Jamison. "They fear that psychiatric treatment will transform them into normal, well adjusted, dampened, and bloodless souls—unable, or unmotivated to write, paint or compose." It may be hard to envision William Blake on the couch describing his visions, or Hemingway droning on to a small bearded man about his cat fetish, but if you can't get your work done because you are suffering from some form of malaise or agitation, avail yourself of help. Writers live inside their heads more than most people. Having someone to let off some of the steam to may not be a bad thing. And more important, creativity is inalienable. No shrink can take it away from you.

No matter how much we may listen to Prozac in our age of feel-good self-improvement, we are still fascinated by altered states, creative genius, mental illness, and suicide, because we all, just once, would like to touch fire. We too want to feel our wings spread as we soar toward the sun. As Anne Sexton wrote in one of her most perfectly realized poems, "I say Live, Live because of the sun/the dream, the excitable gift." Who knew better than she how, in playing with fire, one always gets burned.

PART II.
PUBLISHING

7.
MAKING CONTACT:
SEEKING AGENTS
AND PUBLICATION

WHILE I WAS IN GRADUATE SCHOOL, I RE-
plied to a classified ad in *The Village Voice*: "Sm Lit Agcy Sks P/T
Asst Gram Pk Loc." I took the Number 1 train from Columbia
University's 116th Street station down to Twenty-third Street
and wound my way east to Gramercy Park. Though I knew the
city well, the block took me by surprise, so pristine were the
brownstones, their long, graceful windows with heavy glazing
obscuring the scenes within. Lacquer-black wrought-iron banis-
ters with curlicues and ornate detail garnished the elegant stairs
that led up to the brightly painted doors. I approached with
awe and trepidation; could the smeared address on the news-
print in my now sweaty palm match up with one of these
beautiful buildings?

After college I had taken a job at an investment bank, whose
offices were housed in a midtown tower that boasted the charm
of a cell block. For two years I worked in a cold, impersonal
cubicle where I felt like a rat in someone's cruel laboratory ex-

periment. But now, as I wandered down this tree-lined street, I was transported to a nineteenth-century New York in a Jamesian swirl of excited anticipation. I was greeted at the door by a highly energetic and extremely skinny young woman, who told me to watch my step as we descended into what I would later learn was dubbed the Dungeon, the basement offices of the agency, where the young woman worked with a senior agent. The husband-and-wife team who owned the agency had their large loftlike offices in the aerie above.

The Dungeon consisted of two rooms connected by a long hall lined with bookcases. Every available surface was nearly toppling over with books. In the front office, a wall of manuscripts, file cabinets, and a Xerox machine held court. In the back were two desk areas, one looking long abandoned, piled high with old files. The other desk belonged to the senior agent, a beautiful woman with an extraordinary sense of stillness and grace, whose bulletin board was decorated with exquisite scraps, postcards, pieces of art, book jackets, and a variety of trinkets that I was eager to examine but tried to act nonchalant about. In comparison with the investment bank, where the only pieces of "art" allowed on the walls were framed tombstones from completed mergers, this office teemed with the life of the mind and creativity I had always craved.

The senior agent asked me why I wanted the job, and I explained that I hoped to acquire some worthwhile experience by the time I finished graduate school and that I had always imagined myself in either teaching or publishing. As she would later tell it, she tried everything she could to talk me out of publishing, but I only grew more smitten as she explained my various clerical responsibilities. Finally I felt bold enough to ask about one of the book jackets on her wall. I can still see the small, hand-tinted photograph of a young boy leaping a precipice at its center, and I admired it.

"Oh, do you like it?" she asked, removing the dust jacket from the wall. "It's one of mine."

Confused, I asked if she was a writer too.

"No, no. One of my writers," she laughed. "The jacket is for one of my authors, one of my *clients.*"

I didn't completely understand what she meant, and feeling a bit foolish for not understanding, I didn't pursue it. What I did know was that I was falling in love with the atmosphere; as I dared to look around the small room, I realized that every inch of available space was crowded with books. Finally, I was shown through a back door that led to a gorgeous garden, where I imagined lovely literary teas being served in the late afternoon. After I assured the senior agent that neither the low pay nor the long haul from Columbia would present any problem, she offered me the job.

A lot of people would have balked at the sheer amount of paperwork, the stacks of files that needed to be weeded out and sorted through, but I was a sponge soaking up every piece of information I could. It was all fascinating to me: the letters to publishers that accompanied the submissions, the rejection letters from the publishers, some so kind and apologetic, some deeply involving and full of interesting ideas about how the author might improve the material; others were terse, and still others were extraordinarily arrogant and unnecessarily hurtful. (One of my jobs was to send the rejection letters to the writers, culling those that might entice the razor blades out of the medicine cabinets.) I loved reading the letters the agents dashed off to clients, urging them on: *Great new chapter, keep up the good work.* Or the longer editorial letters offering structural advice, ideas about character development, or in one case, the suggestion to rewrite the novel from an entirely different point of view.

I marveled at the telexes we would receive from the UK and Spain, Japan and France. The foreign editions of books that arrived in their travel-weary cartons always looked a little hilarious with their incomprehensible titles and bad graphic art. Sometimes an author would drop by in the flesh, which always thrilled yet slightly embarrassed me. Somehow the real people behind the books, behind the files and letters and royalty statements, always seemed a little less glamorous than they had in my imagination. And then there was the retinue of foreign publishers and movie scouts and foreign agents who paraded through the office in search of projects for their own purposes. I'd often listen in on these meetings while I pretended to be otherwise engaged, filing royalty reports and mailing checks.

I did every kind of office work imaginable, but the most exciting and heady responsibility by far was reading. The first time the owner of the agency asked me if I read, I was taken aback. *Did I read? What was he thinking?* What he meant was did I want to read manuscripts from the unsolicited pile, a Pisa-like tower threatening to crash down at any time. When I replied in the affirmative, he handed over a manuscript box from the top of the pile and told me to bring it back with a reader's report. I so clearly remember reading those pages. It was over the Jewish New Year, and I sequestered myself with a blanket in a hammock off the side of the house, away from my family. I read all four hundred pages and took elaborate plot notes. Then I worked on a reader's report for most of the next day, describing the plot, the tone, the setting, the quality of the writing. On some level I knew that the book was terrible, obvious and clichéd in every way, but I felt in awe of the task and the attendant responsibility. Who was I, after all, to judge this writer? Who was I to pass judgment on this Joe Shmo who couldn't draw a convincing character or punctuate to save his life but who had, after all, written an entire novel? It was more than I had ever managed.

When I proudly handed in my four-page single-spaced report the following week, the owner took one look at it and said, "Do you really expect me to read this?"

Naturally, I was taken aback.

"Look," he said, "just tell me one thing. Did you like it?"

Did I like it? I didn't know what my liking it or disliking it had to do with anything. I had written a four-page critical report, a plot summary, an analysis of the author's intentions, and an assessment of the writing quality. *Did I like it?*

"No." I shrugged. "Not really."

"Then get rid of it," he said. "Write a rejection and I'll sign it."

I went back to my desk in the rear office and told the senior agent what had happened. I was more than a little agitated. I had spent the entire holiday working on the report, and on top of that I had the awful feeling that this guy's future was in my hands. *Who was I?*

"He didn't even want to read the report," I told her. "He just wants me to get rid of it."

"Well, kiddo," she said, "welcome to the real world."

I lost my publishing virginity that day. And I would lose it again and again at the hands of agents when I started my own eventual climb up the editorial ladder. One of my first mentors in the business referred to literary agents as necessary evils. In today's conglomeratization of publishing houses, they are more necessary than ever—and perhaps more evil. But even fifty years ago the need for good author representation was apparently keen. It was none other than legendary editor Maxwell Perkins who suggested that a young Putnam editor named Diarmuid Russell, who had been fired for taking the author's part in a dispute over a contract, join up with Henry Volkening and start a literary agency. Perkins felt there was a shortage of good agents, who could not only help clients sell their work to publishers but advise them in literary matters as well.

If there was a shortage fifty years ago, Perkins would no doubt be alarmed today at the glut. We now have all manner of agents: the mega-agent, the power agent, the boutique agent. We have West Coast agents, rugged northwestern agents, right-wing agents, old lefty agents, gay and lesbian agents, horror agents, Canadian agents, academic agents, psychology and self-help agents, wunderkind agents, science agents, political agents, journalist agents, pop culture agents, celebrity agents, and good old-fashioned plain literary agents. Some agents have become so powerful in their own right that they are widely known only by their given names. Like Cher, Sting, and Madonna, the most powerful agents in the book business are known as Mort, Lynn, Esther, and Binky—and of course the late great Irving Lazar, known to all as Swifty. (Lazar was so dubbed by none other than Humphrey Bogart after he made three deals for the actor in one day.)

Agents come in all stripes and colors, and it is impossible to generalize about the work they do or the services they provide. But the first question all aspiring writers ask is whether or not they need one. And the answer, quite plainly, is yes. Once in a great while a writer is fortunate enough to be discovered, but most are in the unenviable position of relying on others to provide what they most desire: dissemination of their work. Eudora Welty was one of the rare exceptions. The very first two short stories she sent out, "Death of a Traveling Salesman" and "Magic," were published in a small husband-and-wife-run magazine called *Manuscript*. The couple wrote to her saying that "'Death of a Salesman' [*sic*] is one of the best stories that has ever come to our attention—and one of the best stories we have ever read. It is superbly done. And 'Magic' is only slightly short of it in quality."

Welty was ecstatic. "Is this the way it happens?" she wrote. "You just put something in the mail and they say okay. If they paid me a million dollars, it wouldn't have made any difference. I wanted acceptance and publication." She then had the continued good fortune of being contacted by Diarmuid Russell, the Putnam-editor-turned-agent, who had heard of her from a

Doubleday editor who had recently made a trip through the South in search of new talent. According to biographer Ann Waldron, Welty had never heard of literary agents before Russell contacted her, and she was unclear about their role, but she signed on nonetheless. It was more than a year before Russell was able to sell her first collection (even in the 1940s publishers were loath to take on short-story collections without the promise of a novel to follow). Still, he was convinced of the quality of her stories and sent them out repeatedly. "At times he feared his new client would lose confidence in him, as he seemed to be unable to convince editors how good her stories were," Waldron writes. "Eudora reassured him that she would not be 'bitter' if he never sold the stories, just impressed if he did."

❧

Every writer has to figure out how to make his way in the world, how to find support through patronage or publication. Every writer struggles each time he sends some new pages out into the world. If you're just starting out, I can tell you that editors do respond to well-written cover letters and to opening sentences that bring a manuscript to life. In fact, an editor can usually tell from a cover letter the person's facility with words. Some letters are so stiff and stilted they are almost painful to read. Others use the language to keen and clever effect, within the lines a promise of what is to come.

When I give writing workshops, I use two exercises to make the point of how important that first impression is. I distribute two handouts, the first a packet of query letters and the second a packet of first pages from actual manuscripts received from agents as well as over the transom. I ask the students to determine two things based on the letters and sample pages: would they invite the writer to send his or her work, and would they continue reading the novel based on the first page? In every workshop I've conducted, the students are in almost unanimous agreement about which manuscripts they wanted to continue reading and which letters piqued their curiosity.

Evaluating manuscripts, like grading papers, produces a bell curve of what appears to be natural ability. It quickly becomes clear which papers are the most accomplished, which letters the most inviting. Indeed, an editor enjoys nothing more than being startled awake by a particularly witty or moving letter or reading the fresh pages of an extremely well-written manuscript and finding that the world recedes as she becomes more deeply involved in the pages. "I try to remind my students that most of the editors I know are not opening that envelope hoping to find another story like the ten thousand they've already seen," said Michael Cunningham. "They're hoping to find something alarming, brilliant, and unprecedented."

Too many writers, in trying to secure the services of a literary agent or publisher, simply do not do their homework. The best way to get an agent's or an editor's attention is to write an intelligent and succinct letter. And then send it to the right person. Too many aspiring authors send blind letters of inquiry in the vain hope of piquing the recipient's interest. These letters, which agents and editors receive by the dozens, both depress and astonish me. What's depressing is how much misguided energy goes into these efforts. What's astonishing is the sheer industry. Because writing is such a personal endeavor for most people, some forget that the relationship is a professional one. Editors and agents are turned off by letters chock-full of misspellings (including the recipient's name), or those that assume a relationship where none exists. Query letters that sound as if they were penned by Crazy Eddie instead of a thoughtful writer tend to get deep-sixed. Just as the reading public judges books by their covers, we judge manuscripts by the accompanying query letters. And if you can't write a good, crisp sentence by way of introduction, it's doubtful that you'll inspire any interest on the part of the recipient.

Over the years I have received any number of gifts or gimmicks included with query letters or manuscripts intended to butter me up, amuse me, or entice me, including chocolate cigars, a stained-glass pendant, baby booties, ribbons, flowers, a pair of dice, a five-dollar bill, a bottle of patchouli oil, numerous author photographs (sometimes topless of the men), a box of Band-Aids, a box of Kleenex, a pack of cigarettes, and a bottle of wine. In one six-month period I received a monthly package of what looked like outsider art, usually a soda can decorated with clay, buttons, twigs, and so on. When no letter of explanation or manuscript arrived as part of what seemed like an elaborate scheme to get my attention, I was advised to call personnel and turn over each piece of "art" as evidence in case a crazed writer ever decided to come and claim his work or go postal along editorial row, blowing everyone away in a fusillade of pages and buckshot.

Just to make matters perfectly clear: Please resist the temptation to do any of these outlandish things. Also, do not use colored paper (it doesn't copy well) or scented paper; and no joky attention-getting opening lines, no sob stories, no crazy fonts, no overly long explanations of what follows, and no ridiculous threats or overstated marketing statistics. Be sure to double-space your manuscript (most of us are going blind), don't bind it in a three-ring notebook or any other way (we usually like to carry a chunk home to read, and binding makes copying a hassle as well), always paginate (fear of strong winds), don't attach stickers or drawings (they're just silly), don't print out double-sided pages (again, they're a pain to copy).

I am always struck by the writer who, with no credentials per se, blithely compares his work to any number of current or past bestsellers. As if! Every writer who proposes a book of oral reportage swears that he's the next Studs Terkel. Those who want to describe a year in the life assure you that they are the next Tracy Kidder. Every lawyer is the next Turow or Grisham. Every feminist tract is the next Backlash. And now, every Civil War novel in the land promises to be the next Cold Mountain. Just once I'd like to see a writer make a humble promise or estimation of his expectations. Just once I'd like to see a writer compare his or her work to a book that isn't a commercial blockbuster. Or better yet, let the publisher draw the conclusion based on the quality of the work. I promise, a simple, dignified letter with a clear statement of your intent and credentials will win more affirmative responses than any gimmick or hype. Remember, Terkel, Kidder, Turow, Grisham, Faludi, and Frazier were once nobodies too.

Don't address your query "Dear editor" or "Dear agent." Do your homework and find the right person's name. Read the acknowledgments in books that you love or that are in the category you hope to break into and see if an editor or agent is mentioned. If none is listed, call the publisher and find out who the book's editor was. Ask who the agent is. Get a list of three or four agents or editors. Just as you would seek out a specialist for a medical problem, find the right agent for your genre or specialty.

When Susan Sontag finished the first book she felt was publishable, in 1963, *The Benefactor,* she made a list of publishers. "Farrar, Straus was my first choice, because they had just published *The Selected Works of Djuna Barnes,*" she recalled in *Conversations with American Writers.* "New Directions was my second choice, because they published many more writers I admired, but somehow I had the impression that they were more inaccessible. Third was Grove Press, because they were publishing Beckett. I put the manuscript of *The Benefactor* in a box and left it at Farrar, Straus and Giroux. Two weeks later I got a call, was asked to lunch by Robert Giroux, who offered me an option that turned into a contract. I spent several months reworking the book and they published it."

Sontag's story of her first publication is made even more remarkable by the fact that thirty-six years later she is still with the same publisher. By seeking those whose work she respected and responded to, and leaving her small package without much flourish or craven exaggeration, she found herself a home. While these stories are rare, when a writer finds me and mentions that he has read and enjoyed one or more books that I have edited, I am not immune to the flattery. I may not connect with his work in the end, but I would encourage that writer to send me his work after he went to the trouble of seeking me out. Unfortunately, most of the unsolicited mail that editors and agents get comes from people who clearly have not taken the time to research the playing field. In other words, if you go to the trouble of writing to editors and agents, at the very least target your search through some careful investigation of what the house publishes, what that editor has worked on, or whom the agent represents.

And then, *don't call*. I cannot emphasize this enough. Editors and agents are on the phone most of the day, for that is the way we conduct business. Most can't even return all their calls in a single day and by necessity prioritize them according to their urgency or importance. And in terms of urgency, returning the call of an unsolicited author ranks very low. Yes, you can have the last laugh when your book stays on the bestseller list week after week, and those who took weeks to return your calls are fawning all over you. But as an unsolicited writer you're at the bottom of the barrel. Plus, if you are calling to see if the agent or editor has read your work yet, I can promise you she hasn't. No one reads a manuscript, loves it, and doesn't call the author. She'll call if she's interested, or she will send it back. This may take up to six months, but if you supply a self-addressed stamped envelope, your material will be returned.

If you think that calling will get your manuscript closer to the top of the pile, think again: chances are it will have the opposite effect, and you'll be branded as a nudge. All editors and agents already have enough nudgy authors to deal with. In addition, unless you were referred, the editor probably has no idea who you are. Most editors and agents don't read their slush or unsolicited query letters. They depend on their assistants to pass along anything that might be of interest. And an editor will not take kindly to anyone who hassles his or her assistant. The *only* reason to call an editor or agent who is sitting on your manuscript is if another party is interested. Once you're "in play" the picture changes. It's not unlike that dating syndrome, where you go for months without so much as a phone call, and then, when you finally start seeing someone, your dance card suddenly fills up. Competition is quickening, and just a whiff of it often spurs both agents and publishers to act.

Writers always ask whether they should multiply submit. The answer is yes, unless you hope to work with an agent who has expressly stated that he or she will not read a multiply submitted manuscript. I recommend sending your work out to a half-dozen people, unless you have a good referral or contact at an agency or house; otherwise you could spend a year making three or four single submissions. However, I also recommend that you make the most of your multiple submissions by paying keen attention to the responses. And I would mimic the strategy our high school guidance counselors suggested for applying to colleges: one submission that is a reach, two that are in range, and one "safety school." Try an agent at one of the big power firms, a couple at medium-sized firms, and one who is out on her own. And if you're also trying publishing houses, try a big conglomerate, a couple of smaller houses, and a regional or academic press if that makes sense.

Just as when you are buying a first home, you are extremely vulnerable when seeking an agent or book publisher, and you might feel that if only you better understood the protocol, the process would be less fraught with anxiety. For instance, the long silence that follows the submission of your work can be maddening; frustration and paranoia tend to run high. Every now and then an editor will receive a call from an extremely irate author who cannot believe that no one has jumped on his opus or that months have passed and his highly explosive nonfiction proposal remains untouched on the unread pile. Many writers become agitated, and some turn hostile, as if those of us in the corridors of publishing were deliberately trying to sabotage their careers. Granted, nothing is more frustrating than waiting for a response for weeks or months and then getting only a form letter. However, a form letter is all that any agent or editor owes you. After all, you are seeking professional, not educational, services.

If you receive only form letters in response to a query, then you should take a good look at your approach. Chances are that it needs serious refining, revising, or rethinking. And before you waste any more of your own time, you should seek out educational services in the form of a writing workshop, a course on proposal writing, or perhaps a freelance editor or copyeditor to review your work and offer specific help. Such services are advertised in journals such as *Poets & Writers* and *Writer's Digest.* If you do receive some personal notes from editors or agents, take this as a very good sign. Perhaps an agent has even offered to read a revision should you make some changes. As with love, all you need is to find one person who believes in you.

Edith Wharton confesses in her autobiography that when she sent out her first tentative submission of a few poems to the leading magazines of the day, she was clueless about how to do it. "I did not know how authors communicated with editors, but I copied out the verses in my fairest hand, and enclosed each in an envelope with my visiting card!" After a week or two, she received word that all three poems had been accepted. "As long as I live I shall never forget my sensations when I opened the first of the three letters, and learned that I was to appear in print. I can still see the narrow hall, the letter-box out of which I fished the letters, and the flight of stairs up and down which I ran, senselessly and incessantly, in the attempt to give my excitement some muscular outlet." As if this weren't heart-stopping enough, the editor of *Scribner's* magazine, Edward Burlingame, invited Wharton to share more of her work. As she recounts, "He not only accepted my verses, but (oh, rapture!) wanted to know what else I had written; and this encouraged me to go to see him, and laid the foundation of a friendship which lasted till his death."

✦

More than a few writers whom I've met at conferences have complained to me that it's harder to get an agent than it is to interest a publisher, which is surprising, given how many agents there are. Some tell horror stories of agents who agree to take them on but never return their calls. Agents who, after making a few submissions, lose interest if the project doesn't sell and stop submitting it. Agents who take months to read new work. Agents who care only about making the deal and don't act as advocates for the book. Agents who fail to sell the au- thor's foreign, audio, film, and serial rights. The worst accusa- tion I ever heard was of an agent who reportedly held on to an author's advance monies and royalty payments until the author threatened to sue. As in every profession, there are a few people who give the industry a bad name, but unless you already have a publisher interested in your work and feel reasonably certain that you can handle any disputes that may arise, you should spend whatever time and energy it takes to secure the services of a good agent.

Do not, however, let an agent's interest in you or your work keep you from taking certain precautions. A writer is entitled to a reasonable amount of information when he or she signs on with an agent. You should ask who else the agent represents, what books he or she has sold and to what publishers, what his or her percentage, or cut, is, and what, if any, additional charges will be billed back to the client, such as the cost of messengers, copying, and foreign submissions. You need to know what the contractual obligation is between you and the agent and whether you are required to sign a contract. As a client you should be apprised of the general game plan, including where the agent plans to send the book and whether he plans to send it out to just a few publishers or widely. If the first six publishers turn it down, will the agent give up, advise you to revise, or keep plugging until he finds one? What plans does he have for the exploitation of secondary rights, meaning film, foreign, audio, and electronic rights? I know some young writers who are afraid of their agents, who don't want to bother them or appear needy and insecure. It's understandable that they don't want to alienate the first person who actually seems to like their work. Still, you should feel a bond of trust with the person representing you and your work. If at all geographically possible, meet with any agent who expresses interest in representing you and bring a list of questions. Whether through letters, conversation, or an actual meeting, it should become clear if the agent is interested in your long-term career or just a one-night stand.

For as long as I live, I will never forget an incident at the agency where I first worked. The owner, an extremely hard-working man with many successful commercial clients, loved literary fiction and went to great lengths to sign up writers of literary quality, even though their earnings were meager by comparison with others on his roster. After sending one young woman's first novel around for nearly thirty submissions over a two-year period, he persuaded her to write it from a different point of view, based on the advice of some of the more thoughtful rejection letters. The author spent a year on the revision, and the agent started to send it around again, first to the editors who had said they would reconsider the work if it was revised. And again he sadly began to rack up another pile of heartfelt rejections. He was up to the twenty-second turndown when, late one night, while I was putting in some extra hours in the back office, the phone rang. The agent had wandered downstairs with a pile of manuscripts and letters for the following morning, and I heard him take the call. Then I heard what sounded like sobbing. When I came down the hall to see what was wrong, my boss, who hadn't realized I was there, became flustered and embarrassed. Then he laughed and said, as he removed his glasses to wipe away an escaped tear with the heel of his hand, "We got an offer, we finally got an offer."

Writers complain that there aren't many agents left who will keep submitting a book with that kind of tenacity, though I would argue that those willing to stake their name and reputation on a literary novel will go the distance. After all, no one takes on a quiet literary novel because he thinks it will make him rich. He takes it on because he loves it and hopes that the writer will develop over time into an author of some esteem. Some might argue that fewer agents take chances because fewer publishers take chances and because there are fewer publishers period, and all of this is true. What's critical is that you feel you can trust your agent's judgment and ability to do her job. If you don't, then the relationship will prove to be a grueling and excruciating exercise in torture.

Much of the unhappiness and pain that arises in an author-agent relationship seems to stem from a lack of trust or from frustrated expectations. Some writers only want their agent to sell their book and do their bidding. And yet they are always second-guessing the agent's strategy or choice of submission. Others crave camaraderie; but more than friendship, they sometimes want their agent to be all things: father confessor, brother, and champion. Some authors want their agents to be mind readers, offering help and encouragement when they need it, leaving them alone when they don't. Some authors want to belong to a certain agent's stable because his list is full of well-established, successful writers, but once there they feel like small fish in a big pond. Others want to be big fish, then wonder if their agent has enough clout to get the best deal.

Often the agent is the first reader of a writer's work, and the author relies on him as heavily as, if not more than, his editor for feedback. And some agents do indeed edit. Furthermore, editors tend to jump from house to house, and sometimes the most continuity a writer can get is from the relationship with his agent. It's extremely important to have an agent who not only knows your publishing history the way a doctor knows your medical history but who understands how you work, what you need, and how to present your work not only to the publisher but to the world at large as well. The best agents provide this service and then some. Some have even been known to lend money to clients in advance of their publishing payments, as agent Harold Ober often did with the wayward F. Scott Fitzgerald. But that is going above and beyond the call of an agent's duty. Still, no matter how many wonderful agents there are, their reputations, like those of mothers-in-law, are sullied. "Ten-percenters," as agents are referred to in *Variety*, aren't known as the world's great humanitarians.

Agents are often accused of venality, even when a client is the driving force behind their demands. When the newspapers report that a certain writer got an enormous advance, agents never fail to hear from clients who want to know why they didn't get as much. And writers who are represented by powerful agents sometimes imagine that they aren't getting the star treatment they are certain the bigger clients enjoy. I think a certain level of resentment or jealousy or envy naturally accrues because the agent always takes a percentage of the earnings. And in any job that involves commissions, one party is always beholden to the other to a certain extent, and these arrangements can become strained. No matter how grateful a writer is to have her first, second, or third book sold, at some point she either believes she deserves more money or imagines that a new agent can get her a better deal. Or she just gets tired of her agent the way a married man may suddenly find himself flirting with a cocktail waitress at an airport bar.

Every year we witness one or another high-profile defection of a writer to a new agent. Always the circumstances are acrimonious, as they should be; money, sometimes lots of it, and ego are at stake. The most notorious case in recent history, and one that will take some doing to top, is that of Martin Amis, whose highly entertaining novel *The Information* details the exceedingly healthy spirit of competition among writers. Taking top honors in the ever-amusing art-imitating-life category, Amis's much-publicized defection from his longtime British agent to the American agent Andrew Wylie (who travels under the moniker of "the Jackal") kept writers, agents, and publishers on both sides of the Atlantic knee-deep in gossip for weeks. *The New York Observer* referred to the melee as "a stew of literary envy and bad karma worthy of the most stomach-churning, self-flagellating moments in *The Information*." The bad karma referred to the fact that Amis's longtime agent just happened to be married to Julian Barnes, Amis's oldest friend in the literary world. And ratcheting it up a notch from there, apparently Amis based the buffoonish best-selling writer at the novel's center on none other than Barnes. "The friendship did not survive the business rupture," editor Gerald Howard wryly noted in the *Review of Contemporary Fiction*, pointing out that "the novel might be described as a demonstration that hatred of one's peers is so powerful a force in the literary world that they can cause writers to behave approximately like Tonya Harding."

Sometimes agents jump ship too, as in the much-publicized 1989 departure of Lynn Nesbit, the head of ICM's literary department, to join forces with lawyer Mort Janklow. A story entitled "Royalty Wedding of the Year," which appeared in *Manhattan Inc.* magazine, described the merger as the "marriage of Mass and Class." Nesbit is famous for her literary authors: her first bestseller was *The Kandy-Kolored Tangerine-Flake Streamline Baby*, by Tom Wolfe. Later, she sold Donald Barthelme's first short story to *The New Yorker*. And in 1968 she took on an unknown first novelist called Michael Crichton. Janklow's stable consisted of Judith Krantz, Sidney Sheldon, and Jackie Collins. "Mort sells the equivalent of heroin in books," commented his competitor Andrew Wylie. "One damages the body, his books damage the mind." But Janklow, as a result of having worked with some of the best-selling authors of all time, was able to see, from what Wylie dismissed as his beach-blanket perspective, the international and marketing opportunities for promoting authors. Though publishers have been slow to apply the tools of marketing and publicity to literary authors, instead leaving their futures in the hands of the critics, they have finally begun to see how promoting an author can pay off.

"Publishing used to be a sort of mom-and-pop operation," Janklow commented in *Manhattan Inc.* "It's going through a transitional phase. It's becoming more international. There are big changes in the retailing and distribution. The marketing side is vastly improved. Publishing is becoming a very serious business. There is the growth of the idea that it is not unliterary to sell the product." And he said this long before the proliferation of superstores, coffee bars, Amazon.com, readers' guides, and reading groups, before Brian Lamb's *Book Notes* and C-Span, before Oprah and Imus and Charlie Rose. What Janklow didn't say, but what he certainly must have seen, during the decade when he brilliantly joined forces with ICM's top agent, was that this would be the decade of the agent. Now, more than ever, people are interested in the art of the deal. And the bigger the deal the better.

No agent exemplifies said art better than Irving "Swifty" Lazar, who, in his day, made deals for the likes of Noël Coward, Tennessee Williams, Clifford Odets, Lillian Hellman, and Ernest Hemingway. Acclaimed editor Michael Korda's reminiscence of Lazar in his *New Yorker* article "The King of the Deal" portrays a larger-than-life character whose business feats and philosophy were part Attila the Hun, part Yogi Berra. Lazar, one of the first truly bicoastal agents, became well known for his undaunted bravado and for making deals and offering projects by famous actors he didn't actually represent, then exacting a commission if his fishing expedition proved fruitful. Lazar had three advantages, according to Korda, that kept him on top for fifty years. The first was his extraordinary access to anyone and everyone; the second was his staunch refusal to deal with underlings, going straight to the top instead; the third was his insistence on a quick answer. "Even now, if I tell Irving that I want to think something over or discuss it with someone else," writes Korda, "he will snap, 'Never mind, I can see you're not interested.'"

I think every industry needs its Swiftys, its Jackals, just as it needs its elder statesmen, its iconoclasts, its rising stars. We need people who defy convention just as much as we need those who uphold it. Every time an agent challenges conventional wisdom and gets a good deal for her client, whether it's better terms or a bigger advance, then she has moved her client's cause forward. Every time an agent discovers a new writer and through careful grooming and presentation offers publishers an absolutely irresistible property that sells for more money than anyone imagined, it's a victory. But most agents struggle along, just as everyone else in the industry does. While their financial risk is small in comparison with the publisher's costs of development, manufacturing, and distribution, their reputations are at stake, as is their livelihood—for their clients can walk out at any time. And like everyone else in publishing, agents deal with the residual effects of disappointing sales, bad reviews, selling slumps, loads of rejections, and unearned-royalty statements.

However, they can also profit from an unexpected windfall in ways that turn most editors green, especially when their participation has been critical to the book's success. *The New York Observer* recently profiled a group of hot young agents, all under the age of thirty-five, with the headline "The Baby Binkys." It sounded like the name of a new children's television program, but the assembled group was as serious as a heart attack. "So it goes these days," the article lamented, "when the agent has eclipsed the editor as the author's main crutch in the perilous, bottom-line-driven publishing world." Still, when the salmon-colored *Observer* hit the desks of editors around town, the reactions were as various as the personalities who people the industry. Some editors panicked because they didn't even know or had never lunched with some of the "hot" agents listed and immediately reached for their phones to set up dates. One agent reported that his calendar was booked solid for five months of lunches after the article ran. Other editors were chagrined: those profiled would certainly milk their fifteen minutes for all it was worth, trying to exact even speedier responses and bigger advances from the largely beleaguered editorial corps. We were officially in the era of the agent.

A fresh-faced college graduate might surmise that becoming an agent is a better goal than trying to become an editor, especially if he's intrigued by the financial incentive. There was a time when actors' salaries, ballplayers' contracts, and author advances were private matters. No longer. Whenever a large deal is struck, the story is all about the agent and the size of the advance. Who the writer is or what the book is about is often secondary. Everyone wants to report that his deal was the highest amount paid for a celebrity book, the most money paid for a first novel, the largest movie option, and so on, as if book deals were sports records, there to be broken.

On the other side of the equation is the great story of the late golf pro Harvey Penick, who was considered the crème de la crème of golf instructors and who kept a lifelong record of advice in the form of homilies in a little red leather notebook. According to ICM agent Esther Newberg, writer Bud Shrake saw the potential in Penick's work and helped the golfer pre-pare the material. Newberg shared it with Simon & Schuster publisher Charlie Hayward, an avid sports fan. Hayward, she said, "took about 25 seconds and offered $90,000." Newberg called Penick's wife, since Harvey was nearly deaf by this point, and told her that Simon & Schuster was interested in publish-ing the book for $90,000. His wife said she needed to discuss the offer with Harvey. When she got back to Newberg, the golfer's wife said that they had talked it over and wanted very much to go forward with the book. She explained that they would get a second mortgage on their home to come up with the ninety grand. It's amazing that the news didn't kill Penick when he finally understood that the publisher was going to *pay him*. And as if that weren't enough, *Harvey Penick's Little Red Book*, published in 1992, went on to become the most successful sports book of all time.

But the day that stays with me as emblematic of the sea change taking place in the industry came when one literary writer whose work I loved was making the rounds of publish-ers with her agent. The agent planned to move her author from the small regional publisher where she had gotten her start to a major New York house. It was a bit of a coup for me to get the agent to send the new manuscript, as I was still relatively untested. I was more than a little excited about the meeting, which was to be attended by some of the company's brass. The writer was from the South, and after an exchange of niceties about the weather and how New York was a far cry from her hometown, she placed both hands on the table and asked if we could get down to business. Yes, of course, we told her; what is it exactly that you are looking for in a publisher? "The Maxwell Perkins stuff is great and all that," she drawled, "but what I want to know is how y'all are going to break me out?" She had had her share of editing, now she was looking for a publisher to show her the money. This was ten years before the hit movie that made everything perfectly clear: Maxwell Perkins has been supplanted by Jerry Maguire.

8.

REJECTION

REJECTION IS A FACT OF WRITING LIFE. IF you are still unpublished, you probably suffer from the misconception that publication in and of itself will cure everything that ails you. But the pain of rejection doesn't stop the day a contract arrives. In fact, when you sign your name on the bottom line of your publishing contract, you may be signing up for more disappointment than you ever dreamed imaginable. Saint Teresa's dictum "More tears are shed over answered prayers than unanswered ones" should be hung on the wall over every writer's desk. Sometimes being rejected may mean being spared. But try telling that to a hungry writer with some fresh pages in hand!

If you are just starting out, try to look at rejection as a ladder. The first rung is made up of form letters, the preprinted kind that offer some trite condolence about why your work isn't right for the literary journal, magazine, or publishing company. The next rung might still be form letters, but now an editor has scrawled a note: *Try us again!* Usually the signature is illegible, a common tactic to keep the writer from getting his hopes up by imagining that he might actually develop a relationship with the editor or, worse yet, try to call. James Dickey, in a *Paris Review* interview, said that the world of publishers and agents might just as well have been in the outer part of the solar system, so foreign were they to him. "I just knew that I liked to write and I had some ideas that I thought might work out as poems. So I wrote them, then sent them around. As they say, I could have papered my bedroom wall with the rejections. . . . I sent poems in and I kept getting back these form rejections. In 1948 or 1949 I remember with wonder I saw a true human handwriting on a rejection slip. It said, 'Not bad.'"

The next rung may seem like a small step, but it is the equivalent of a moon landing: the personal letter. At this stage it may be a very short letter, but the point is that it is absolutely *not* a form letter. Fourth rung: they don't want *this* story or project, but the editor or agent is actually inviting you to send more work! Fifth rung: bull's-eye! Then those magic words: *We are pleased to inform you* . . . Very few writers are catapulted into the land of publication without amassing rejection slips. If you are not one of those fortunate few, take heart as you climb. As frustrating as a close call can seem, it does mean that you're on the right track. And chances are, if you stick with it, that close call will eventually become a full-fledged acceptance. Unfortunately, it's easy to become agitated and lose heart, especially when you drop back a rung. For instance, after receiving personal notes for a while from a book or magazine editor, you may suddenly find a form letter in the mail. Or worse, just as you have finished the sixth draft of your novel and are preparing to send it to the editor who had sent you a few encouraging notes or provided some editorial advice over the years, you discover when you phone the publishing house that she has joined the Peace Corps. The one person who had appreciated what you were up to is off somewhere in Somalia. No note, no call. Just up and gone. *Somalia! Somalia!*

These things do happen, and often it is a matter of luck, good or bad, that appears responsible for any given access or denial to the coveted moment of acceptance. I have always felt fortunate in having been strongly influenced by my father, a self-made man who is a living example that with hard work you can accomplish anything. Absorbing his worldview, I came to believe that people were neither lucky nor unlucky. Life was more like a game of odds in which you could increase your chances of winning simply by doing more than the next guy. It wasn't about being in the right place at the right time but about being in a lot of places at a lot of times, showing up even when the odds seemed lousy. How this applies to writers is somewhat obvious, but I'll belabor the point: submitting your work fifty times or revising it as many times as you have to may be what separates the sung from the unsung.

There is no better story in publishing history than that of mega-best-selling writer John Grisham. His first novel, *A Time to Kill*, which he wrote in the predawn hours over a three-year period while he juggled a high-stress sixty- to eighty-hour work-week and a young family, was rejected by dozens of agents before he found one who would take it on. His agent then submitted the book for a year, also amassing a pile of rejections, before finally placing it with the now defunct Wynwood Press for an advance of $15,000. The book had a 5,000-copy first printing. "I bought 1,000, and another 1,000 were sitting in a warehouse," said Grisham in a 1993 *Publishers Weekly* interview. "So you know not many were out there." Not exactly an auspicious debut.

But as is his habit, Grisham started his next novel the day after he finished *A Time to Kill* (and more important, long before the world responded with its resounding yawn). That next book, *The Firm,* had a rather different publishing trajectory. While it was on submission to publishers, a copy leaked out to Hollywood, and Paramount paid $600,000 for the movie rights before a single publisher made an offer. "News of the deal lit up phone lines on both coasts," reported *Publishers Weekly.* "Within two weeks, Grisham had a contract with Doubleday, one of the many houses that had passed on *A Time to Kill* two years earlier."

Grisham's success looks like the stuff of fairy tales. Ten years and ten books later he is still the number-one-selling author in the world, and his record-breaking first printings nearly top three million copies. You might say that John Grisham got lucky, but I would posit that hard work, persistence, his habit of starting a new book the day he finishes his last, as Anthony Trollope always did, account for Grisham's success. Luck is winning the lottery. Writing draft after draft, and sending them out over and over again, is sweat.

In a witty and useful essay in *Poets & Writers* magazine, author Bill Roorbach puts it this way: "Luck is a fine thing for a writer, but take note: Good writing creates luck. . . . By the time most good writers start to publish work regularly, they've amassed many hundreds of rejection slips, in all shapes and sizes. . . . Ping-Pong, my writer friend Bob Kimber calls it. You shoot a manuscript out, they shoot it back; you whack it back out there, it comes back. As long as you've done the honest work and know that what you're offering is good stuff, you have every reason to play the game." So, do people stop whacking their pages out there because they get discouraged, or are they too lazy to keep working at it?

What sometimes looks like laziness in writers is often a camouflage for a range of feelings, including fear and vulnerability. If, after giving up in your efforts to find publication, you catch yourself thinking that the John Grishams of the world are merely lucky or well connected, if you begrudge others their success, feeling that you are once again outside the sweet-smelling bakery with your nose pressed up to the glass, understand that the sticky buns are within reach. If Grisham hadn't pinged his pages out there one more time, he wouldn't be the writer with the most cake.

*

No one suffers as much as the rejected writer. If he isn't beating himself up, he is expending a fair amount of energy feeling slighted and neglected and in some cases downright robbed when a writer of similar age or background makes it. He doesn't stop to consider that the other writer may be worthy; the very fact that others are able to get published is like

salt in the wide-open wound of a writer's psyche. I meet a lot
of people at writers' conferences who exude woundedness. I
can tell they have made an attempt to get published and have
failed thus far. They are full of yearning yet lack confidence.
Some would rather talk about writing than write. Some are desperate for contact with other writers. Others are suspicious,
guarded, or weary, and a few are downright hostile. They seem
to think that the publishers and agents present are on enemy
ground; who wouldn't feel that way after being rejected time
and again?

After attending one such conference, a group of editors and
agents gathered for dinner, and naturally we started to gossip
about the attendees, those who showed promise and those who
seemed hopeless. I felt implicated in the judgments we so easily tossed off; after all, I had been one of those seekers who had
attended writers' conferences before throwing in the towel and
going into publishing. I took workshops, even got my MFA,
though a part of me felt that writing programs were a joke, just
a place to bide your time and stave off entering the real world.
One of my literary heroes, Truman Capote, said in an interview, "The last thing in the world I would do was waste my
time going to college, because I knew what I wanted to do. . . .
The only reason to go to college is if you want to be a doctor,
a lawyer, or something in a highly specialized field. . . . If you
want to be a writer, and you are a writer already, and you can
spell, there's no reason to go to college."

Much as I agree with Capote's sentiment in theory, I still
feel a huge compassion for those seeking the community of

writers and advice about getting published. The fact is that many students of writing programs get invaluable advice about their work and even direct access to agents and editors. However, any statistics would show that most of the people attending any conference or writing program will never become published writers. Even if your portfolio gets you into a writing program, once there you have only entered another Darwinian system that will naturally weed out the weak from the strong. Not the better writers per se, but the ones who won't quit.

When Gordon Lish (aka Captain Fiction), famous for his outrageous conduct, used to harangue the students in his marathon-length writing classes about their staying power, sometimes even mocking the rare student who'd dare to get up to go to the bathroom, calling him a puppy who couldn't hold his water and piss with the big dogs, many of the attendees thought him certifiable. Others let their bladders nearly burst during the six-hour marathon sessions. The method may have been mad, but Lish treated his job as seriously as a drill sergeant's. He knew that most of us were likely to get killed out there, that the world of ten thousand things, as he called it, was indifferent to our sentences, and he wanted to toughen us up. He scrutinized our sentences with all the coldness and lack of interest of the real world. His was not a workshop, it was boot camp, and more than a few grunts couldn't hack it.

I think the best advice to writers attending a conference or beginning a writing class is to ascertain where you stand in relation to the other participants and learn from those who are a step or two ahead. Like finding a tennis partner whose ability is a notch above your own, you will play better if your partner's game challenges yours. All you really need during those long years when rejection may get the better of you is one friend with whom you can share your work, one fellow writer with whom you can have an honest exchange. Just as Wordsworth befriended Coleridge, as Hemingway used Fitzgerald, so did Welty rely on Porter, and Kerouac on Ginsberg—writers need one another. Some have formed loose associations, such as the Bloomsbury writers, the Algonquin Round Table, or the Beats, thus establishing powerful networking channels, a literary manifesto, and a platform from which to be heard. For a number of years following graduate school, some friends and I put together our own magazine and held monthly poetry readings. Eventually we all became too busy, and our mutual purpose eroded as we made diverse career choices. But for that brief period we felt as if we were part of something important that involved our identity as writers.

If you don't have a writers' group, start one. You can't expect the publishing community, either agents or editors, to stand in for personal instruction and feedback. Some writers, even those who are quite accomplished, rely their whole lives on a person or a small group of trusted writing friends for feedback and support. I was shocked when I discovered that an established writer whom I had signed up relied on no fewer than five writing friends for a critique of her manuscript before turning it in to me, her editor. And as she started refuting some of my editing, she'd recall the comments of one friend or another. I wanted to tell her that I didn't edit by committee, that too many chefs spoiled the word soup, especially when she'd cite an ex-boyfriend's reaction. As if he'd tell her the truth! But I was also aware of how important this circle of friends was to her survival as a working writer; they were more than readers, they were also engaged in the struggle and thus provided shelter.

Still, no matter how valuable I think a writer's conference can be, especially for a writer who has yet to find a community, when I attend as a representative of the publishing world I automatically feel on edge. Suddenly I am staring at all those rejection letters I dinged back at writers. Week after week we editors churn them out: *Not right for our list, Not our cup of tea, Better luck elsewhere, Good luck with your work.* And suddenly we're face to face with the cup of tea. Better luck elsewhere is sitting in the front row and asking if I'd be interested in her memoir about incest. What the hell am I supposed to say? It feels like the *Titanic;* I want to take everyone, but the goddamn raft will sink.

❧

Writing is nothing if not a long-distance race. The same kind of hubris that can cripple a runner who doesn't properly train can also derail a writer from reaching his goal. And just as the expert runner can tell the novice from a mile away, usually from his spanking-new running suit, the editor can spot the writer manqué. These are the people who invariably give editors the most trouble, who badger us constantly to help them, who make a million excuses or apologies for their work, or lack of work, and whom we wind up carrying down the mountain in a body bag. These are the writers who want to sell us on a book idea but balk when we suggest that they first try it as a magazine-length piece. It's like wanting to get married without having gone on a date.

Before attempting to publish a book, you can do any number of things that will help make your work more rejection-proof. If you are a nonfiction writer, try placing op-ed pieces on your topic, or publishing a magazine piece, or better yet, a series of articles. Perhaps you could get a regular column in a local newspaper. If you want to be recognized as an authority, you probably need to get an advanced degree and publish in the professional journals in your field. Think about offering classes to gain a local following, as Clarissa Pinkola Estés did with her storytelling and myth workshops before publishing *Women Who Run with the Wolves.* John Gray had been running successful seminars for years before *Men Are from Mars, Women Are from Venus* took up what seemed like permanent residence on the national bestseller list. Some writers even go so far as to self-publish, so determined are they to spread their word. In the last few years, major publishers have gotten wind of some successful self-published books and have acquired the rights and published them nationally. In each case, whether it was *Conversations with God, The Celestine Prophecy,* or *The Christmas Box,* the authors' determination, elbow grease, and missionary zeal kept the dream alive long enough for someone else to finally pick up the ball and run with it. When I address writing conferences I always ask the participants to think about how badly they want it. Is having a book published worth taking out a second mortgage, filling up the trunk of your car, and schlepping books from mall to mall?

Novelist E. Lynn Harris self-published his books about relationships among straight and gay African-Americans after the major publishers had turned him down. He loaded his car with copies and brought them to local beauty salons, where he rightly guessed he might find an audience as well as a pretty good word-of-mouth network. His books caught the attention of a local bookseller, who in turn mentioned them to a publisher's sales rep, who brought the novels back to the home office. The company took up Harris's novels, all of which have gone on to become national bestsellers.

If you insist that you want to write only in book-length form, that writing magazine articles or running workshops doesn't interest you, then write your book proposal or even the complete manuscript and see how far you can get with it. Perhaps the power of your ideas, the strength of your prose, the irresistible appeal of your style will garner you a publisher. Not so long ago, a *Newsweek* article featured the nature-versus-nurture debate and used as its centerpiece a recently published book called *The Nurture Assumption* by Judith Rich Harris. "This petite, gray-haired grandmother hardly seems the type to be lobbing Molotov cocktails at one of the most dearly held ideas in child development," the article explained. What fascinated me was that the sixty-year-old author had no academic affiliation and no Ph.D. In fact, she was thrown out of Harvard in 1961 "because her professors believed she showed no ability to do important original research." Thirty-eight years later, Judith Rich Harris made the cover of *Newsweek*. Naturally, her adversaries claimed that her work was irresponsible. Still, Harris, who clearly never gave up, had the satisfaction of seeing her ideas disseminated and debated.

There is always more than one way to skin a cat, as the expression goes, and if you've got great writing/communication skills, something new or necessary to say, focus, drive, and a certain amount of quixotic self-belief, then I believe you will be heard from. Obviously, writing a novel and writing a self-help book are entirely different endeavors, but as an editor I will venture to say that all authors, at heart, are not so different from one another. All are driven by a desire to share their stories and ideas and to connect with people. All believe in the power of the written word and in the power of the book. The novelist wants to change people's lives by transporting them into a story; the journalist wants to find the story hidden in plain view; the self-help author wants to help people effect change in their lives. The greatest compliment any writer can hear from a reader are the words *Your book changed my life.*

As much as writers and agents complain that the publishing industry is interested only in bestsellers, the truth is that most of us live for the unexpected runaway successes. Sure it's fun to publish big celebrities (that is, until they treat you like the peon you are), but nothing compares with discovering an unknown writer working on an obscure topic and seeing that book come to fruition and meet with success in the marketplace. Whether it's Dava Sobel's quirky historical narrative *Lon-*

gitude or David Sedaris's hilarious essays in *Naked*, on everything from his nervous tics to his mother's cancer, the gratification of seeing a book break out is enormous, and it's what keeps everyone in publishing going. Every time an editor lifts the top off of a new manuscript box, listens to its cardboardy hiss, and takes her first intoxicating whiff of the fresh pages within, there is, if only momentarily, that renewed hope that this one will be it.

Unfortunately, the pressures of the publishing world too often diminish that feeling of hope, and editors, in dealing with the sheer number of submissions alone, don't have time to stop and smell the pages. We rely on a body of conventional and received wisdom about what sells and doesn't sell (which is thankfully proved wrong from time to time) and develop a shorthand to evaluate and reject projects. In combing through the minutes of editorial meetings where editors and publishers gather to consider the week's offering of projects, one sees the same phrases repeated over and over. Encoded within them are what I call editorial rejection euphemisms: *not right for our list* (get it out of here), *pacing problems* (boring), *exhaustive* (academic/ boring), *somewhat heavy-handed* (preachy), *not without charm* (too precious), *nicely written but ultimately unsatisfying* (plotless), *under-developed characters* (totally stock), *nice sense of place* (is this about anything?), *not enough tension* (mind-numbingly slow), *feels familiar* (yet another road-trip / coming-of-age / ugly-duckling / dysfunctional-family novel), *entertaining* (overwritten), *crowded marketplace* (not another!), and my personal favorite: *too special* (which of course means it won't sell).

It is incumbent on you to make your proposal or novel as bulletproof as possible. Anything can sink it, so take precautions, go the extra mile. Have it professionally copyedited if you're nervous about grammar, punctuation, spelling. Try to get endorsements from experts in the field before you seek a publisher. If your project comes with a blurb or introduction by a nationally regarded specialist, it will naturally attract more attention. Get feedback from other writers. If you're pitching a nonfiction idea, it's important to study the competition and in your proposal explain why your book is different, better. Sometimes the title alone will distinguish your book from the rest of the pack. Sometimes a catchy, clearly targeted title can make a project almost irresistible. Enticing readers is the Holy Grail of titling: A good title will go a long way, and if the book's contents live up to the promise of the title, you just may have something destined to sell for years. Lots of books are acquired without a title or with a bad title, but a brilliant one can improve its chances of acceptance.

Also, don't make the mistake of writing to publishers in what I call a proposal voice; this isn't a grant you're applying for—there's no need to pad the thing with high-minded promises. Editors and agents primarily want to know whether you can write and what the voice of the book will be. Write the proposal in the voice and style in which you have written or plan to write the book. Over the years I have witnessed too many writers who take the opposite approach, believing they must compose their ideas in the most basic terms. They are writing, they tell me, for the lowest common denominator. When I ask who they imagine reading their book, they invariably reply: everyone. No one seems to think that his subject matter is limited. Rather, everyone thinks that Oprah, if only she heard about the book, would plug it, no matter if it is about vegetation along the Merritt Parkway, overcoming halitosis, or the power of wishful thinking in Jane Austen's novels. The desire to popularize your ideas is neither uncommon nor wrong-spirited. It becomes problematic only when you imagine yourself somehow above your constituency in the process. So where do you pitch your book, or rather what is the right pitch? My advice is to write the book you want to read. Write the book that takes everything you've got. Don't imagine an audience of more than one. Don't try to outsmart the market.

If the *What to Expect When You're Expecting* authors had listened to publishing wisdom, which usually asserts that readers want expert medical advice only on medical topics, they never would have written their vastly successful book, now a staple on every pregnant woman's bedside table. And the authors have gone on to write a series of books that cover the child's early years. They wrote in a style of friendly authority, like that of a girlfriend who always reads ten books on every subject, a voice that women could trust. When Jonathan Harr set out to write *A Civil Action*, it's likely that more than a few people tried to discourage him. Who wants to read about kids who die of leukemia? Who wants to read about toxic poisoning? It took Harr many more years than he had planned to write the book, and he must have lost heart many times as each extension on his deadline came and went, as the money dwindled to zero,

freakishly mirroring the life of his main character, Jan Schlict-
man, who went broke trying the case. The success of Harr's
book pays tribute to an author going for broke and writing his
book with as much integrity and grit as a person can muster.

On the fiction side, the same holds true. Whether you are
writing literary fiction, a potboiler, a thriller, or a romance, you
must appeal to something real in the body of human experience. Always write with an ideal reader in mind. No writer was
more blunt in her appreciation of her audience than Jacqueline
Susann, who said that she wrote for the women who read her
on "the goddamn subways." "I know who they are," she continued, "because that's who I used to be." Susann understood
that the fantasy she created fed an intense envy and curiosity on
the part of her readership, women who dreamed of expensive
jewels, star-studded parties, and suave men with slow hands.
But she also gave her readers what they needed by making all
her rich and beautiful characters suffer. "That way the people
who read me can get off that subway," she said, "and go home
feeling better about their own crappy lives."

Susann's own life was more than a little crappy, though she
worked hard to conceal both her personal suffering from breast
cancer and the pain of having an autistic son. Some people
might dismiss Jacqueline Susann as just a trashy writer, but I
believe her success is underlined by her identification with her
audience. She never wrote down; rather, she wrote her heart
out.

I like to tell people to write for their mentor or their fiercest
critic. Write to the very top of your form. When rejection

comes, and it will, at least you will know that you did your best work. Every moment you spend explaining away the hurt of a rejection, telling yourself it wasn't your best work, is a moment that fails to advance your cause.

_≫_

If a wad of rejection letters is all it takes to get you to quit writing, then accept the consequences, but understand that it was you who gave that wad its power.

Every now and then an editor will get an irate letter from a writer for whom the rejection letter was the straw that broke the camel's back. The writer will rail against the rejection, quote the editor back to himself, and insist that the criticism is misguided. Some writers question whether the editor actually read the book, noting that the pages barely look riffled through. Some will demand a rereading, so convinced are they of the editor's subterfuge. According to Robert Hendrickson's wonderful book of literary anecdotes, _The Literary Life and Other Curiosities,_ one author wrote an editor who had recently turned down her story, "Sir, You sent back last week a story of mine, I know that you did not read the story, for as a test I pasted together pages 18, 19, and 20, and the story came back with these pages still pasted; and so I know you are a fraud and turn down stories without reading them." The editor replied, "Madame, at breakfast when I open an egg I don't have to eat the whole egg to discover it is bad."

Accusatory letters from rejected writers are depressing. It's impossible not to feel for the writer, to empathize with the helplessness, the depth of despair. Yet to answer these letters would be to invite madness. Most editors throw them out and pity the poor soul—though at some of the publishing houses where I have worked, such letters are posted on a communal bulletin board, which, in its collective desperation, resembles the wall of fugitives staring out at you in the post office. I like to believe that writing the letter and shooting it off in anger at least reclaimed some piece of dignity for the writer. The author must know on some level that an angry letter won't get him anywhere; but I like to imagine that it helps him get through another day, that it enables him to reclaim his writer's soul by saying, *You cannot erase me—I reject the rejection.*

Naturally, editors prefer to get letters thanking us for our time and asking if we might be willing to look at some future work. This, dear reader, is a better strategy. Unless you have received a form letter, it doesn't hurt to write a thank-you note. However, do not mistake a polite letter of rejection for a letter of encouragement. Every editor has experienced the sad submission of a writer who includes the rejection letters of other editors, all of which are clearly kiss-off letters, as proof of the project's appeal. The writer imagines that the sentences of faint praise are actually words of encouragement. True, some editors do get off on rejecting people, showing off their smarts and exercising their power, but most of us are truly uncomfortable saying no to people. I've often suspected that part of the reason why editors take so long to decline on projects, apart from never having enough time to consider them, is linked to how uncomfortable we are rejecting and disappointing people, whether it's the agent who has submitted the work or the un-known soldier who wrote it. Plus, we've all seen enough books that have been notoriously and strenuously rejected throughout the industry that nevertheless go on to bestsellerdom or critical acclaim.

Just as you shouldn't take a polite letter for an encouraging one, don't let a harsh letter do more damage than necessary. Maybe the editor writing it was just dumped by his wife, or ac-quired more than her share of projects, or lost the office foot-ball pool. It's hard not to focus too deeply on a rejection letter, or any correspondence from an editor, because it's often the only feedback you have, but I beg you not to spend more time with rejection letters than the time it takes to read and file them away. Do not paper your bathroom walls with them, as one woman I went to writing school with did; do not wear them down to a fine talc with your worrying fingers. Do not study them like the *I Ching*, hoping to draw symbolic meaning from the arrangement of letters on the page. Trying to figure out what the editor or agent *really* meant or felt is not useful unless she has offered some specific constructive criticism that resonates with you. Even if it is shattering to learn that the editor whose response encouraged you to totally revise your novel is now in the heart of Africa, you should have revised it only if you be-lieved it was the best way to fully realize the story.

Never do anything just because an editor tells you to. I have heard too many writers complain to me or absolve themselves of responsibility for a bad idea or a revision by saying that an editor told them to do it that way. No matter how desperate you may feel in your efforts to secure an agent or editor, don't go along with their advice unless you believe that it is right and sensible. It can be hard to decide when to stand your ground and when to capitulate. Most writers work in isolation for so long that they no longer have perspective. What's most important in the dance of submitting your work and getting it rejected is figuring out how to use the process to improve your material, and thereby your chances of having it published. "It is not too much to say that how well a writer copes with rejection determines whether he has a genuine literary vocation or just a literary flair," writes esteemed editor Ted Solotaroff in a superb essay called "Writing in the Cold." "Rejection along with uncertainty are as much a part of the writer's life as snow and cold are of an Eskimo's: they are conditions one has not only to learn to live with but also learn to make use of. . . . The gifted young writer has to learn that his main task is to persist."

The only writers I ever feel contempt for are those who announce that unless their work is accepted for publication they won't keep writing. Perhaps they save themselves lifetimes of grief, but I find the attitude astonishing in its arrogance and naiveté about what the world wants or owes anyone. The world is a mysterious place, and as far as I can tell, no one really knows why we all dance around certain texts and parade them through our streets. One thing, however, is certain: the only person whose rejection really counts is your own. No matter how many people return your work, the only one who can send you packing is yourself.

9.

WHAT
EDITORS
WANT

ASKING WHAT EDITORS WANT IS A LITTLE LIKE asking what women want. Even if two editors were to say that they wanted a literary novel or narrative nonfiction, cutting-edge psychology or a four-hankie tearjerker, if they each received the same proposal or novel, there is no guarantee that they would respond the same way. Although particular editors become known for loving and choosing certain kinds of books, an extraordinary number of variables affect any editor's taste, judgment, and response, and these are subject to change based on everything from the weather, her workload, her feelings about his colleagues, and the length of time since her last acquisition.

Some editors are hired with a particular mandate: to bring in celebrity books, sports books, business books, commercial fiction, health, or how-to. And some publishers are likewise focused. But for the average editor who works for a trade press, chances are she does a variety of books in what we call general adult trade, and whether those genres are broken down into rigid or fluid categories depends on the person and the press. For instance, if someone is known as a health editor, her opinion of a literary novel is considered less valuable than her assessment of a diet book. Whereas if she is the doyen of crime fiction at the company and claims to have found the next James Ellroy, chances are she will be supported in the acquisition. Generally an editor becomes known as an expert in a certain field after she has a certifiable hit, a book that either sells exceedingly well or that walks away with one of the big literary prizes. An editor does not exist without her authors; as the coach of any championship team acknowledges as he enters the winner's circle, he's only as good as his players.

When I started as an editorial assistant at Simon & Schuster, I was fortunate to be a fly on the wall of a publishing house that still had at its editorial helm two editors whose reputations were built on books that inspired awe. At one end of the corridor was Alice Mayhew, who shepherded the publication of one of the century's most important political books, Bob Woodward and Carl Bernstein's *All the President's Men,* a book that electrified the nation, if not the world. The other end of the hall was occupied by a man of slight build with a showman's glint in his eye, and I soon discovered that Michael Korda had worked with both Jacqueline Susann and Carlos Castaneda, two writers I had eagerly devoured as a high school student during the seventies. As far as I was concerned, these two editors were a part of history, and I felt both shy and giddy when our paths crossed in the long corridor known as editorial row (also known as Death Row, as the house was famous for its swift removal of any editor who didn't pull his weight and for its tyrannical leader who, fortunately, was housed many floors above).

Everyone who works with books is in one way or another attempting to become a part of publishing history. Just as the author hopes for immortality through publication of his book, most people in publishing hope to work on a book that touches people, entertains them, enlightens them, or changes them, a book that shapes the national dialogue or becomes a part of the lexicon. Over time, many book people become disenchanted and cynical about the business, but even the most hardened tend to soften when their company produces a runaway bestseller or a surprise success, a book they feel proud to be associated with.

During that same first year as an editorial assistant, I watched as Simon & Schuster discovered one such book on its list. It was by an academic from the University of Chicago, and it went against the grain of the political-correctness movement that was suddenly mushrooming on American campuses. Even more surprisingly, the book's initial printing was so small that when a rave review by Christopher Lehmann-Haupt in the daily *New York Times* vaulted it onto the bestseller list, no one was more astonished than the publisher. "Allan Bloom fools you in his remarkable new book, *The Closing of the American Mind*, which hits with the approximate force and effect of what electric-shock therapy must be like," began the critic. "By turns passionate and witty, sweetly reasoned and outraged, it commands one's attention and concentrates one's mind more effectively than any other book I can think of in the past five years." Lightning had struck!

It was very exciting to be at Simon & Schuster during that time, even though I obviously didn't have anything to do with the book or its success. There was a palpable sense that a book could still be a force of nature. In a world of $40 million movie budgets and Madonna, of Reagonomics and The Gap, this little flare from the pristine campus of Great Books Land was making headlines. One late night during a Scrabble game that I played each week with two other editorial assistants, I wondered aloud if the editor was enjoying his success, imagining what it might feel like to have a book on the bestseller list and stirring national debate. "He didn't bring it in, you know," one of the assistants retorted with a sneer. I didn't understand—he was the editor of record. My friends, who had been assistants for a year or more before I arrived, quickly filled me in. The acquiring editor, the man who had signed the book up, had left the company to run his own division at another house. We debated whether the editor who was responsible for taking the book through the publishing process was any less important than the one who brought it in. Finally, the assistant with the most seniority explained with an air of great wisdom and world-weariness that ultimately it was the person who signed the book, the acquiring editor, who mattered.

Signing up authors or acquiring projects is ultimately what separates the assistant editor from the person in the next cubicle who winds up going to law school or getting that graduate degree after all. The aspiring editor has to acquire a project of her own if she ever wants to be promoted, get out of a cubicle and into an office, be paid a salary she can actually live on without sharing an apartment with five roommates, and be granted a business card and an expense account and all the other accouterments that seem so unattainable when one starts out. If you surveyed a random group of editorial assistants, it quickly would become clear which ones were secret writers, hoping to use the job experience as a jumping-off point for their own careers; which ones, too in love with Literature or some romantic notion of how the world should work, would never cut it in the grueling, competitive environment; and those who brought just enough book smarts, good taste, marketing savvy, and social skills to succeed in the age of corporate publishing.

The year I entered publishing, 1987, an article entitled "Nobel House" appeared in *New York* magazine, about the estimable independent publishing firm of Farrar, Straus & Giroux. (Even the name sounded more like a tweedy old law firm than a book publisher.) Most of my favorite poets were published there, and I salivated as I read about the care with which the house treated its authors, its commitment to quality and literature. According to the article, the firm took an almost perverse pleasure in publishing books with little or no audience ("FSG prides itself on its often brazenly uncommercial titles"), spending as much time on an unknown Polish novelist as on Tom Wolfe. According to the article, Roger Straus, the publisher, was famous for "barb-trading" with Dick Snyder, the head of the house where I worked, saying that "he cried for the trees sacrificed to produce

Snyder's books." In describing FSG's appeal, various authors, including Philip Roth and Alice McDermott, weighed in with praise, remarking on the accessibility of everyone who worked there. Scott Turow said, "Everyone there is a standout, from the amazingly literate salespeople to the publicity department. Long before my book was a success, they were all spectacularly kind to me at every turn." Walker Percy said of cofounder Robert Giroux, "He's a man of great good taste. One writes with a sense of who your reader is, and Bob Giroux is my imaginary reader." But the quote that really impressed my youthful, idealistic soul came from the production director, who explained that FSG still used metal type to set their books instead of film, which is less expensive and the way all the other houses have gone. "We feel typefaces in metal have a nicer look, more expressive," she explained.

Everyone who comes into book publishing has a special re-lationship to books, understands their mystery and their power, even if their careers take unexpected turns and don't end up the way they had planned. In certain respects, the climb up the ed-itorial ladder is not unlike the writer's quest for publication. The apprenticeship is long. Many, if not all, of the ideas and manuscripts a young editor brings to the attention of his supe-riors are rejected. He often wonders if it's worth it, especially when he watches a fellow assistant who seems to be the soul of corruption get a leg up. Advancement is not guaranteed, and whether an aspiring editor sticks with the long hours and largely uncertain future often depends on whether he is en-couraged by more senior people in the company.

I had the good fortune of finding a mentor, either directly or from afar, at every publishing house where I worked, and from each I gleaned some inspiration. At Houghton Mifflin I had the privilege of working with Ruth Hapgood, a beautiful woman with nearly translucent skin and long white braids that were always neatly pinned into a bun. Ruth introduced any number of health gurus to the public long before alternative medicine took off. At her retirement party, Ruth, never long-winded (a virtue in and of itself in the publishing business), thanked people for their friendship and collegiality. She told us not to worry about her, she had enough dreams for six people. But then she became quiet, searched out our faces as she scanned the room, and said in a lowered voice, "All of you are the children of the book. Remember who you are."

I never forgot the admonishment or the phrase "children of the book," and I like to think of it and to remember Ruth when cynicism in the business runs high, when people seem not to remember what they are trying to do or why they chose this low-paying, thankless field. I like to think of it every time a book I have sunk my heart and soul into vanishes without a trace, or when a beloved author gets a hideous review in the paper of record and I want to rail against the powers that be for giving my kid a bad grade: *She deserves better than that! She worked so hard!* But I especially like to think of Ruth every time a new college graduate finds her way into my office for an informa- tional interview and tells me with complete sincerity, when I ask her why she wants to become an editor, that she loves books. I want to tell her to run for the hills, as the senior agent

I once worked for had tried to warn me. I want to tell her that the surest way to kill that love is to work in a publishing house, just as going to writing school will surely kill the aspirations of any number of writers.

Yet, somehow, no matter how beleaguered the world of editing has become, no matter how short a book's shelf life in today's market (Calvin Trillin's now-famous line is that the life of a book is somewhere between the milk and the yogurt), no matter how uncertain the future of any publishing career today, none of us can ever forget the feeling of first discovering the majesty of reading. (Roger Straus III, son of the cofounding father of Farrar, Straus & Giroux, claims to have had his first "literary orgasm" at fourteen while away at boarding school, when he discovered "The Lovesong of J. Alfred Prufrock." Who doesn't remember that moment?) Working as a book editor brings with it the possibility of re-creating that feeling through the discovery and nurturing of authors. The joy of working on a manuscript, holding a finished book that one has helped shape, is not unlike the midwife's joy for those who believe that communication through the written word is miraculous.

❧

As a junkie craves a fix, an editor gets off on the thrill of discovering a new writer. There is even something vaguely amatory about the whole mating dance when an editor is in pursuit of an author, especially one who is being vied for. I have heard authors complain of editors who were far more attentive before they signed them up than after, almost as if the conquest were the point. Sometimes an editor will go for months without reading anything that inspires him, that makes him stay up past his bedtime or miss his bus stop, or causes his throat to constrict. Whenever a fellow editor starts to complain about how long it's been since he's acquired a book, it reminds me of how my friends and I used to lament how much time had transpired since we last got laid. And as with sex, the longer you go without it, the greater the chances are that you'll lower your standards. Acting out of desperation—whether with partners or projects—all too often ends in disaster.

After an editor has won the hot project being offered around town, she's a bit like a lioness after capturing her prey, lazily chomping on the spoils from the kill, her tail absently smacking flies off her rump as she surveys the savanna, certain no other game is on the horizon. But the editor who loses one project after another, either because she can't find support in-house, or because the advance goes higher than she is allowed or willing to bid, starts to feel and act just a little too hungry. After a few months of this, she will jump on anyone's bones, all judgment and perspicacity out the window. When I left one publishing house for a decidedly more commercial company, the editor-in-chief who had been my boss for four years took me aside as I was packing up my office and said he would like to offer one small piece of counsel. I couldn't imagine what he was going to say. "One word," he said, leaning in: "patience."

An editor newly arrived at a publishing house feels enormous pressure to make that first buy, to plant the flag, and this often means trying to acquire a big-ticket item. Added to the pressure is the likelihood that if one editor feels all hot and bothered when she reads the proposal, chances are a half-dozen other editors around town feel the same way. Before copying machines, agents used to send manuscripts out one at a time. Xerox is as much to blame for the present competitive climate among publishers as any cultural shift. One suspects that electronic submissions, which have already reared their ugly heads, will speed the process even more. This is fine if it achieves efficiency, if it spares trees, and all that. But no matter how fast we can transmit material, the fact is that writing and editing, if done well, are extremely slow processes. And it strikes me that taking a certain amount of time to consider a project is warranted.

The editor who nurses a Maxwell Perkins fantasy of discovering great authors, having three-martini lunches, and making gentleman's agreements will be sorely disappointed to discover that in today's publishing climate it's eat or be eaten. The publishers themselves have recognized that they must merge and solidify operations and distribution lines or risk disappearing altogether. Just ten years after the *New York* magazine article about Farrar, Straus & Giroux, the house that prided itself on its independence was bought by the German conglomerate Holtzbrinck. About the same time, Bertelsmann bought Random House; Warner had already bought Little, Brown; Pearson bought Putnam and merged it with Viking Penguin; HarperCollins bought William Morrow; and as in the Agatha Christie title, then there were none.

Now more than ever, editors are under tremendous pressure

to acquire. And with fewer houses, the number of players is always being reduced, as if publishing were a game of musical chairs. The editor who can find a project of quality or commercial potential and edit it well will no longer survive on those skills alone. She has to be faster, more clever, and more resourceful than the editor next door as well as the editor across town. She needs to have the clout to convince her publisher to pay as much money as will be required to win the next big book at auction when the asking price escalates in competitive bidding. It's tremendously exciting to be a part of such a feeding frenzy, raising the bid with every round like a poker player pushing all his chips to the center of the table.

Some editors feel perfectly at ease in this gambling game; *It's not my money*, they tell themselves. But it's not as if an editor has free rein to spend; most editors have to have the publisher's authorization to make even a modest offer. And yet, as we see over and over again, when one too many of those big books bombs, heads tend to roll, whether it's the editor's, that of someone higher up on the food chain, or personnel cuts across the board to get budgets back in line. Some editors are more fiscally responsible than others. They get nervous spending a lot of money on a project, almost as if the money *were* their own. In fact, nothing relaxes them more than when the agent calls at the end of a long auction and they hear the word that spells relief: underbidder.

Some people in publishing think an editor has to spend big to earn big. Others prefer to put their eggs into several smaller baskets and hope that a couple will hatch into bestsellers. Still, everyone wants that big book, which is why every six months or so a *New York Times* article claims that the industry is going down the tubes, neglecting the midlist, failing to support writers in midcareer, failing to develop new talent. Media-driven conglomerates are blamed for expecting unrealistic returns on their investments, more on a par with Hollywood profits than book royalties. And yet when the industry's health seems most threatened, journalists and pundits love nothing more than to point the finger of blame at editors, who, they claim, no longer edit, as final proof that the sky is falling.

In fact, heavy-duty editing is a fairly modern phenomenon. Before Max Perkins came along, very little was done to manuscripts. The policy at Scribner's, where Perkins worked, was decidedly hands off. In a letter from senior editor William C. Brownell to Edith Wharton, the company's editorial policy was made clear: "I don't believe much in tinkering, and I am not *suffisant* enough to think the publisher can contribute much by counselling modifications." So it was more than a little unorthodox for the young Perkins to respond to an unknown writer's novel, entitled *The Romantic Egoist,* with extensive suggestions for revision. This was a manuscript that had bounced from editor to editor, each of whom had found it unpublishable and attached his opinion: "Couldn't stomach it at all," said one; "Hard sledding," wrote another.

As Perkins's biographer Scott Berg explains, editors at Scribner's felt it beyond their purview to offer criticism of manuscripts they declined. "But Perkins's enthusiasm impelled him to comment further." After one revision, the writer paid a visit to

Perkins, and while it is not known what happened, the young writer set off and began another round of changes, including switching the narrative point of view from first person to third. Seven months later a complete revision landed on Perkins's desk. Every one of his suggestions had been taken, including the transposing of the story's point of view. The title page, also revised, now read *The Other Side of Paradise.* According to Berg, Perkins brought the novel to the monthly editorial meeting for "his third assault." Once again the editor was met with a dismissive attitude by the more senior staff, and it looked as if he was going to give up when Charles Scribner entreated him to explain his point of view. "My feeling is that a publisher's first allegiance is to talent. And if we aren't going to publish talent like this, it is a very serious thing." Perkins argued that Fitzgerald would get another publisher and attract other young writers to that firm. "Then we might as well go out of business," he said. "If we're going to turn down the likes of Fitzgerald, I will lose all interest in publishing books." Smart young editors have been using the same argument ever since to convince the old fogies that they risk losing business if they lose touch with the next generation of readers.

❧

If editing has become a luxury in today's world, because of the accelerated pace of publishing and the pressures on editors to spend their time acquiring, it is no less important in the life of a book. No matter what anyone may ascertain about an editor's abilities, it is finally the writer who knows whether his editor has a gift for language, an understanding of structure, a grasp of the dynamics of plot, pacing, tension, and resolution. Only the writer knows if his editor edits. The best editor is a sensitive reader who is thinking with a pencil in her hand, questioning word choice, syntax, and tense. An editor is someone who probes the writer with insightful questions, who smooths transitions or suggests them where none exist. A good editor knows when the three pages at the beginning of a chapter are throat-clearing. *Start here,* she'll mark in the margin, *this is where your book begins.* And she'll know when you should stop, spare you from hitting your reader over the head as if your point were a two-by-four.

In a 1946 speech to welcome and introduce Maxwell Perkins to the students in NYU's publishing course, Kenneth D. Mc-Cormick, then editor-in-chief of Doubleday, described the great editor as "more a friend to his authors than a taskmaster, he aided them in every way. He helped them structure their book, if help was needed; thought up titles, invented plots; he served as psychoanalyst, lovelorn adviser, marriage counselor, career manager, moneylender. Few editors before him had done so much work on manuscripts, yet he was always faithful to his credo, 'The book belongs to the author.'" When the quality of editing is attacked, and editors who don't know a restrictive from a nonrestrictive clause are held accountable, I like to remember that Perkins, the man who became synonymous with great editing, by his own admission was a terrible speller who used punctuation idiosyncratically.

A good editor should be able to go as many rounds as a

writer needs to get his revision just right, though an inverse equation often rules: those books that require the most work may be least improved by editing. Often the editor has to work hardest on a book that was mediocre to begin with, and, after she labors over everything from structure to grammar, soup to nuts, the book is still only readable. The finest writers, often perfectionists, tend to require the least amount of an editor's time. I think most editors would agree that nothing is more satisfying than working with a writer whose quality of mind and ability with prose are exquisite and well matched. As the first editor I ever worked for said, after finishing his line-edit on a very fine biography that was eleven years in the making, "It was like polishing silver."

Editing is a science and an art. There is a basic architecture to every book, and if the author has a wobbly narrative leg or an insufficient thesis to stand on, the editor must find the blueprint or create one. What an editor learns as she gains experience is that while no two manuscripts are exactly alike, certain predictable patterns crop up, and as with math problems, the more experience you have, the more readily the solutions appear. I have often applied my understanding of the formal structure of poetry to the books I work on. At the beginning of my career, I found it difficult to hold a many-chaptered book in my head, but when I imagined each chapter as a stanza and used my knowledge of how a metaphor builds throughout the argument of a poem, it was easier to keep the bigger picture in mind as I helped the writer shape sentences, paragraphs, chapters. Every prose writer has his own rhythms, from sentence structure to the length of paragraphs and chapters, and the editor must help him use that form to its most powerful effect, just as Perkins was able to see that Fitzgerald's novel would work when written from a different point of view.

The art of editing is a dance one engages in with the author to help him achieve the best results. Before an editor can cut a paragraph or a page, she must establish trust. Suggesting that a writer delete his words is excruciating for some, and the exci-sion must be made with delicacy. Sometimes this means the use of subtle queries in the margins: *awk? right word? believable? trans? rep?* Of course, what the editor means is: *totally awkward, terrible word, completely unbelievable, how the hell do you expect the reader to make a transition when you haven't,* and *this is so damn repetitive I feel like killing myself.* But if the editor wants the writer to address these problems, she will find it useful to flag them with lightly pen-ciled queries. Likewise, she will pepper the manuscripts with appreciation: *lovely phrase, great word, nice transition.* An editor builds trust with an author through the careful attention to his pages. The comments and queries become a net beneath the writer so that he feels emboldened to risk the high wire, to the thrill of the crowd below. The editor says, *I won't let you fall.* The editor says, *I will catch you.*

I had the unique experience of editing the work of an autis-tic woman. Dealing with her absolutely literal mind and repet-itive thought process was an astonishing test of patience, but it was not without rewards. Helping her translate her pictures into words enabled me to see the world through her eyes. Though she told me more than once that she couldn't understand the subtle cues that the rest of us trade in as part and parcel of our basic communication skills, it took a while before I stopped trying to politely urge her to stop repeating herself. Finally I wrote in big, dark letters in the margins: BORING. REPETITIVE. YOU HAVE TO MAKE A TRANSITION HERE. And she got it. Or I suppose you could say, I got it.

The editorial dance between author and editor isn't complete until the author takes the marked-up manuscript away and goes back to work, taking, the editor hopes, her suggestions and improving upon them. When editors talk about percentages, they mean how much of their editing the writer took. According to the editors I speak with, the percentage varies greatly, though I think it would be very difficult to continue editing if you didn't feel that writers were mostly appreciative.

❦

Only a writer knows for sure whether an editor is making a serious contribution to and improvement of his work. Only the writer really knows how good an editor is on the page. While industry watchers are eager to point out how few editors edit, they never report on those books that were nearly rewritten by editors or that were cut to within an inch of their lives.

The reason is twofold: first, once the book is published, the editor's marks are invisible. Second, the idea of authenticity is central to our literary culture. Don DeLillo rightly counseled his friend Gordon Lish, whose editorial contribution to Raymond Carver's success has been hotly debated, to take a big step back from the fray: "There is no exposing Carver," DeLillo wrote. "Even if people knew, from Carver himself, that you are largely responsible for his best work, they would immediately forget it. It is too much to absorb. Too complicated." He further explained that readers wouldn't fault Carver for relying so heavily on his editor as much as they would resent Lish for sharing the credit.

For an article about the true provenance of Carver's work for *The New York Times Magazine*, writer and former editor Dan Max visited the Lilly Library at Indiana University to see first-hand the extent of Lish's editing in the archives. "What I found there, when I began looking at the manuscripts of stories . . . were pages full of editorial marks—strikeouts, additions and marginal comments in Lish's sprawling handwriting. It looked as if a temperamental seven-year-old had somehow got hold of the stories." Max charted what reads like a classic father-and-son story through the correspondence between the two men, in which the son, suffocating under the father's controlling hand, yearns to break free. While the father, astonished at the son's lack of appreciation, clings more fiercely. At first, Carver is deeply grateful to Lish, telling his editor in a 1971 letter, "Took all yr changes and added a few things here or there. . . . You've made a single-handed impression on American letters. . . . And, of course, you know, old bean, just what influence you've exercised on my life." Ten years later, when Carver is at the height of his fame and struggling to wrest his sentences from Lish's mighty blue pencil, he finally writes, "I can't undergo that kind of surgical amputation. . . . Please help me with this book as a good editor, the best . . . not my ghost."

"An editor does not add to a book," Perkins warned a group of students toward the end of his career. "At best he serves as a handmaiden to an author. Don't ever get to feeling important about yourself, because an editor at most releases energy. He creates nothing." It's hard for an editor to remember that all he has done is release a little energy when he has discovered a writer, nurtured him for years, rewritten him in some cases, and gotten him ready to meet the world. It's hard to remember that $e = mc^2$ when the writer in whom the editor has invested the breadth and depth of his creative attentions and on whom he has staked his reputation says, *Stop, you're suffocating me.* Perkins, too, had learned the hard way.

It was during the writing and editing of Thomas Wolfe's second book, *Of Time and the River,* that the relationship with the brilliant and complicated writer began to devolve. Wolfe was adding 50,000 words a month at a fevered pitch, and Perkins apparently pulled the book away from him, fearful that the writer was on the brink of breakdown. Years later, in an article for the *Carolina Magazine,* Perkins wrote, "I, who thought Tom a man of genius, and loved him too, and could not bear to see him fail, was almost as desperate as he, so much was there to do. But the truth is that if I did him a real service—and in this I did—it was in keeping him from losing belief in himself by believing in him." Perkins read the manuscript in its entirety—one million words—and set about delineating the two separate story cycles within. The work they did together was legendary, and in thanks, Wolfe dedicated the novel to him, despite Perkins's attempt to discourage him from doing so:

To Maxwell Evarts Perkins
A great editor and a brave and honest man, who stuck to
the writer of this book through times of bitter hopelessness
and doubt and would not let him give in to his own
despair . . .

Two years later that dedication would be used against Wolfe
in a piece that ran in the *Saturday Review* called "Genius Is Not
Enough," attacking Wolfe for not having the "critical intelligence" to have pulled off his novel without the help of his editor. Scott Berg suggests that even as Wolfe lashed out against
critic Bernard De Voto to anyone who would listen, the piece
struck the very deep vein of his terrible insecurity, and he grew
to resent Perkins for being the bearer and enabler of his terrible
secret. The relationship never rebounded; the two exchanged
letters that suggest the emotional wreckage of a love relationship come undone. No writer, no matter how grateful, wants
his mother forever straightening his lapel as he gets up to accept
his prize.

✻

No reviewer ever says, "By God, this book was well edited,"
though reviewers seem to have no compunction about slam-
ming editors for not doing more, when they have no idea how
hard an editor may have tried to eliminate a character or help
an author with his tone. If a book is basically solid and the author insists on keeping certain elements his way, the editor usually accedes. It's the author's book after all—though some editors

will make a last attempt to get the author to make changes, even going so far as to pull what I call the Jewish Mother caveat, insisting, *The changes are for your own good,* or *We just don't want you to get hurt,* or *I won't say I told you so.* Still, it doesn't make it any more pleasant when the reviews come in exclaiming, *This book sure could have used an editor.* Once, after a book I worked extremely hard on received such a notice, even my own mother called and asked why I didn't edit it. *Mom!*

One of the great thrills for an editor is to have a revision come in that feels transformed. It may be the result of a complete overhaul or of just getting a whole lot of tiny details finetuned, but suddenly the writing sings where before it had only hummed. In describing the editorial process, editor and writer Charles McGrath said of Robert Gottlieb, an editor who has worked with some of the finest writers of the last few decades both in publishing houses and at the helm of *The New Yorker,* "Bob has an uncanny knack for putting his finger on that one sentence, or that one paragraph, that somewhere in the back of your mind you knew wasn't quite right but was close enough so that you decided to worry about it later. Then you forgot about it, or you convinced yourself that it was okay, because it was too much trouble to change. He always goes right to those places. It's an instinct. He and I share a belief that if you take care of all the tiny problems in a piece, all the small attention will somehow make a big difference. Sometimes I think that's just a touching faith of ours, and that, in fact, nobody ever notices whether, say, you use the same word twice in a paragraph. At other times I'm convinced that the details are all that matter."

Editors and authors are happy to crow about their successful unions. One rarely hears about the books that didn't live up to expectations, the relationships that fell apart or ended badly, as the Perkins–Wolfe collaboration eventually did, and the Carver–Lish affair decades later. For every author devoted to his editor, many more feel short-changed, cheated, slighted, forgotten. An editor's stable of writers tends to resemble a family of siblings in which a clear favorite emerges, in which the hard-working, dutiful ones never feel appreciated, while the ones who drive their parents to distraction also win their hearts. There are some writers whom the editor banishes and some who preemptively banish themselves.

I have learned from experience that the only way to deal with sibling rivalry is not to engage. For instance, when a writer asks what else I'm working on, I try never to tell him. In the first place, he doesn't really want to know, and in the second place it's a trick question. What he's really trying to determine is whether his book is the most important on my list. Authors know that their editors are working with a number of other writers at the same time, but they still want to feel unique, and in this way being an editor is not unlike being a shrink. You know your therapist has other patients, but you're the most interesting, right? She likes you the best. And just as a shrink sees a person at his most vulnerable, editors see a side of authors that no one else ever should: we see them at their most needy, their most egomaniacal, delusional, paranoid, insecure, and arrogant. We are on the receiving end of false flattery and buttering up, as well as tantrums and sulks.

It is the dream of most editors to amass a group of writers and work with them over their writing lives. This has become a nearly impossible feat in an age when authors and editors jump ship in the quest for better advances and salaries, respectively. Sometimes an editor moves on because she needs to be seen in a new light, just as an author sometimes needs to be reimagined by a publisher who has no history with him or her. Everyone has reasons for moving on, and it is not necessarily a bad thing to do so, but at the same time I have known no greater joy than to watch a writer develop from book to book, to see her prose and imagination stretch, her ambition fueled, to be both surprised and delighted that someone whose abilities I thought I knew so well had a book inside her I never dreamed possible. This, too, is what editors want.

Today's acquisitions editor must walk the high wire of trying to get the best projects into the publishing house, convince her colleagues of their merit, spin the books in-house as effectively as possible with the marketing and publicity departments, and pull whatever strings she can with reviewers, magazine editors, television producers, movie and foreign scouts, and bookstore buyers to give the book a fighting chance in a market crowded with a million titles vying for the same space. On top of that—and usually after office hours, when the phones aren't ringing, deals aren't pending, and colleagues aren't appearing at the door with some new crisis or deadline—she must edit the manuscript so that there will, in fact, be a book at all.

❧

Every now and then everything works out: everyone at the company loves a project as much as the editor does; she is al-

lowed to top the high bid and win the book at auction. The author turns out be a lovely, hardworking person who takes all
editorial suggestions, including a new title that everyone agrees
is brilliant. The art director presents a jacket that is so beautiful
and original and right for the book it takes everyone's breath
away. The editor introduces the author to the director of publicity, who then wants to send him to every bookstore in America—he's that promotable.

When the editor sends the manuscript to key people in the
marketing department and on the sales force before the sales
meeting, it is met with universal approbation. Marketing wants
the author to meet with key booksellers in advance of publication and decides to make up T-shirts and posters for key buyers. The sales force recommends the book to all their accounts
and requests that the publisher produce an advance reading
copy to get booksellers excited. First serial rights are sold to *The
New Yorker.* Barnes & Noble selects the book for its Discover
program. Borders writes it up in its newsletter. It's a staff pick
at many independent retailers. Steven Spielberg buys the movie
rights. All the top newspapers give the book glowing reviews.
Thomas Pynchon comes out of seclusion to rave on the front
page of *The New York Times Book Review.* Oprah selects it for her
book group (the grown-up equivalent of getting a gold ticket in
your Willy Wonka chocolate bar). The book appears on the
bestseller list, climbs, and stays there for a record-breaking number of months. The book is nominated for this, shortlisted for
that. The editor signs up the author for his next two books. She
gets a big bonus at the end of the year and feels like Cinderella

at the ball, with midnight nowhere in sight. And for a brief while, she doesn't wake up in a cold sweat wondering when she's going to be fired. This, too, is what editors want.

Every year one or two books seem to have their stars thus aligned, and all of us in publishing watch as that much-longed-for ideal, a book that achieves both critical and commercial success, materializes. The above scenario, or a close approximation, could have been written in recent memory about Wally Lamb, the only author to have *two* books selected by Oprah for her book club. Or about Arthur Golden, whose first novel, *Memoirs of a Geisha*, was ten years in the making as the author struggled to find the right voice. "I had to throw out my entire 800-page draft," Golden recalls, "and start from scratch." The novel has sold more than a half-million hardcover copies, has been on the *New York Times* bestseller list for over a year, has been translated into twenty-three languages, and has been optioned by Hollywood with, yes, Steven Spielberg slated to direct. Or about *Cold Mountain*, another book that was nearly a decade in the making, and that defied industry convention as well as pressure from the national bookstore accounts to put a Civil War image on the jacket, displaying instead a beautiful abstract painting. The book eventually sold more than a million hardcover copies *and* won the National Book Award.

People in publishing are students of the industry, watching these seemingly blessed publications and keeping tabs on them the way a veteran gambler plays the ponies. We know the history of every book that breaks out and track its rise on regional, chainstore, and distributor bestseller lists. We know the amount of the advance, the editor, the agent, the number of copies the publisher first printed. We track the ad campaigns, roughly tallying how much the publisher is spending. We read the reviews and debate whether a good review is also a selling review, whether a negative review has any impact once the book has momentum. Sometimes we even make time to read the book amid all the submissions we have to read and manuscripts we have to edit just to see what the fuss is all about.

We tend to feel kindly and generous toward some successes, deeply chagrined and mingy about others, depending on who is involved. One editor I know, in talking about rivalry and jealousy, among editors, put forward the theory that every one of us has a bête noire, a person of reasonably similar position and taste, who drives us to distraction and with whom we are highly aware of being in competition. And in that spirit we crowd the fax machines on Wednesday nights like a group of shaggy dogs at the nearby OTB, waiting for the advance copy of publishing's ultimate racing form: the *New York Times* bestseller list.

It's easy to forget, in this ultra-accelerated culture of ours, where even fusty book publishing is caught up in the national fervor for celebrity and where the value of all things is equated with their dollar value, that what most editors truly want is good books. No matter how much it may seem otherwise, no matter how many mediocre or just plain bad books get fed into the great machine, most of us are in awe of a brilliant manuscript and will do everything in our power to see that it reaches readers. No matter how competitive editors may be with each other or with their authors; no matter how little or how much they edit; no matter how beleaguered or esteemed—editors are a breed apart. And in a world threatening to go electronic, our pencils and Post-its and erasure shavings sometimes seem as antiquated as the letterpress and quill pens of yesteryear. But editors are still the world's readers. And thus the eyes of the world.

10.
WHAT
AUTHORS
WANT

"MY DEFINITION OF A GOOD EDITOR IS A man I think charming, who sends me large checks, praises my work, my physical beauty, and my sexual prowess, and who has a stranglehold on the publisher and the bank," said John Cheever, in what might be the truest words ever uttered by a writer when asked what he wanted from his editor. All writers have a fantasy of who their editor will be and what the relationship will be like. In the best cases, the pairing is as mutually agreeable as a good friendship, in which each party feels ennobled by the other's company. And in some cases the relationship does grow into a friendship and may become intimate or personal. After all, when an editor gives a writer a contract, the effect can be no less intoxicating than the words every lover hopes to hear: *I choose you.* Not only does the editor want you, he is staking his reputation on you. Unfortunately, many such pairings do not survive the first rush of excitement, when the thrill of acquisition is overshadowed by the reality of day-to-day work. More than a few author-editor relationships have fallen apart when disenchantment sets in. But in the best of all worlds, somewhere between Cheever's fantasy and reality, a mutually beneficial relationship is forged.

"The first thing writers want—and this sounds so basic, but you'd be surprised how un-basic it is in the publishing world— is a quick response," said Robert Gottlieb in a *Paris Review* article entitled "The Art of Editing," which serves as a case study on the editorial process from the author's point of view. A number of Gottlieb's authors were tapped for accounts of their experiences working with him. Most editors would cringe at the thought of being thus dissected by their authors, but the comments from this roundtable of literary lights make it clear that Gottlieb has in abundance both the gift of language and the psychological acuity to handle each author's individual needs. In simply understanding the need for a speedy response and providing one, Gottlieb lays the foundation for trust, which is the basis of any healthy working relationship with a writer.

Most writers are simply too paranoid and prone to magical thinking to imagine that silence from an editor is anything but a death knell. Writers are desperate to hear from their editors once they've turned in pages. Some even try to force their way into the office and have the editor read their pages while they wait. This way madness lies. In my very early, inexperienced years, I once let a writer pull this stunt. I proceeded to read while she sat across from me, pretending to be distracted by the other books on the shelf and the collage of pictures on my bulletin board. But every time I so much as twitched my lip, she burst out of her seat and demanded to know what had made me smile. If I furrowed my brow, she'd lunge across the desk and demand an explanation, as if I were a suspect in a major crime. At one point I laughed, and when I looked up in anticipation of her inquisition, she just smiled and gazed out the window, as if suddenly supremely confident of her powers. Only ten seconds later she asked, "Where are you now?" and "What was the line that made you laugh?" Since then, when others have tried to get me to read while they waited, I have flatly refused, explaining that they won't be able to sit with every person who buys their book, and gauge the reactions. Reading, I like to remind them, is not a team sport.

"Once they've finished a new manuscript and put it in the mail," continued Gottlieb, "they exist in a state of suspended emotional and psychic animation until they hear from their editor, and it's cruelty to animals to keep them waiting." Most writers become fairly agitated awaiting a response from the editor. Some have been known to decompose completely during the waiting period. They are parents anxiously pacing outside the intensive care unit, who care about just one thing: *Is my baby going to make it?* What they often don't realize is that in today's publishing climate, editors are required to do far more than edit their books. They must serve as mini-publishers for each of their titles, which means that their time and energies are always stretched exceedingly thin. As a result, taking on a new author can sometimes feel like adding an eleventh child to a family of ten. Happy as Mom is for the new baby, she's not sure where she'll find the time to nurture her or the food to feed her. The new baby doesn't give a fig for the ten before her, she wants all of Mom's attention now.

When editors sign up a nonfiction project, they usually give the author twelve to eighteen months to finish the book. During this time some authors want or expect a great deal of attention, even when they aren't producing any pages. As I grew more experienced with writers, I realized that like small children, they work best with some guidelines and boundaries. To that end I hold fast to two rules. The first: no pages, no lunch. Having concrete work to talk about is by far the most productive use of an author-editor meeting. Second: call before sending chunks of manuscript. Forewarned, I can give an author a reasonable estimate as to when I will get back to him. There is nothing more disconcerting for an editor than to have four hundred pages of a manuscript show up without warning. It's not that we don't want to edit the manuscripts, it's just that it's like having out-of-town guests show up uninvited for the weekend.

Editing requires a kind of deep immersion, a total concentration, and the best among us average five to ten pages an hour. It's possible to pick up some speed if the manuscript is really clean, but it's slow, painstaking work that demands complete concentration. In addition to the actual time it takes to edit, time that few of us can take during the workday, one needs to create the mental space. And sometimes an overanxious author can unwittingly crowd that space by calling too often. I am completely sympathetic with the anxious writer, and doubtless there are editors who are negligent in the extreme, but if you basically trust your editor and are impressed with the authors and books she has worked on, try to diffuse your anxiety in some other way.

Not all writers are so dependent on their editors for assurance; some are even disdainful of any interference. The master himself, Vladimir Nabokov, was more than dismissive in describing how he felt about editors and their services. "By 'editor' I suppose you mean proofreader," he said. "Among these I have known limpid creatures of limitless tact and tenderness who would discuss with me a semicolon as if it were a point of honor—which, indeed, a point of art often is. But I have also come across a few pompous avuncular brutes who would attempt to make a 'suggestion' which I countered with a thunderous 'stet.'"

Some authors crave the blue pencil. They seek out those friends or readers who are unafraid to be completely honest, whose opinions lead to improvements in the work. Edith Wharton described one friend with whom she had a lifelong literary affair whose critical response she credited for both sharpening her prose and helping her see the world anew. "I suppose there is one friend in the life of each us who seems not a separate person, however dear and beloved, but an expansion, an interpretation, of one's self, the very meaning of one's soul," she wrote. "Such a friend I found in Walter Berry. . . . He alone not only encouraged me to write, as others had already done, but had the patience and the intelligence to teach me how. Others praised, some flattered—he alone took the trouble to analyze and criticize. . . . Once I found my footing and had my material in hand, his criticisms became increasingly searching. With each book he exacted a higher standard in economy of expression, in purity of language, in the avoidance of the hackneyed and the precious."

I have known authors who were truly dependent on and grateful for feedback, while some paid only lip service to the editorial process. When I came up against tremendous arrogance in a writer, I realized that usually more than the words was being defended. Perhaps his work had been mangled by a previous editor or decimated by reviewers. No matter how much bluster a writer produces, he still wants to be loved, to be read, to be praised. It's no coincidence that famous older writers are often assigned to young, eager editors. At the end of their careers, these writers are often resistant to any editorial suggestions, but they still need someone to kick around. And no one on earth is more slavish than an eager associate editor newly assigned to a literary lion. Until, of course, he gets eaten for supper.

Writers want to be catered to. And who can blame them? Having survived the deprivations and degradations of being an unpublished aspiring nobody, why shouldn't you hope for a little . . . delicacy? I remember one fiasco in which a young editor had done a line-edit for the editor-in-chief and had composed a letter to be signed by her, all of which is fairly standard practice. Said chief reviewed the letter, made some changes, signed it, and had the letter sent to the author with the manuscript without having reviewed the assistant's line-by-line work or comments in the margins. When the package arrived, the writer, believing that the running commentary was from the

chief herself, went ballistic and threatened to take his book
away from the company. As it turned out, in his inexperience,
the young editor had made a number of marginal notations that
would give most writers an aneurysm: *Pretentious! Hello? Incoherent!* and, my personal favorite, *Repetitive! Repetitive!*

Eliciting revisions requires more than delicacy; it requires a
certain understanding about the writer's general temperament
and well-being. Some writers are dead serious about their work
and defend each word. Some are deeply analytical and need
only be presented with reasons to make changes. Others work
on instinct and feeling; they traffic in nuance and tone. Some
authors are humorless. I usually like to have a trial run of editing around seventy-five pages to see how an author responds
before continuing on the entire text. Almost in a reversal of the
authorial anxiety that attends handing in pages, I'm always anxious about the author's response. Will he or she take to my editing? When I hear about author-editor relationships that have
run aground, it is usually the author who is cited as the malcontent. But it is also true that some editors fail to realize that
an author needs more than the benefit of line-by-line editing; he
needs someone who has the sensitivity to build confidence in
the writer as he revises his text.

✦

In order to calm a writer's nerves sufficiently and give him the
necessary assurances that he has indeed come in from the cold,
the editor has to figure out what he needs to feel safe and to
stay productive. Is this a writer who just needs to be pumped

up with encouragement? Or does he like a spanking? Does he need to be read the riot act, or will a measured response convey the problem? I now cringe recalling some of the ways I allowed authors to run roughshod over me. One of my first editorial experiences was with a highly neurotic woman who had been signed up to write an oral history even though she had no research skills. After six years she still hadn't turned in a page, and when her editor left for another company, she was assigned to me. The editor-in-chief went on at great length about what a privilege it was for me to get a project of this caliber. I smelled a rat.

I knew the project was going to be a colossal headache from the moment I first laid eyes on the writer. Actually, she looked fairly normal—it was the two brown shopping bags from Bloomingdale's that she schlepped in that told me she would ruin my life. She spoke nearly nonstop for over two hours about her project and her inability to judge the value of her transcripts, which constituted hundreds of unedited interviewing hours. She was completely uncertain as to whether anything she had transcribed was usable. I promised I would read through the transcripts—1,400 pages' worth—and highlight the best material. Her desperation and my naiveté conspired in such a way that she left feeling better, while I remained—the two brown Bloomie's bags now in my court. I retrieved the pages and stared numbly at the dot-matrix type. I spent the next three weekends alternately cursing myself out for having agreed to read the transcripts. I never did see the fruits of my labors because I took a new job before the manuscript was completed—if it ever was.

As I grew more experienced and confident, I learned how to ward off writers who hadn't brought their material to a reasonable level. You have to read unedited transcripts only once to know that life really is too short. I also began to see that writers often were looking for more than editorial or professional advice, and while I was sometimes uncomfortable making some of the bigger decisions, such as how to end the book or what the author should do next, I realized that writers often wanted my mediation. In describing her editorial relationship with Gottlieb, Cynthia Ozick identified the unspoken transference that tends to occur between a writer and an editor. "An editor is often a father figure, a mother figure, a kind of ministerial figure . . . someone who stands in authority over you and has something to tell you."

For me, as an editor, the transference was often mutual. More than once when a writer, especially a first-time author, handed in his pages, I felt they were presented with the innocent hope and pride of a small child offering a first art project. And sitting amid a sea of folding chairs at a reading, watching my author read from her book, I often felt that she was giving her first recital, my heart in my throat as she worked her way through the sections that I alone knew had given her trouble.

Writers sometimes need an hour of an editor's time, and what they want has very little to do with fixing sentences or correcting proofs or requesting ads. They want and need hand-holding, and no matter if they have loved ones, friends, esteemed colleagues, and extremely expensive psychotherapists, few people understand what they are going through or share the same level of investment as the editor or agent. "Sometimes I feel like I'd make a lot more money," said Eric Simonoff, an agent, "if I charged an hourly rate, like a psychotherapist."

Authors want an editor who knows what he is doing and who, like a good host, never lets his guests know that they have overstayed their welcome. I remember attending a cocktail party in London at the home of one of publishing's grande dames. It was during the first week of a six-week editorial fellowship to learn about British publishing. The first thing I learned was that everyone in England still smoked and drank. The parlor was filled with smoke and the sound of clinking glasses as editors and writers crowded together. But at precisely eight-thirty, our hostess began to shuttle various conversation circles toward the door by corralling people, her arms encircling the waists of her guests in a firm grip, drawing them near and exclaiming in hushed tones, as if to deliver some juicy gossip, "Have you *ever* known a party to go on this long?" So conspiratorial was her affect that people felt absolutely compelled to down their sherries and get a move on. Her powers of persuasion, not lost on a single guest, most certainly contributed to her reputation as one of London's most formidable editors.

"An editor has to be selfless," says Gottlieb, "and yet also has to be strong-minded. If you don't know what you think, or if you're nervous about expressing your opinion, what good is that to a writer? I remember working on a book of John Cheever's and feeling there was a minor problem with the ending. At first I thought, Who am I to be telling John Cheever to change the end of his novel? And then I thought, Well, I'm the editor he chose, and I can't, out of cowardice, withhold what I think. I'm not forcing him to do anything. I'm saying, This is what I think is wrong, and it's up to him to decide whether to take my advice or not. As it happened, he immediately got the point and found a solution."

What goes on between a writer and an editor is as mysterious and alchemical as a marriage. Some relationships are terrifically sadistic, abusive, and malcontent, while others are filled with mutual respect, adoration, and appreciation. But what most writers want, it seems to me, is to feel secure. They don't want surprises. They don't want to be kept waiting. They want their criticism meted out along with praise. They want to know why you don't like this, and some want to know how to fix it, while others want to be left to their own devices. Most have such deeply ambivalent feelings about what they deserve and how good they are that they are often bouncing between their desire for approval and fear of rejection. Then again, if they didn't struggle with issues of need, attention, disapproval, isolation, and social life, chances are they wouldn't be writers.

"It took me some time," said Gottlieb, "when I was a very young man, to grasp that a writer—even a mature, experienced one—could have an emotional transference on me. But of course, it makes sense: the editor gives or withholds approval, and even to a certain extent controls the purse strings. It's a relationship fraught with difficulty, because it can lead to infantalizing and then to resentment. Somehow, to be helpful, an editor has to embody authority yet not become possessive or controlling." Novelist James Salter explained in a *Publishers Weekly* interview that he and his Random House editor, Joe Fox, became friends over the years. "I found him authoritative, but he also had that nice quality of saying, 'All right, if that's what you feel.' I think a good editor does that, unless you're obviously headed for the cliffs."

Writers want to know that they are not alone. After the long struggle to find an editor and a publisher, a writer wants to feel that finally he has found some protection, some support. A contract is symbolic of many things, not least of which is the implied commitment of another person to see you and your book through, to walk you down the aisle the way a father walks his daughter on her wedding day. The writer wants a relationship with his publisher, and the physical embodiment of that relationship is usually the editor. Cynthia Ozick describes her editor as a combination of muse and guardian angel. "Now, very often when I am writing, I have something like a bird sitting on my right shoulder, a watchful bird looking over my shoulder at what I am doing. I want that bird's approval—I have to get it. It is a very critical bird, who is in a way a burden, but also grants me *permission*." Most writers want that bird to help. To tilt its head this way or that as they peck out their pages. They want their editor to leave bread crumbs, Hansel and Gretel-like, a trail that shows the way but that vanishes as surely as those scraps of bread across the forest floor.

❧

In my experience, most writers are happy to be shown the way or provided with a solution, especially if the manuscript is in some kind of trouble. Almost every book I have ever worked on needed help with the pacing and structure. The challenge of sustaining a certain pace and rhythm throughout an entire book can be staggering, and most writers are too involved with the details to see where the story flags. I like to imagine the narrative as journey. Just as a trip feels shorter on the way home, a phenomenon all school-age children remark on, even though it is exactly the same number of miles as the trip away, the reader expects that time will pass more rapidly as the book heads toward the finish. Once we know the way, the scenery rolls by like so much wallpaper. Your editor should help you see when the writing has turned into wallpaper.

When readers speak of being hooked from the first page, what they most likely mean is that the writer has earned their trust. It's a silent and immediate pact that the reader doesn't even realize he is making. In just a few introductory sentences we know whether we are traveling by Concorde or ocean liner, whether we need seat belts or life preservers. And more important, whether we want to go along for the ride. No matter what genre you are working in, keeping the narrative moving will keep your reader, and it is the editor's job to address those sections where the tire is leaking or, worse, is completely out of air.

The best editors call attention to those parts of the book that have been bothering the writer, if only on an unconscious level. One editor told me how he won the contract for a book over another publisher who was willing to pay much more money. The author, who was a perfectionist, had let her agent submit the book even though she had a number of reservations about the story and was uncertain how to resolve these out-standing issues. The publisher who was willing to make a hand-some two-book deal felt that the manuscript was ready to go. The other editor recited exactly what he felt was wrong with her book and how he would restructure it to solve the prob-lems. His criticisms were identical to her own, and it was worth it to this writer to both delay publication and take a smaller ad-vance to have her book handled by an editor whose feelings and ideas about it were synchronous with her own.

Questions of how to handle the passage of time are easier to cope with once a structure has been decided on. Like the foun-dation of a house, a book's parameters, once set, dictate only so many ways to build. Usually within the first two or three chap-ters, all the major decisions of any consequence have been made, whether or not the writer is aware of his choices. Mat-ters of tone, tense, point of view, time frame, syntax, style, and narration are like the pipes and electrical lines: you may not see them buried beneath floorboards and behind Sheetrock, but you can depend on them to bring you light and water. Books tend to be constructed either chronologically or thematically, with many variations on the theme. But even if you don't have a narrative per se, your book needs to find its inner logic so that the reader does not feel she is entering a hall of mirrors. Begin-nings, middles, and ends, no matter how they are shuffled, are the ways in which we organize our lives.

Not all writers have an innate sense of structure. As a young editor, I used to think that those who couldn't structure their books were somehow inferior to "real" writers or people with "natural" ability. I imagined that skill in the handling of time was akin to having an innate sense of rhythm in music, and that you either had it or you didn't. I've since revised that notion, having worked with brilliant authors over the years who committed all kinds of time crimes and didn't see the structure their own sentences and paragraphs suggested. I have also worked with writers who were flummoxed when it came to connecting two scenes or collapsing a week's events into a day to advance the narrative more swiftly. Whether you want to chronicle a lunch hour, as Nicholson Baker did in *The Mezzanine*, or have your main character worry about a single dinner party, as Virginia Woolf did in *Mrs. Dalloway*, or concern yourself with a single day—June 16, for instance—you must find and adhere to a specific structure. If you plan to write an epic covering many years and many lands, such as the *Odyssey* or the *Ramayana*, you will need to chart an entirely different course. Are you concerned with one terrible century, one terrible summer, one terrible night?

In her collection of essays and reviews *The Eye of the Story*, Eudora Welty articulates the importance of time and how it functions: "Time can throb like a pulse, tick like a bomb, beat like the waves of a rising tide against the shore; it can be made out as the whisper of attrition, or come to an end with the explosion of a gun. For time is of course subjective, too. ('It tolls for thee.')" A good editor—whether for fiction or nonfiction—crouches like a coach on the edge of the track, his stopwatch grasped tightly in hand, clocking a writer's progress as each sentence strides toward the finish. Sometimes merely breaking a long paragraph in two can take a few seconds off a writer's time. Sometimes breaking apart a long chapter can give a feeling of movement and breadth. A writer can use paragraphs and space breaks the way a poet uses stanzas, each one setting forth a new beginning, signaling to the reader that we are going through another door. A good editor knows that paragraphs, space breaks, new chapters, and part divisions are far from arbitrary. Just as a driver uses directional lights to signal his turn, a writer uses these devices to say, *Here, this way, come with me*, or *Take a breather, refill your glass, get into your pj's and then we'll read one more chapter.*

❧

Any writer doing work of real interest is by necessity going out on a limb, taking chances with either the content or the style of his material. Does the limb hold, or does it break under the strain? Will the writer wish, months or years from now, that someone had stayed his hand? Of course, the writer must decide what to include and what to leave out, but a trustworthy editor can make all the difference. John le Carré said of his novel *A Perfect Spy* that it was his most autobiographical novel and the one closest to his heart. "It skates along the edge of a great deal of childhood pain and stuff. Bob [Gottlieb] pointed out the places where he felt that the fiction became so autobiographical that it became embarrassing—where he felt that I had really spilled into private experience and had thrown away the mask. He was terribly good at that. What we left on the cutting room floor still makes me blush."

Most writers swear up and down that they want the whole truth from an editor, but this is rarely the case. While the editor should be able to tell the writer everything that's on her mind, especially where the book fails, few writers can handle the truth, which is why an editor's good bedside manner cannot be overvalued. At no time is this put to the test more than when the relationship ends. After I had been editing for half a dozen years or so, I found myself spending countless hours at the computer trying to explain in detail why a beloved author's book wasn't "cohering" and thus why I had to reject it. It was an exercise in the gravest diplomacy. There could be no doubt that I was rejecting the manuscript, yet my criticisms had to be couched in language that wouldn't devastate the writer. I had been putting off sending the letter, despairing of the consequences. Not only was I the author's editor, I was her friend as well. And now I had to tell her why the book was no good, a response that most writers internalize instantly: *My book is no good, ergo I am no good.*

Some writers, however, reject the rejection. When Paul Theroux's editor took him out to lunch to turn down his seventh novel, he told the young writer that he didn't believe in the book and couldn't publish a book he didn't believe in. As Theroux describes the scene in *Sir Vidia's Shadow,* he lashed out in response, "You publish lots of crappy books. If you turn this down you'll lose me as an author. I'll go to another publisher. I'll never let you publish another book of mine. And all it's costing you is two hundred and fifty quid. This lunch is costing you thirty!" When the publisher replied that he'd publish the book if Theroux twisted his arm, Theroux snapped, "That's it, then. That's all. Forget it—I want my manuscript back." Then he confessed to wishing he could shove his publisher in the path of a car. Doubtless a lot of authors have the same wish.

Theroux's response seems healthy to me—healthier, in any case, than letting one editor shatter your belief in yourself. Some writers, angry at the powerlessness of their situation, especially when no other publisher is waiting in the wings, begin to feel that editors are arrogant at best, sadistic at worst. But the truth is that most editors fear confrontation of any kind and feel terrible about turning down an author, especially one with whom they've developed a relationship. And though few admit it, an editor may begin to question her taste and judgment in light of these decisions, especially when, after letting a writer go, she sees his next book break out. When the new publisher makes a success of a writer who has been languishing, the feeling industrywide is often one of astonishment. Turning a writer's career around is extremely difficult, given how much an author's previous sales track has come to dictate the level of support bookstores are willing to give. But sometimes a new team of publishing people can, with the right book, relaunch a writer with savvy and brio and make lemonade where others saw the pits. It must feel like sweet revenge to the writer, and sweet revenge is something nearly all writers want as well.

When I had to turn down my friend and author's book I was a wreck. A much more senior editor stopped by my office and noticed my agitated state. When I explained what I was facing, he ran to his office and returned with an envelope, which he flipped onto my desk. Then, without a word of explanation, he ducked out again.

The letter inside, a single-spaced carbon copy typed on a manual, was dated nearly thirty years earlier. It was the most moving, generous, and intelligent editorial letter I had ever read. It explained in exquisite detail why certain characters in the novel were not believable and how the writer might make critical changes to ensure their verity. It spoke of pacing, setting, and style. It spoke of bringing the book's deepest themes into relief through the restructuring of flashbacks. The editor also felt that the book needed to be told in the third person so that the novelist could make the wife's point of view more convincing. He spoke of the beauty of the prose but wondered if it wasn't overshadowing the simple human gesture at the book's core. In essence, the editor had opened the chest cavity and held the heart of the novel, carefully outlining the necessary surgical procedure to resuscitate it. But more important, he wrote in a spirit of friendship and respect for the author's great literary accomplishments and beseeched him to consider his advice so that this book would maintain the author's reputation in the literary world. In closing, the editor harked back to the half-dozen books the two had already worked on together and hoped that this novel, with the major overhaul he was suggesting, would be his best yet.

After I finished reading the letter, I returned to the senior editor's office and slumped down in the chair facing his desk, which held little more than whatever the editor was reading at that moment, a pencil, a dictionary, a shabby lamp with a wooden base, a box of cough drops, and the manual typewriter on which the letter had presumably been composed. Most editors of his accomplishment surround themselves with walls of books and framed jackets of the renowned titles they have worked on. His modest furnishings and half-filled shelves betrayed none of his extraordinary experience in publishing some of the greats. I told him the letter was the most amazing editorial response I had ever read. I said I was humbled by how much I still had to learn in terms of corresponding with writers and how this editor had walked that very fine line of telling a writer his book was not good enough while filling him with hope and ideas and confidence to tackle the revision.

Finally I asked what happened, whether the writer took his suggestions. As it turned out, he had taken his book elsewhere and gotten it published on the strength of his name. The book was a colossal failure and the two men never spoke again. I asked the older editor if he felt vindicated. In answer, he lowered his eyes, shook his head, folded the letter, and returned it to the drawer. I ventured that the writer was a fool for not taking his advice and reiterated that I had never read anything like his letter. "Well," he explained with his characteristic wit, "I guess it's a little like telling a guy you think his wife is ugly."

I turned my friend's book down with what I thought was a great deal of tact, but my result was no better. The rejection was a bitter pill, and we didn't speak for some time. I give her a great deal of credit because she finally confronted me and accused me of abandoning her and our friendship. She was right. I was so preoccupied by my own sense of guilt and disappointment that

I failed to reach out to her. She struggled with the book for a number of years and revised it many times, throwing hundreds and hundreds of pages away before finally feeling satisfied. After a change of agent, the novel was submitted again, along with a brilliant collection of short stories. I tried to convince the publisher I worked for at the time to make an offer, but I didn't have the support. Another publisher made a handsome offer for both books. When I called to congratulate my friend, she started to describe her new editor in glowing terms. Even after everything we had been through I felt jealous, as if watching an old lover go off in the arms of another. Yet I think the writer and I were both a little relieved as well. Now, finally, released from the professional pressure, we could just, to carry the metaphor, be friends.

⚜

The only thing writers want more than getting into print is staying in print. No matter how well your book is received, there are no guarantees that it will have staying power or will not be supplanted by the next big thing. Martin Amis, in a *Paris Review* interview, summed up the attitude of most writers toward their fellow authors. "I feel generally resentful of younger writers," he said. "You're not thrilled to see some blazing talent coming up on your flank. Dislike and resentment of younger writers is something fairly universal among writers." Even when a writer's stature and currency are as assured as anyone's can be—and Amis certainly enjoys more literary distinction and reported financial gain than many—I find it fascinating that his eye would still be trained over his shoulder. "The older writer," he elaborated, "at some point, is going to lose touch with what the contemporary moment feels like." As one of the most successful upstarts, who upstaged not only the older generation of writers but his own famous father as well, perhaps Amis is more attuned to the Oedipal threat than most.

Editors are likewise prey to the rivalries and jealousies that each new generation of editorial talent brings. I will never forget the week I lost two projects at auction for books by hot young writers to editors ten years my junior, both of whom were newly promoted and highly touted. They had both been editorial assistants at the company where I had previously worked, and I felt like something of a mentor to them. Now my kid sisters had walked off with the prize. I complained bitterly to an agent friend, who reminded me that I had had my moment and was now a well-established editor with a stable of writers. Isn't that what I had always wanted?

It is impossible not to be envious of a young writer whose first novel seems for the moment to captivate all the world. I remember one writer guiltily confessing to feelings of sheer joy when he heard that someone with whom he felt highly competitive was suffering from an extended bout of writer's block. Another writer told me that she couldn't write for three months when a rival novelist's book was in the spotlight. She felt she was by far the better writer, but knew that the other's work would always prove more popular with the critics and enjoy better sales. Her jealousy was killing her.

Writers want justice. They want some insurance that their

drive, their will, their hope and delusions, their madness and profligacy, and their fierce self-belief will produce work of lasting value. What writers want is to be taken on their own terms, to have their books praised or panned according to their own stated or implicit goals, not according to the whim and prejudice of critics who say they should have attempted something different, more in keeping with the critics' ideals or notions. "Writing a book is a horrible, exhausting struggle, like a long bout of some painful illness," wrote George Orwell. "One would never undertake such a thing if one were not driven by some demon whom one can neither resist nor understand. For all one knows that demon is simply the same instinct that makes a baby squall for attention."

No matter how lonely or driven the writer, no matter how many others he would gladly trample or shove in front of an oncoming car so that his own words could emerge triumphant, what writers finally want more than good editing and smart marketing and ten-city tours and two-book contracts and appreciation (make that worship) and lucrative movie deals and hoity prizes are readers. Loyal, avid readers.

11.

THE

BOOK

THE PUBLISHING PROCESS MIGHT BEST BE described as everything that happens between the writing of the book and its reading by the public. No matter how well or poorly a publisher readies a book for the marketplace, there are finally only two people, the writer and the reader, and the opportunity they have to connect through the power of words on the page. It is easy to forget how truly intimate the encounter is between writer and reader.

Most first-time authors are woefully unprepared for what to expect when they're expecting to publish. Some publishers prepare a booklet about the process that they give their authors along with the contract. But somehow even the best author's guides, with their descriptions of clearing permissions, formatting text, and reviewing page proofs never fully convey exactly what happens once a book is accepted for publication. Some writers, so grateful for a publishing contract, are reticent about asking what the process entails. Others, full of information from writer friends or expectations nursed over those many months and years waiting for publication, come with a good deal of knowledge, as well as a lot of misinformation heavily laced with fantasy.

Journalists, who are used to speedy responses, especially if they work on dailies or weeklies, are often shocked when they discover how slowly the wheels of book publishing turn, from editorial responses to production schedules to selling cycles. Publishers ideally like to have nine months from the time the book is completely edited to its publication date, during which time the book is copyedited, designed, typeset, proofread, and manufactured. At the same time, sales representatives are criss-crossing the country taking orders, publicists are attempting to get advance bookings, and marketing people are working with bookstores and other avenues through which to sell or market the book.

Most of the disappointment that a writer experiences in having a book published can be traced back to his initial expectations and how well he was informed about the publisher's plans. What most writers don't understand, but learn all too quickly and painfully, is that landing a contract and being published do not guarantee the fulfillment of all their hopes and dreams. In fact, getting onto a publisher's list just means that your book will be physically produced and catalogued for booksellers to evaluate. Whether booksellers actually order your book depends on a great many factors, most of them not in your control, such as what other books are being published that season, whether booksellers perceive the category as glutted, whether they are skeptical about the author's credentials or ability to interest the media, and sometimes whether they hate the jacket. They know they can always order the book after publication if they discover that they've passed on something that is gaining momentum. But an initial lack of interest will affect how the book initially is perceived and performs. No matter how many times an editor walks a new author through the process, until he finally goes through it there is little the editor can do to quell his fears. And in many cases, authors' fears are justified, especially when they begin to sense that getting published may not be everything they had imagined.

One doesn't have to work in publishing for very long to know that a great deal of time is spent in letting people down gently. I had been an editorial assistant but a few weeks when I fielded my first author-in-distress call, from a woman in her mid-thirties whose first book had been published about six weeks earlier. She wanted to know what was "happening" with the book. I told her I'd pass her message along and gather what information I could. What I discovered after talking with her editor, my boss, was that the first printing was very small, that the sales force didn't feel it distinguished itself enough from other books in an already crowded category, that publicity had been able to get only a couple of local radio interviews, and that reviewers weren't biting. All told, the book was DOA. When I asked my boss if there was anything we could do for the author, he shrugged. It wasn't that he didn't care; it was more that as a seasoned professional he knew when and how to call his shots. Much as he liked the author and this project, he understood that its viability in the marketplace was negligible unless something truly miraculous happened. When I asked why he had signed it up, he explained that he had believed in it, the author's credentials were solid, and she had a worthwhile message. What I didn't understand then was that you just can't know if that message will translate to a wider audience until you've put it out there.

At the time I was extremely upset by all of this. The woman had sounded desperate on the phone, and I had promised to call her back with an update. I pressed my boss about how to handle it. He explained that her expectations were out of scale for a book on the health-care system. It was a good and important book, but as the sales force and publicity departments had discovered, there wasn't much of a market outside of health-care administrators. The book clearly wasn't going to sell, and it didn't take much to realize that everyone whom I tried to get answers from was evading the questions.

When I finally screwed up the courage to call the author back, I told her, as I was instructed by the publicist, that the publicity department was still trying to get reviews and that we might get a break in one of the professional journals. Like many authors I've worked with since, she believed that the critical silence in response to her book was personal. "They hate me," she cried. "I can't believe no one's going to review it. I put four years into this book." Not knowing what to say, I asked her about her research and about the process of putting the book together. (In college I had been good at talking people down from bad acid trips, and my skill returned in force.) After listening to her passionate description, I asked if any good things had happened since she had written the book. As it turned out, writing it had given her the confidence to stop teaching and work full-time in the health-care profession, which she truly loved, and the book had helped her land a fast-track job in that field. I told her that I thought her personal accomplishment was tremendous and that the book had clearly done more for her than she realized. Most of all, I told her, you did it. For every person who writes a book there are thousands who believe they could. She seemed buoyed by our conversation, and I had gotten my first real taste of an author's unhappiness.

Somewhere between the acceptance of a manuscript and actual publication, a great deal happens, or doesn't happen, that greatly influences how well the book will be received, by both critics and consumers. The unpredictability of the business—whether reviewers or bookstores support the book, whether it will get a break or remain ignored—is what makes the process both maddening and thrilling. Still, if publishers didn't think they knew what they were doing on some level, paralysis would ensue. There is a famous story of an expensive consulting firm coming into a publishing house in the mid-eighties, just as the merger fever of that decade started to have its impact on the book business. The consultants spent six months interviewing employees at every level, analyzing distribution lines, warehouse systems, accounting practices, and profit-and-loss statements. After crunching numbers and systematically breaking down operations, they came up with the following recommendation: Since 10 percent of the titles account for 90 percent of the revenues, why doesn't the company publish only the 10 percent that are profitable—that is, only the bestsellers. A clever-sounding strategy. The problem, the publisher explained to the consultants, was that we never actually know which is which.

Although some publishers improve their odds by specializing in particular categories and becoming extremely adept at packaging, marketing, and distributing one kind of book, most of the trade houses still produce a fairly eclectic list every season, with a range of fiction, literary and genre, and a range of nonfiction, including how-to, self-help, and lifestyle titles. Most publishers take their cue from the marketplace and produce books according to current trends and tastes in everything from jacket design to trim size—that is, the height and width of the book page. There are a handful of tried-and-true formulas for packaging books that seem to have currency. Go into your bookstore and examine a dozen books in any given category: parenting, business, health, literary biography, and you will easily ascertain how a certain look dictates the general style in which the titles are presented. Most publishers adhere to tried-and-true formulas. For instance, a health title will usually have an all-type jacket on a white background, lending it an air of seriousness and authority—the idea being that people looking for medical advice want a package as reliable as an aspirin bottle. Some publishers will depart from the conventional look in an attempt to set a book apart or break it out, while others leave well enough alone; if ain't broke, don't fix it.

All of these decisions fall under the general heading of positioning. And as publishers prepare a book for the marketplace they engage in a series of meetings to focus that effort. Once an editor has a complete manuscript, or one that is close enough that the book will make it into the next catalogue and selling season, she prepares a variety of materials about the book, such as sample pages, author credentials, and tip sheets with marketing handles and comparison titles. These are circulated to key people in various departments within the company, such as sales, publicity, and marketing, to acquaint them with the project. This process varies from publisher to publisher, but all follow the same general trajectory. Having worked at four different companies over the course of my career, I have learned that the particular emphasis in a house generally emanates from the publisher's own career path. In other words, if the publisher worked her way up through sales, she will tend to put the most emphasis on selling. If she came up through publicity, she will tend to focus on how the media will react and how to secure promotion for the book; if the publisher has an editorial background, he will focus on the book itself and on the writer. This is what people mean when they call a publishing house sales-driven, or marketing-driven, or editorially driven. There is always an emphasis on one part of the process, and that emphasis influences everything from the size of the first printing to the jacket.

❧

One of the most visible ways in which a book reaches its market is through its jacket, and the jacket or packaging meeting is usually the first in the process. In some publishing companies the art director won't even think about starting the jacket until he has a manuscript to read. Other publishers begin work on their jackets with nothing more than an editor's description of the material. I used to think it was blasphemy for an artist to work on a book without having read it, but I have to confess that the very best jackets are not always as a result of the designer's having read the book. Sometimes reading the manuscript can be a hindrance, leading to a jacket that is too literally conceived.

Everywhere I've worked, I have witnessed the most acrimonious behavior surrounding a book's jacket art. While most people are somewhat circumspect about commenting unfavorably about the content of a book (especially to the editor of the project), everyone has an opinion on the jacket and feels perfectly qualified to offer it. Usually, when a jacket is displayed at this first meeting there's an immediate rush of enthusiasm or adverse reaction. The worst, however, is when the unveiling is met with a pregnant pause. A famous art director at a major company was known for ripping jacket comps in half when an editor took too long to respond.

Jackets, like faces, can tell you quite a bit about what's inside. When an editor and author see a jacket for the first time, it's like looking in the mirror. If the reflection doesn't radiate the qualities you believe your book possesses, it will be disappointing, maybe worse. Some authors don't care what is on their jacket as long as their name is prominent. Others take the art personally and cannot separate from it. One author, in a moment of supreme anguish over a jacket image she hated, threatened to pull her book from publication. As her editor I completely understood her dilemma; I take supreme pleasure in the presentation of books, so much so that if the jacket on a book I am reading strikes me as wrong, I have to remove it. Other people cannot even tell you what the jacket of the book they are reading looks like. They don't judge books by their covers because they are interested only in the content.

Most people fall somewhere in between those extremes, and the presentation and marketing are aimed at that person, who may or may not pick up your title for any number of reasons, most of them subliminal. The person who walks into a store with a specific subject in mind—a book on accounting or bedwetters or flower arranging—shops with diligence. Another has either read a good review or perhaps had a book recommended to her, and she will likewise make a fairly concerted effort to find that specific title. But many people come into the bookstore feeling vaguely hungry though uncertain what they're in the mood for: Chinese, Italian, maybe a burger. They look around. Sniff. Hover over the display table stacked high with its spanking-new eager offerings. A jacket, a title, an author—some combination of these elements will beckon and the prospective buyer will pick up the book. He may examine the back, the flaps, he might even read a first line or paragraph. In the end he may not buy the book, but the packaging did its job by enticing the browser.

Why are so many authors unhappy with their jackets? And why are there so many bad jackets? The two main reasons involve the usual suspects: time and money. As soon as a pub-

lisher comes up with the first pass at a jacket design, he has
started to spend money. The meter is running. The editor hopes
against hope that the first few designs will come close to some
ideal in her mind's eye, because once that clock starts, the options shrink. If the author hates the jacket and the publisher
loves it, or if the budget and deadlines are used up, the editor
can be in the unfortunate position of having to convince her author that it's a great jacket or, taking a more politic stance, that
it's *right for the book*.

I once worked on a memoir by a young woman whose
childhood cancer had caused facial disfigurement. A poet, she
wrote with haunting beauty about her condition, universalizing
the particulars of her rare illness. We all agreed on a literary
treatment for the jacket and farmed it out to a top designer. He
returned with three mock-ups: one incorporated a mask, which
had been an element in the story, but here it made the book
look like a thriller. The other jackets used bandages in different
collagelike patterns, which made me think of mummies. Time
was growing short, and we had spent a small fortune with no
jacket to show for it. Then I returned from lunch one day to
find a photographer's portfolio on my desk. I didn't see any note
attached, and I opened the box. Staring up at me was a black-
and-white photograph of a young girl, her face obscured by the
piece of cellophane she was looking through. I knew in an instant that this was the image we had been looking for. It perfectly captured the inner landscape of the writer's life as she
grappled with the loss of something as basic to one's identity as
one's face.

As it turned out, the photographs were part of a submission by an Irish photographer who collected the tales of Tinkers in the Irish countryside. Although I was unable to convince my company to publish the book of pictures, I did persuade the photographer to contribute his photograph for my author's jacket. The little Tinker girl was often mistaken for the author herself, so perfectly did the image convey the book's interior.

Publishers do not as a rule rely on any kind of market testing, apart from showing the jacket to various people in the office and canvassing their reactions. Unlike the magazine world, where marketing can afford to test jackets in different geographic regions, publishers make their decisions either on their own or by some quorum of their choosing. Needless to say, sometimes the process works, sometimes it's disastrous. The most obvious but most overlooked reason why so many authors complain about their jackets is that an art director is generally responsible for anywhere from fifty to a hundred titles per season. It's not like marketing a new low-fat tortilla chip or breath freshener: every book is a product unto itself and requires a unique package. Art directors are under tremendous pressure to produce an enormous amount of original artwork, and often they work under the most arduous conditions—without a manuscript to read, with an editor who may not provide clear direction, with an artist who may be temperamental or blocked, and with a publisher who may be completely inarticulate about why he doesn't like a design yet has no ideas to offer.

The worst mistake you can make is to let an author's spouse or partner create the jacket. In my opinion, spouses or partners

shouldn't be allowed to do anything for the book, just as sur-
geons are not allowed to operate on their loved ones. I once in-
herited a project at the jacket stage. It was a memoir about a
marriage, and the author's husband was a freelance artist. Naturally she wanted him to produce the jacket, and the previous
editor had agreed. When the husband's design came in, it was
awful. The author insisted that she loved it, and it would have
been most awkward to say anything to the contrary. Fortunately,
the sales force rejected the jacket at sales conference and a new
one was created for publication. Much later, the author confessed to me that she was relieved that the original jacket didn't
fly; she actually didn't like it either, but was afraid to hurt her
husband's feelings.

In a letter to his editor, F. Scott Fitzgerald complained vociferously about the jacket for his novel *Taps at Reveille*, which
followed *Tender Is the Night*, citing no fewer than six people who
commented on its awfulness. Having spent so much time trying to create charming characters, he said it was "discouraging"
to be stuck with an artist who couldn't draw better than his five-
year-old daughter. He added that he didn't want to sound un-
grateful or be a pest but was writing on the "off-chance" that
what he had been shown was a sample and that there was still
time to try again. It may prove comforting to some writers to
know that authors at every level and for all time have felt themselves ill served by their jackets.

The best way to avert jacket disasters is for an editor to
glean from an author what exactly is in his mind's eye and to
have some discussion before a line is drawn or penny spent. As

the author's in-house advocate, the editor can communicate the author's wishes to marketing and the art director as well as squash any really stupid ideas on the author's part. It's hard to let go and trust that you will like your jacket and that everything will be okay. Find out from your editor when the process starts and tell her what jackets you like and give a rough idea of what you envision. If you actually have a photograph or a piece of art in mind, share it with your editor. If there is a style of type or a color you absolutely hate, let her know. Publishers prefer their authors to be happy. But they don't have the time or resources to give an author an endless number of choices, unless that author is a bestseller. I promise you, Tom Clancy, Mary Higgins Clark, and Stephen King aren't chuntering about their jackets. Sometimes it seems that we'd all be better off publishing the French way: all type, no bother.

❧

Once the jacket art is under way, the next series of meetings involve marketing, publicity, and sales, and this is often where an editor can "make or break" a book. Sometimes the attendees have been given some sample material from the book, but more often than not the editor's presentation of the book and the author are all they have to go on. The editor will have produced a title sheet with biographical information, a brief description of the book, competitive titles, the author's track record if there is one, marketing ideas, and probably the most important element: the sales handle. This is your whole book boiled down to a sentence, and in recent years Hollywood parlance has slipped into publishing lingo with a vengeance. According to a *New York* magazine article called "How to Make a Bestseller," Knopf characterized Jane Mendelsohn's *I Was Amelia Earhart* as "*Jonathan Livingston Seagull* meets *Blue Lagoon*." An editor at Grove described the recent novel *Shooting Elvis* to a reporter as "*Thelma and Louise* meets Tarantino."

But what's worse is if a book can't be easily boiled down. If the editor can't say "Oliver Sacks meets *Pride and Prejudice!*" or "*Catcher in the Rye* meets *Blair Witch Project!*" or "*The Rise and Fall of the Third Reich* meets *There's Something About Mary!*" then it's harder to put the book over in bookstores, where a rep sometimes has but a few seconds with a buyer to make a point. Likewise, the publicist may have to pitch the book to a television or radio producer in twenty seconds or less. The problem with boiling a book idea down is that it reduces it to a single essence, and the best books consist of many essences. Still, in the world of sound bites, it's critical to get a good, juicy one.

Sometimes the editor is too close to the book to make a good, clear presentation. If she is mired in editing it, she may give a long-winded, confusing plot description when all that's called for is a witty anecdote and some salient points that are not on the fact sheets. The best presenters I have seen either have breathtaking erudition, making whatever they talk about seem highly intelligent and worthy, or they are showmen, with vaudeville cunning in their blood.

During my Simon & Schuster internship, I had the privilege of watching each of the company's editors present his or her books at a presales conference. Each editor clearly had his own style and ability to communicate the value of the books, but some of the presentations seemed to implode. Unfortunately, most editors aren't showmen. They wouldn't be editors if they were. Editors tend to be introverted and self-conscious. But in today's world, where presentation, spin, and perception seem more important than anything else, a book may hit the skids in a meeting if the editor can't put it across. There's nothing worse than the dead silence following a botched presentation for a book.

On the other hand, I will never forget the feeling in the room when S&S editor-in-chief Michael Korda—king of the showmen editors—arrived to present his list. The room came to attention. I had only glimpsed him in the halls until then, but every time I saw him, either turning a quick corner or disappearing behind closing elevator doors, I'd think of the British recommendation for exiting the Tube: Step lively! As he entered, it was clear that he relished the moment, taking his seat and smoothing his pink silk tie as he surveyed the room the way an actor assesses the crowd. He was there to present one of his best-selling diva authors. "Look, folks," he finally said, smiling with the impish grin of a schoolboy caught red-handed. "I haven't read a word of it yet. I doubt she's written one. But it's going to be fabulous. And it's going to sell." And of course, he was right.

✤

Most people know a good title when they hear one, but as publishing wisdom goes, a good title is one that sold. Sometimes, as the writer is working, the right title can help bring the entire work into focus. In Larry Dark's anthology *Literary Outtakes*, which collects a wonderful variety of life on the cutting-room floor, Amy Tan tells how she originally thought to use the title *Wind and Water* for her first book, after the Chinese belief in *feng shui*, the balance of the elements. "The words 'The Joy Luck Club' had never struck me as unusual or remotely literary. It was a social club my father had named and to which my parents and their friends belonged for as long as I could remember." The club's name may have sounded ordinary to Tan, but upon reading her manuscript, her agent seized on *The Joy Luck Club* and sold the book with that title. Tan found that as she continued to work on the book, the club and its members became increasingly vivid to her. "I sometimes wonder what would have happened if I had not changed the title. Because now I realize that a title is not simply an ornament that graces a book jacket. For me, the title gave shape to the stories, provided the necessary force to pull the whole book through from beginning to end."

It's at the publishing meetings that titles and subtitles are tested. This is about as close to market research as publishing gets, when the various departments, including sales, publicity, and marketing, react to a given title. One person or another may voice a complaint about a title or ask for a new subtitle. Again, study the competition if you are seeking a title. If the book is self-help, the title or subtitle should offer some promise or hope. If it's a how-to book, the gimmick should be part of the subtitle. A survey of diet books shows that most put the message into the title, such as *The Seven-Day Rotation Diet, The Carbohydrate Lover's Diet, Sugar Busters!* and so on. Recently a diet book called *The Zone* became a huge bestseller. That title could have been used for a thriller, science fiction, science—almost anything. It was a gutsy move not to put the diet concept in the title. I think a lot of publishers would have rejected the title because it didn't follow the formula. Perhaps one of the reasons *The Zone* worked so phenomenally well, especially among male consumers, who don't generally talk about diets and dieting as much as women do, was that it deemphasized dieting and had a macho ring.

Sometimes getting the title right comes down to the wire. Peter Benchley claims to have tried more than a hundred titles before settling on *Jaws* twenty minutes before going to press. As he tells it in *Literary Outtakes*, "I had toyed with a lot of Françoise Sagan–like stuff, such as *A Stillness in the Water*. My father goaded me onward with splendid solutions like *What Dat Noshin' on My Laig?* Then there were *The Jaws of Death* and *Leviathan Rising* and *White Death* and *The Jaws of Leviathan* and *Death in the Water* and *Shark!* and (the French used this one for their version) *The Teeth of the Sea*, and *Summer of the Shark* and on and on and on." Finally, Benchley and his editor decided that they should pick a single word. The only one they agreed on was *Jaws*. "I ran the title by my family and my agent. Everyone hated it. I didn't think much of it either. But what the hell. . . . nobody buys first novels anyway."

Best-selling author James McBride struggled to find a title for his memoir about being a black son raised by a white mother who kept her Jewish roots secret. After his editor rejected his suggestion "A Bird Who Flies," he wondered, in a letter to her, how much the title mattered. If it's good, won't people buy the book, he asked. As the press date for the publisher's catalogue approached, McBride and the editor brainstormed. The laundry list they came up with included the usual range of dull solutions ("My Mother's Life") and occasional howlers ("Bagels and Blues") born of complete exhaustion. At the last moment, however, the title appeared. It came, as some of the best do, from a line in the text, a beautiful snippet of dialogue that captured both the big picture and the nuances within the memoir. Once, when the young McBride had asked his mother what color God was, she replied, "The Color of Water."

After books are titled and jacketed, the next major meeting in the publishing cycle is called presales, and once again it's a gathering of all the departments, but now the in-house sales people are joined by the regional sales representatives from around the country. Once again each book on the list is presented, and this time the various parties have a chance to read some of the text and react to what we call the numbers—the planned first printing or number of books the publisher hopes to advance in the marketplace.

The sales conference, the culmination of all the planning and preparation of the list, is a bi- or triannual meeting at which all the reps now gather along with the in-house people, who present the next season's list of books and attempt to communicate what is best about each of them. The sales meeting is where, year in and year out, those people in the collective endeavor of selling books come together. There are roasts and banquets, service awards and special author appearances, extramarital affairs and brawls. The abstemious drink and the nonsmokers smoke. After days of presentations, computer training, and long nights in the hospitality suite, many people, battle-fatigued, let their hair down. Most authors are aware of this thing called sales conference, and fear that the one-minute presentations they've heard about reduce all their hard work to some crass or dumbed-down entity. They tend to be wary of the process, which is understandable, given that they are entrusting a group of strangers with what feels like their baby. Also, salespeople are often portrayed as the bad guys, anti-intellectual, anti-literary. Having worked with four different sales organizations, I can attest that this is as far from the truth as you could imagine.

Book salespeople are among the biggest readers in the world. And their mission is to get books into stores, a very different prospect from getting Ultra-Brite toothpaste into aisle B of their supermarket. Bookstores are as individual as the people who run them, and book reps are keenly attuned to the idiosyncrasies of bookstore owners and their communities of readers. Just as the author faces rejection, the sales rep is on the front lines of rejection at the doors of the marketplace, and is often responsible for persuading a wary buyer to try a few copies of an unknown writer. A rep may also know about a special promotion, a competitive title, a creative way another book in the same field was marketed, and may help formulate a publisher's selling strategy. In more than a few cases, reps have picked up on a regional success and brought the book to the attention of the publisher, who then brought the book to national recognition. Though only a handful of titles may dominate a sales conference, most reps are religious about studying their catalogues, reading the books, and tailoring their presentations for each individual account. Sales conference is the place where a company's identity and culture are created, and this, too, is in the service of selling books.

Unfortunately, in our accelerated culture, where there's so little time to read and digest books, it's no wonder that authors, especially literary writers, fear that their books will get lost in this process. It's important to remember that most people fall in love with reading through fiction and that most people in publishing love great writing. First novels still hold out that promise of first love. And contrary to popular opinion, if a sales force lights on a first novel or a work of literary nonfiction and feels passionate about it, the book can get an incredible push backed by genuine enthusiasm, even when the monetary commitment seems relatively small. "Money doesn't necessarily matter," explained agent Lynn Nesbit in a *New York* magazine article entitled "How to Make a Bestseller." "There has to be a buzz within the house, and of course, they might only get behind one book a season." That buzz usually starts with the sales force. The rep with his ear to the ground is the closest link between the publisher and the reader.

❧

While all the meetings are going on, the manuscript is also being physically prepared for publication. It will be copyedited, a process that the best writers appreciate. I have authors who insist on using the copyeditor they worked with previously, so profound is their respect for that person's careful eye and command of grammar, punctuation, syntax, and other nuances of language, and so deep their gratitude for having been spared embarrassing errors. For the writer who truly loves language, a trip to the copyeditor is like a week at Canyon Ranch spa. You come out looking younger, trimmer, and better groomed, and standing straighter. It is true that some copyeditors will, in their efforts to bring a piece of writing into accord with house style, fail to appreciate a writer's particular quirks of style, and in these instances, the editor needs to step in and referee. In general, however, copyeditors are unsung heroes, the men and women who stand as the last line of defense against the fall of civilization, so fierce and exacting is their protection of the English language.

After the author reviews and corrects the copyedited manuscript, it is designed and set in type. Page proofs, the typeset pages, is a stage that never fails to excite me, no matter how many times I shepherd a book through production. Usually, one of the company's designers consults with the editor about the typeface, the design of the title page, and the page layout, and the editor in turn shares the designed pages with the writer; in some cases this is a contractual obligation. But it's when the entire manuscript is set in type that one truly senses the book coming into being. Type is a powerful element. In his remarks on receiving the 1998 National Book Foundation Medal for his distinguished contribution to American letters, John Updike paid tribute to the typeface used in his books, explaining that his editor, Harry Ford, was "a perfect knight of the print world, an editor and designer both, who gave me a delicious striped jacket and an elegant page format, in the typeface called Janson, that I have stuck with for over forty books since. To see those youthful willful hopeful words of mine in that type, with Perpetua chapter heads set off by tapered rules, was an elevated moment I am still dizzy from. The old letterpress Linotype had a glinting material bite that all the ingenious advantages of computer setting have not quite replaced."

There is nothing more disconcerting than finding a typo in a book. It's an affront. We all hope that the proofreader who is paid to comb the book for errors is meticulous, but the author also has this last chance to read his pages and make minor changes and corrections. There are many stories of writers rewriting their books in the final hour of the page proof stage, causing great unhappiness all around. Once a book is typeset, any major changes, especially those that affect pagination, are costly and time-consuming to fix. It can be disastrous if a book "slips," meaning it was scheduled to publish in a certain month but because of production delays, often caused by heavy or late author changes, is pushed back a month or more. By this time the book has been sold to the stores, it's on their computer systems, and it's scheduled for warehousing and distribution. If delayed, it may be bumped from special in-store promotions, and media engagements may not be rescheduled unless the author is a powerful person or celebrity. All told, a delay in a book's production usually puts it on a roller coaster of potential disasters.

The final addition to the jacket is the flap copy—the de-

scription of the book, written by either your editor or an in-
house copywriter—and the blurbs, which have become de
rigueur for the backs of jackets, even though almost everyone
knows that the business of blurbing is a game of six degrees—
or fewer—of separation. I thought blurbing would finally cease
and desist after *Spy* magazine ran a monthly item called "Log
Rolling in Our Time," in which they outed any number of fellow back scratchers in the act of mutual admiration.

The reason blurbs won't go away is simple: consumers inherently distrust manufacturers. Why should anyone believe
the publisher? Of course we're going to tell you that the book
is good, and more important, that you should buy it. No matter how much money is spent on advertising, Americans tend
to trust personal experience or expert endorsement; we've been
ripped off too often. While some consumers are among the literary cognoscenti, know who's slept with whom, and thus can
deconstruct the connections that bind a book with its blurbers,
most readers don't know that A is friends with B, who was
taught by C, who was married to D, who went to school with
E, and so forth.

Sometimes the blurbs are most effective in-house before the
book is even published, which is why editors circulate the
blurbs to everyone in the company in the months before publication. When an editor can show his or her colleagues that an
extremely famous author has endorsed his first novelist, people
take notice. A domino effect is created as the blurb is then for-
warded to bookstores and the media as a way of saying: Pay attention! No matter how much any editor hates sending bound

galleys to famous writers, trolling for blurbs (it is, after all, a huge imposition and favor), it's thrilling to actually land the endorsement of a famous writer, especially when he or she doesn't know the author from a hole in the ground. And there's nothing like a good blurb to settle the nerves of a prepublication author.

The blurbs, the flap copy, the author photo—all these elements join the jacket art to create an overall effect that the publisher hopes will attract and intrigue the consumer. Every few years there seems to be a backlash against the importance of author photos or the corruption of blurbs. Still, it's hard to resist the trend. Even university press books are starting to jazz up the flaps and back ads. It's obvious when a publisher is trading on an author's physical beauty to sell the book, and while this strikes most people as venal and banal, given that it's literature we're trying to sell, it's impossible not to be intrigued by a gorgeous photograph.

In his oral biography of Truman Capote, George Plimpton calls the author photo for Capote's first book, *Other Voices, Other Rooms*, the most famous book-jacket portrait in contemporary letters. "It caused as much commotion as the book itself. Truman, dismayed by the negative comments, said he had been cajoled into the languorous pose, which in fact he had suggested himself." If Capote was making love to the camera in his author photo, with his saucer-wide eyes staring straight out, David Foster Wallace, the hottest young writer of the current decade, perfectly projected his postmodern ambivalence with fame and its discontents by averting his eyes and tilting his head downward, away from the camera, making no contact with the viewer. And the shmatte atop David Foster Wallace's head struck me as the ideal prop, silently dubbing him the crown prince of grunge literature.

If an author looks like George Eliot, chances are her picture won't be emphasized on the jacket. However, when an author's photo is incorporated into an ad campaign, it's usually because he or she is stunning. Most recently Sebastian Junger, author and hunk, complained bitterly that people were focusing on his looks. Somehow it's hard to feel sorry for him after he posed open-shirt, his torso extended in all its washboard definition over the prow of a ship, for *People* magazine's "Most Beautiful People" issue. If you want people to accept your book on its own terms, irrespective of your looks or personality, then you might want to think twice about how and for whom you pose. You're never going to catch Thomas Pynchon vamping for the glossies.

When all is said and done, there is nothing quite like seeing your book for the first time. Whenever the two first copies of a book from the bindery arrived in my in-box, I always took a few minutes to examine one of them, carefully removing its jacket to make sure that the spine had the right title and name. I'd check the endpapers, the title page, a few sample pages. Then I would write a note to the author, urging him to take a moment before the world reacted and take pride in his accomplishment and in the thing itself. No matter how many compromises were made along the way, no matter what happens in the future, a book is a thing to behold.

12.

PUBLICATION

"MOST BOOKS COME INTO THE WORLD WITH the fanfare of a stillborn," wrote James Purdy, in a line so dark and forbidding one feels the need to avert one's eyes. Publishing a book can be a cruel joke on the uninitiated. Every author hopes that publication will improve his life, if not transform it in some miraculous way that usually never materializes. Sometimes even a successful publication experience leaves the author in a state of postpartum depression and complete paralysis. No matter how realistic authors claim to be—and many do try to appear rational—all harbor dreams of greatness. This quixotic belief in oneself is critical for a writer's continued existence; as we all know, for every book that wins the Pulitzer Prize or hits the bestseller list, thousands disappear without a trace.

There are very few Cinderella stories in publishing. But consider Alice McDermott, whose first novel, *The Bigamist's Daughter*, was glowingly reviewed on the front page of *The New York Times Book Review* by Anne Tyler—a dream come true for any first novelist. In most cases, a writer would pay for such good fortune by having her second book savaged by critics: *Doesn't live up to early promise! Retread! Better luck next time!* But McDermott's second novel, *That Night*, was again praised on the front page of the book review—lightning had struck twice—this time by David Leavitt, who claimed the novel had a "sense of almost Shakespearean tragedy." It was nominated for a National Book Award and made into a feature film. Novel number three, *At Weddings and Wakes*, made the bestseller list, and McDermott's latest, *Charming Billy*, won the National Book Award and hit the bestseller list. The story of her success is devil's candy for those whose deepest wish is to emulate her, just as surely as it's salt in the wounded egos of those who would begrudge her. (And there's nothing like the National Book Award to stir up grudges.)

As a writer prepares for publication, any number of fantastic scenarios may play out in his dreams. The first misnomer most writers encounter is that highly charged day known as publication day. One seasoned novelist with six books to her credit described the excitement and anticipation she felt as publication day neared for her first novel. She spent the days before her book came out cleaning her apartment like an expectant mother in nesting mode. When I asked her why she was so frantic, she said that on the physical level it was pure nerves, but somewhere in her imagination she dreamed of serving tea to a bevy of journalists who would stop by for a chat about her novel. "I almost bought a tea set," she said, laughing at the folly of it all. "Then the big day comes and nothing, I mean nothing at all happened. The phone didn't even ring. Finally, at four o'clock in the afternoon I put on a hat, scarf, and sunglasses as if I were Greta Garbo and ducked out into a bookshop, didn't see my book anywhere, and skulked out feeling totally mortified."

Tom Wolfe may get a caviar extravaganza at the Pierre Hotel to celebrate the arrival of his newest novel, but most authors have to throw their own book parties or finagle friends into marking the occasion with a celebration. If they are lucky, the publisher will offer to print the invitations and contribute a case or two of wine. But the days of big publication parties are largely over, because they're expensive and don't usually help the sales of the book. My advice to writers is to press friends and family for a fête. It isn't every day that you write a book, even if your publisher hardly notices. In Michael Korda's memoir of publishing, *Another Life*, he tells of the hilarious gaffe made by publisher Max Schuster when he ran into his author Gypsy Rose Lee at '21,' where she was enjoying a celebratory meal for her book. Simon & Schuster had not thrown a party for the famous stripper, and as Korda tells it, when Lee spotted her publisher at the restaurant, she felt awkward about approaching him. Finally she worked her way over to his table. "Max beamed up at Gypsy, and before she could say a word, stammered out to her: 'Gypsy, how nice to see you! You know, I've been thinking about you a lot lately. . . . One of these days, you ought to write a book.'"

If your publication day doesn't mean anything to Don Imus or Katie Couric or Michiko Kakutani, if Tom Snyder and Charlie Rose aren't sparring over who's going to get that exclusive interview, you're not alone. But it doesn't mean you should spend the day skulking around bookstores in dark glasses. (Though after a few weeks of having a book out most authors become heat-seeking missiles, checking every store within driving distance for stock.) In actuality, publication day is a technical term for booksellers. It refers to the on-sale date in the stores and is meant to be coordinated with the timing of reviews. There is almost nothing more frustrating than a fabulous review that runs weeks before a book is available in the stores. Still, publication day sounds like a birthday to most writers, and it's impossible not to have one's expectations aroused, especially after the long months of waiting. This is the time when most writers go into some kind of free fall.

❧

I urge all my writers to get to work on their next project before publication. Working on a new book is the only cure for keeping the evil eye away. After publication, the writer opens himself up to reviewers and critics—or to their glaring silence—and is extremely vulnerable. Even when the press is good, it can be subverting. Scott Spencer, in an interview, recalled that "the public reaction to *Endless Love* immediately put me into competition with myself—'I sure hope the next one meets with that kind of success.' And with that bald-faced utterance, I ripped the pen from my fingers, broke it in half, and basically didn't work for about a year." The great poet Pablo Neruda lamented the effect of criticism in a *Paris Review* interview: "Oh! My critics! My critics have almost shredded me to pieces, with all the love or hate in the world! In life, as in art, one can't please everybody, and that's a situation that's always with us. One is always receiving kisses and slaps, caresses and kicks, and that is the life of the poet."

We expect our writers, like movie stars, to be equipped to handle any kind of scrutiny or attack. Most first-time authors have no experience of handling publicity of any kind and are often caught terribly unaware, both of how to handle the media and of how to deal with the feelings stirred by those attentions or dismissals. If your book is likely to come under attack or is provocative, it is extremely worthwhile for you to spend time being either professionally or casually coached. A good publicist will prepare questions for interviewers and rehearse with you. You can be taught how to steer questions and talk about those parts of the book that put it in its best light.

Few writers are truly gifted at giving readings, and most have panic attacks before doing an interview, whether for radio, print, or television. And nowadays an author who isn't deemed "promotable" can be a liability. I worked with a brilliant academic who couldn't answer a question in less than ten minutes, so accustomed was he to elaborating on his ideas in scholarly journals and among graduate students. When his book came out, he was asked to appear on a few television shows, because the subject of his book intersected with some timely news events. Unfortunately, he failed each pre-interview. One producer summed it up thus: He doesn't give good sound bite.

It's important to plan your readings and selections before you speak in public. Long descriptive passages usually put people to sleep, as does staring down at your book for twenty minutes and reading either too fast or in a monotone. Your publicist or editor should help you select a few sections from the book that

will be effective for the format. I have always loved poetry readings for all the anecdotes that poets share between poems, and
I counsel my authors to do likewise and provide some meaningful stories. After all, anyone can read the book at home. If
an audience has come out to see you, give them something they
won't find in the book.

I once edited a very young and audacious filmmaker's first
novel. He gave his first reading at a downtown New York bookstore. The place was filled to capacity. He showed up almost a
half-hour late in a bathrobe, sneakers, and a safari hat with
hand towels pinned to its edge, obscuring his face. He put a
boombox on the table and pushed the on button. The sounds
it projected were indecipherable, and he screamed over them
for about ten minutes. No one moved. When it was over, a
very anxious employee asked if the author would take questions. He nodded. The first person to venture a question asked
if the writer preferred working on films or books. The writer
jumped over the table, pushed his way through the crowd with
his arms outstretched as if to strangle the man who asked the
question, swearing that he would rip his fucking throat out for
asking that. Then he returned to the front of the room. Now
the bookstore employee looked downright ill and quietly asked
if there were any more questions. Someone in the audience
raised a hand and asked what the writer's next film would be.
Again my writer started cursing and lurching forward. At this,
the clerk said he guessed we'd conclude and asked all those
who'd like to have their books signed to line up. To my astonishment, nearly the entire room lined up, some people with
multiple copies. The bookstore's management was horrified

when they heard about his little stunt and demanded a written apology. His fans, however, clearly loved it. My only regret was that there wasn't any press on hand to blow it up into a full-scale publicity circus and sell even more copies.

I'm not suggesting that you manufacture some ploy to get attention but rather that you examine the possibilities, so that if you have the chance to speak to a group, you can send the audience home with either a book in hand or a story to share. That is how word-of-mouth begins. Sherman Alexie, the Native American novelist, was famous for appearing at readings late and seemingly drunk as a way of confronting the widely held stereotype of Indians. No one who saw Alexie failed to tell his friends about it. If your publisher doesn't send you to bookstores, offer to give a reading or worskshop at your local library, school, church, or even coffee shop.

The more you are able to do on your book's behalf, the better shielded you will be from bad reviews or random acts of cruelty. And I cannot reiterate this enough: get to work on your next project before the reviews begin to come in on the first one. In publishing circles, the inability to come up with a second book is blithely referred to as sophomore slump, but for the writer in slump the pain is excruciating. There is no way to predict how attention or the lack thereof will disrupt your ability to work.

❧

The first signs of how a book will be received are in the prepublication reviews from the trade papers, namely *Publishers Weekly* and *Kirkus Reviews*, as well as *Library Journal* and *Booklist*.

These unsigned, paragraph-length reviews are often harbingers of reviews to come. There is no better feeling for an editor than when faxing off a positive early review to an anxious author and her agent with a quick note: Congratulations on the great review—a sure sign of good things to come. It's more dicey when the review is lousy. Some editors deep-six bad prepublication reviews altogether. Some call the author and commiserate about the stupidity of the review. Often, it's a good occasion for an editor to ask an author if he or she wants to see all reviews, come what may. I've known more than a few writers who claim to want to see all reviews, no matter how bad, only to change their minds when they actually get bludgeoned. I always think it's a healthy choice not to read the bad ones, but many writers are nothing if not masochists.

When Bernard Malamud was asked whether criticism of his work affected him, he replied, "Some of it must. Not the crap, the self-serving pieces, but an occasional insightful criticism, favorable or unfavorable, that confirms my judgment of my work. While I'm on the subject, I dislike particularly those critics who preach their aesthetic or ideological doctrines at you. What's important to them is not what the writer has done but how it fits, or doesn't fit, the thesis they want to develop. Nobody can tell a writer what can or ought to be done, or not done, in his fiction. A living death if you fall for it."

Unfortunately, for some writers, the experience of publication is a living death, or hell, that offers little or no catharsis. Rather than acknowledging the accomplishment or feeling a degree of mastery over a body of material, the writer seems to have opened a Pandora's box of anxiety, guilt, and shame. Feelings of fraudulence continue to haunt some writers throughout their lives. Some writers I have worked with explain that it took three or four books before they stopped feeling like an impostor, and felt they could actually call themselves writers. In her autobiography, Edith Wharton describes her own impostor complex. "I had written short stories that were thought worthy of preservation! Was it the same insignificant I that I had always known? Any one walking along the streets might go into any bookshop, and say: 'Please give me Edith Wharton's book,' and the clerk, without bursting into incredulous laughter, would produce it, and be paid for it, and the purchaser would walk home with it and read it, and talk of it, and pass it on to other people to read! The whole business seemed too unreal to be anything but a practical joke played on me by some occult humorist; and my friends could not have been more astonished and incredulous than I was."

Wharton goes on to describe the feeling of reading her reviews, most of which, she happily reports, were kind and generous. But one eventually came along, she says, that "stiffened her limp spine." This reviewer took the tack that maddens writers most, that of schoolmarm, firmly correcting the writer as if she were some grade-school student. "'When Mrs. Wharton,' the condescending critic wrote, 'has learned the rudiments of her art, she will know that a short story should always begin with dialogue.'" Though Wharton heartily rejected the critic's formulaic approach as entirely bogus, she deeply pondered the critic's response, concluding, "This egregious commentary did me an immense service. . . . In an instant I was free forever from the bogey of the omniscient reviewer."

In Rilke's *Letters to a Young Poet*, he warns his correspondent with the following: "Read as little as possible of aesthetic criticism—such things are either partisan views, petrified and grown senseless in their lifeless induration, or they are clever quibblings in which today one view wins and tomorrow the opposite. Works of art are of an infinite loneliness and with nothing so little to be reached as with criticism."

One bridge that spans the infinite loneliness between a writer and the abyss comes in the form of something far less public than reviews but no less meaningful: author mail. I am always astonished at the depth of feeling conveyed in some of the fan letters my authors have shared with me. One of my authors who was excoriated by the press for her memoir never travels without a suitcase full of mail by individuals who were touched by her work. And even six years after publication, the letters keep coming. Another writer, who was severely criticized in the local press for exposing the foibles of a handful of small-town folk, continues to receive letters from people there, thanking her for finally telling the truth about their lives. One husband-and-wife team with whom I worked canvassed the country to gather stories about girls and sports. The book received only a handful of reviews—parenting titles and sports books rarely get review attention—but they receive daily e-mail and letters from parents who feel their efforts are acknowledged in the stories portrayed in the book. One letter enclosed pictures of a woman's little slugger; the mother described how grateful she was for the book's assurances in support of raising an athletic and competitive daughter. Though my author always appeared the cool, objective journalist, when she shared this letter from Jane Smith, Anywhere U.S.A., her face reddened and I glimpsed a tear well up. Sometimes a single letter can provide an author with the longed-for feeling of being heard and appreciated.

For those who keep living it, the writing life, though never safe, becomes somewhat more predictable. Once you've done enough interviews and read enough of your own reviews, you can begin to predict how your work will be received. "You know, all of this is such a bore," said Philip Roth in a 1990 *Los Angeles Times* interview following the publication of *Deception*. "I wrote a book about adultery and people are very sophisticated about *that* subject until they're involved in it. So I upped the ante and got a little reckless. I wanted to capture the dangerous sense of being in an affair, and that's why I put myself into the book. You'd think people would strike out more independently when writing about my books. Instead of writing what everybody's been writing about for 15 years." What most aspiring authors would give for a taste of such boredom!

Most writers, if they are fortunate enough to be sent out on the road at all, are usually disabused of their fantasies within the first forty-eight hours. Until one learns the drill, the reality of a book tour, for all but the mega-selling author or runaway favorite, is more than a little harrowing. E. Annie Proulx, in a hilarious essay in *The Writing Life* called "The Book Tour," describes a reading in Wyoming where the relatively small crowd appeared rather agitated and kept sneaking looks at papers in their hands. After reading for fifteen minutes, Proulx gave up and headed for the wine and cheese at the back of the room. Immediately "a young woman who had been sitting in the front row got up and read a poem about her first airplane ride, a poem that went on for frozen centuries of time. She barely finished when another one jumped up and launched into a searing description of sex with a teenage cowboy. And so it went, until the entire audience, made up of local writers, had read their stuff."

Reports from the road are laden with tales of woe: the packed bookstore that never received the books or, its converse, the reading where no one shows up while you sit alone behind stacks of your novel; the radio interviewer who keeps calling you by the wrong name or who badgers you for questions during the commercial break, confessing that he didn't read the book and needs you to fill the airtime until Chuckles the Clown shows up. You land in a new city the day your book is panned on the front page of the local paper, or the advertisement for your appearance is printed with the wrong date or time. Then there are the endless flights, the lost luggage, the escort who talks incessantly about her divorce or worse, the book she'd like to write, the hotel that's lost your reservation, and the final insult: a mini-bar with no gin.

And yet, for the author who is scheduled to do only a local book signing, the book tour beckons; almost every author wants to go out on the road. When Terry McMillan discovered that her publisher had no plans to tour her first novel, she

loaded up the trunk of her car with books and hit the pave-
ment, making friends with booksellers across the country. The
rest is history. Today the touring circuit is more crowded, with
some stores hosting three or four authors in a single day. But
just as McMillan refused to let her publisher limit her appearances, writers today have many new ways to provide exposure
for their work.

❧

In today's world, publicity is the key to getting attention for a
book. This was not always the case. In his wonderful *New Yorker*
article "Wasn't She Great?" Michael Korda describes publishing
in 1958, when he began, as "a respectable profession." The business was being run, "for the most part, by men in suits or in
donnish tweeds, with pipes, who were either Ivy League Wasps
or Jews whose highest ambition was to be mistaken for Wasps."
This would all change forever, according to Korda, with the
1966 publication of *Valley of the Dolls* by Jacqueline Susann. "It
brought together for the first time the worlds of Hollywood,
gossip, and Broadway press-agentry, to sell a novel whose subjects included all those things. Jackie, then forty-seven, had
spikey false eye-lashes, a chain-smoker's gravelly voice, and glit-
tery dresses; her feisty, tough-broady image seemed to many
like the beginning of the end—show business vulgarity at the
door of the temple of culture."

Korda goes on to describe the particular magic that was
Jackie, but also points out how she and her husband created a
new way of selling a novel that included shameless self-

promotion, personal appearances, and celebrity tie-ins. Even the word "launch" was new to publishing. But beyond the glitz, Korda also describes a woman who understood that she had earned her success by working it from the ground up. Jacqueline Susann was zealous in getting to know booksellers; apparently she even noted their birthdays in her Rolodex and sent affectionate, handwritten notes to the people who rarely get any attention or thanks: the clerks and managers.

Thirty years later, writers of every stripe, from trashy romance to postmodern literary, want their fifteen minutes, and they want their books to sell. I have heard from more than a few writers that they check their daily "ranking" on Amazon.com, much the way the amateur investor reads the Nasdaq or an inveterate dieter jumps on the scale. *Am I up? Am I down?* Sales figures are to authors what batting averages are to baseball players. Sure, you can have great form, but can you hit it out of the ballpark? Or to put it more succinctly, as Andy Warhol, the deceased priest of the cult of fame, used to say, "Success is what sells"—though I prefer to recall Bob Dylan's Möbius strip of a lyric, "There's no success like failure, and failure's no success at all."

The best advice I can give any author on the verge of publication is: treat your publicist like gold. That, and roll up your sleeves. While most books published by trade houses do get sent out widely for review with a press release, and are assigned a publicist, authors are often unrealistic about how far those efforts can go. Too many authors imagine that having a publicist means having a press secretary, a personal secretary, and a travel agent all rolled into one. Intellectually, most authors know that their publicist is also working on a half-dozen other titles, but emotionally they want total attention. Unless the company has paid a great deal of money for your book and plans to expose it widely through touring and promotion, it is unrealistic to expect your publicist to do much more than send out the book and make follow-up calls. A publicist's job is thankless. And if lightning strikes, if a publicist lands you on *Oprah* or secures a high-profile interview, or schmoozes a book editor until he finally decides to review a book he has been on the fence about, few authors remember their publicist's efforts. Editors are thanked, spouses are thanked, publishers are thanked, but all too often the publicist gets lost in the crowd.

Though few people acknowledge her importance, the publicist is truly on the front lines of any publication. She can hear the distant thunder and knows before anyone else whether producers and reviewers and critics and pundits are clamoring or clamming up. I always instruct my authors to abuse me instead of their publicist if they have to blow off steam. What most writers don't understand is that when they alienate their publicist, they're essentially cutting off their own nose, as the expression goes, because the publicist's job is all about going the extra mile: pitching *your* book when the book review editor is calling about something else, bringing a copy of *your* galleys to lunch with a top magazine editor, mentioning *your* book to a producer trolling for a good segment for her newsweekly. If an author continues to annoy the publicist, harangue her with requests, condescend, or in any other way disrespect her job and position, it is unlikely that that author's book will be on the tip of her tongue when opportunity knocks. There are authors who send daily faxes and e-mails to their publicist, then call minutes later to see if she's received them. Now, some authors will tell you that their faxes and e-mails seem to go into the void. But the publicist has to balance any number of requests and pitches and calls and rejections in the course of her day. She will do a better job if you let her do it. Every minute she is on the phone with you is a minute she is not on the phone pitching your book.

True, not all publicists are created equal. Some have an as-tonishing depth and wealth of contacts and creativity. I have seen publicity campaigns that equal Sherman's March in fortitude and persistence. I have seen creative and strategic plan-ning that has launched a book into the stratosphere. Unfortu-nately, publicity departments also have high turnover and a high burnout rate. Often publicists leave, as do editors, in mid-project, and it's extremely disconcerting for an author who has spent years on his book to discover that it is being reassigned to someone who doesn't seem to have any connection to the material. Yet even if you really bond with your publicist and feel that she will do everything short of selling her own mother to get you exposure, you can't expect the world to flock around when you publish your book. Just because reviewers aren't biting doesn't mean your publicist isn't out there pitch-ing. Think twice before you vent your frustration on your publicist.

This is the point where you have to roll up your sleeves and get to work. I often compare publishing a book to starting up a new business. Just setting up the store isn't enough. People aren't going to come in and shop just because you've put an Open sign in the window. It would be very nice indeed if you didn't have to do anything besides write the book. But if you want it to sell and to reach people, you have to be creative, whether your publisher is willing to push the book or not. Some best-selling books that never get on the usual lists have evangelical authors behind them, authors who either use speakers' bureaus or who set up their own seminars to spread their message. A writer who is out there on the speaking circuit has an avenue through which to sell books outside the traditional channels.

For the nonfiction writer, there are any number of specialized journals, organizations, and newsletters that may be interested in interviewing you and/or reviewing the book. People are more organized than ever before through the Internet, and if you've written a book on a specialized subject, chances are there are groups on-line who would be interested in hearing about it and spreading the word. These avenues may be beyond the purview of your publisher, and this is where you need to apply elbow grease. Perhaps you can negotiate for an additional quantity of your books for publicity purposes, get a stack of press releases, stuff envelopes, and attach labels. I worked with one young writer on a hilarious parody aimed at the college market. He spent a week in our offices flirting with the publicists and sending free copies of his book to hundreds of college newspapers across the country. He got far more attention in

their pages than we were able to summon in the national magazines and media.

In some cases, it's a good idea to hire your own publicist,
especially if you feel that the market for your book is still un-
tapped in the media. I worked with a woman whose book
came out between Thanksgiving and New Year's, and for some
reason we couldn't get her a shred of publicity, though we tried.
Sometimes the holiday season is impenetrable for all but a few
books. The following April the author hired her own PR firm
for an additional three-week push. We supplied books and PR
materials, and the extra effort yielded a few front-page lifestyle
articles, a segment on the TV news program 48 Hours, and a few
more reviews. Though sales didn't improve much, when her
paperback appeared the following fall, the enhanced press kit
and tape from the television program helped pitch her, and as
a result she got on another nighttime newsweekly and received
some higher-profile coverage in the print media. Her paperback
has far outsold the hardcover, which may or may not have been
a direct result of the extra publicity. It couldn't have hurt.

Whether or not you choose to spend your own money on
publicity is a personal decision. For those who will never be
satisfied with the publisher's efforts, I think it's a good idea.
This way you will at least feel that you tried everything and
that your book was given a full-court press—though you should
be forewarned that your efforts might not result in more than a
sales blip. Unfortunately, there are fewer venues and review
outlets for novelists than for nonfiction writers, and hiring an
independent publicist may not yield further press. Norman

Rush lamented the diminishing publicity opportunities for writers in a 1995 essay called "Healthy Subversions," in *The Writing Life*. He writes, "*The New York Times* has recently eliminated the book review column in its Saturday editions, and both *Time* and *Newsweek* now occasionally entirely skip coverage of the world of books. Throughout the daily press the length and number of book reviews are steadily declining, and the process of reviewing is yielding almost everywhere to pressures to make stars or letter-grades or some other reductive ranking device part of the review."

Indeed, all this is disheartening for the serious writer. Every six months or so the whole question of whether the novel is dead or has been supplanted by the memoir is debated in the papers, so acute is the fear that no one will tell us stories about ourselves. Sometimes I think that writers who "lower" themselves to promote their book by appearing on talk shows and bearing their midriffs in glossy magazines are waving the banner for all writers. In a world that seems ever threatened by technology, where books may morph into handheld devices, with pages downloaded at the ATM or through some other Jetson-like invention, it's no wonder that writers want to shout their stories down from the highest mountains. In my opinion, every time a writer gets any ink or any airtime, it's good news.

✻

I recently found my husband's boyhood Cub Scout shirt and proudly admired his patch as den "scribe," with a quill pen embroidered into its center. As a young boy he discovered the love of literature, and according to family lore hoarded his lunch money to buy books. Looking at that faded patch made me wonder if today's Scout gets some kind of Web-site patch instead, if clicking will replace the simple but exquisite act of turning a page.

These are terrifying times for writers and publishers alike. Some contracts demand that authors give up their electronic rights for all time and throughout the universe, so uncertain are publishers of where the future is going and who will control it. I recently had lunch with one of the most successful literary agents of fiction writers, who told me that she burst into tears upon reading that the *Encyclopaedia Britannica* was no longer going to be printed and bound in book form. Her fear of the passing of books from our midst is not without foundation, but I believe reports of the death of books have been highly exaggerated. When asked whether literature as we know it is an anachronism, Isaac Bashevis Singer, in a *Paris Review* interview, replied, "I don't think that literature, good literature, has anything to fear from technology. The very opposite. The more technology, the more people will be interested in what the human mind can produce *without* the help of electronics." Bernard Malamud expressed the same sentiment, though slightly more tersely, when asked if the narrative is dead. His answer bears reprinting. "It'll be dead," he said, "when the penis is."

For every writer who quits and every one who pushes through, for the private diarist and the international best-selling star, the whore and the hermit, there is always the impulse, realized or unrealized, that binds us one to another through the power of language. Every time a person writes, for the public or not, he or she is connected to all who have ever felt that magnificent charge of communication through the written word—whether carved in ancient hieroglyphics or glowing in code across our computer. No matter how often or how vociferously writers are attacked, no matter how many hearts are broken in pursuit of publication or how many authors discouraged in their lonely work, there will always be the brilliant conspiracy between author and reader.

BIBLIOGRAPHY

Amis, Martin. "The Art of Fiction CLI." *The Paris Review* 146, Spring 1998.

Atlas, James. "The Fall of Fun." *The New Yorker*, November 18, 1996.

———. "Speaking Ill of the Dead." *The New York Times Magazine*, November 6, 1988.

———. "Stranger Than Fiction." *The New York Times Magazine*, June 23, 1991.

Beardon, Michelle. "John Grisham." *Publishers Weekly*, February 22, 1993.

Begley, Sharon. "The Nurture Assumption." *Newsweek*, September 7, 1998.

Berg, A. Scott. *Max Perkins: Editor of Genius*. New York: E. P. Dutton, 1978.

Blades, John. "Lorrie Moore: Flipping Death the Bird." *Publishers Weekly*, August 24, 1997.

Blythe, Will, ed. *Why I Write*. Boston: Little, Brown, 1998.

Brent, Jonathan. "What Facts? A Talk with Roth." *The New York Times*, September 25, 1988.

Capote, Truman. *Answered Prayers*. New York: Random House, 1987.

———. *Music for Chameleons*. New York: Random House, 1980.

Carvajal, Doreen. "Read the True (More or Less) Story! Publishers and Authors Debate the Boundaries of Nonfiction." *The New York Times*, February 24, 1998.

Cerf, Bennett. *At Random*. New York: Random House, 1977.

Cheever, Benjamin, ed. *The Letters of John Cheever*. New York: Simon & Schuster, 1988.

Cheever, John. *The Journals of John Cheever*. New York: Alfred A. Knopf, 1991.

Chernow, Ron. "Stubborn Facts and Fickle Realities." In *The Writing Life: National Book Award Authors*. New York: Random House, 1995.

Cheuse, Alan, and Nicholas Delbanco. *Talking Horse: Bernard Malamud on Life and Work*. New York: Columbia University Press, 1996.

Clarke, Gerald. *Capote: A Biography*. New York: Simon & Schuster, 1988.

Coffey, Michael. "Michael Cunningham: New Family Outings." *Publishers Weekly*, November 2, 1998.

Conant, Jennet. "Royalty Wedding of the Year." *Manhattan, Inc.*, January 1989.

Cowley, Malcolm, ed. *Writers at Work: The Paris Review Interviews*. New York: Viking Press, 1957.

Dark, Larry, Ed. *Literary Outtakes*. New York: Ballantine, 1990.

Dickinson, Emily. *Final Harvest*. Boston: Little, Brown, 1961.

Didion, Joan. *Slouching Towards Bethlehem*. New York: Simon & Schuster, 1961.

Dostoyevsky, Fyodor. *Notes from Underground/The Double*, trans. Jessie Coulson. New York: Penguin, 1972.

Duras, Marguerite. *Writing*, trans. Mark Polizzotti Cambridge, Mass.: Lumen, 1998.

Eliot, Valerie, ed. *The Letters of T. S. Eliot*. San Diego, Calif.: Harcourt Brace Jovanovich, 1988.

Ellmann, Richard. *James Joyce*. New York: Oxford University Press, 1959.

Emerson, Ken. "The Indecorous, Rabelaisian, Convoluted Righteousness of Stanley Elkin." *The New York Times Magazine*, March 3, 1991.

Ferguson, Andrew. "A River of Chicken Soup." *Time*, June 8, 1998.

Fitzgerald, Sally, ed. *The Habit of Being: Letters of Flannery O'Connor*. New York: Farrar, Straus & Giroux, 1979.

Garis, Leslie. "Susan Sontag Finds Romance." *The New York Times Magazine*, August 2, 1992.

Getlin, Josh. "Sparring with Roth." *Los Angeles Times*, April 15, 1990.

Gillespie, Elgy. "Carol Shields." *Publishers Weekly*. February 28, 1994.

Ginzberg, Natalia. *The Little Virtues*, trans. Dick Davis. New York: Arcade, 1989.

Giroux, Robert, ed. *Robert Lowell: Collected Prose*. New York: Farrar, Straus & Giroux, 1987.

Goffman, Erving. *The Presentation of Self in Everyday Life*. New York: Anchor, 1959.

Goldberg, Natalie. *Writing Down the Bones*. Boston: Shambhala, 1986.

Goldstein, Bill. "King of Horror." *Publishers Weekly*, January 24, 1991.

Gottlieb, Robert. "The Art of Editing." *The Paris Review,* Fall 1994.

Green, Jack. *Fire the Bastards.* Normal, Ill.: Dalkey Archive Press, 1992.

Hendrickson, Robert. *The Literary Life and Other Curiosities.* San Diego, Calif.: Harcourt Brace, 1981.

Howard, Gerald. "The American Strangeness: An Interview with Don DeLillo." *Hungry Mind Review,* Fall 1997.

———. "Slouching Towards Grubnet: The Author in the Age of Publicity." *Review of Contemporary Fiction,* 1997.

Hughes, Ted. *The Birthday Poems.* New York: Farrar, Straus & Giroux, 1998.

Hughes, Ted, and Frances McCullough, eds. *The Journals of Sylvia Plath.* New York: Dial Press, 1982. Reprint, Anchor Books, 1998.

Ishiguro, Kazuo. *The Remains of the Day.* New York: Alfred A. Knopf, 1989.

James, Caryn. "Auteur! Auteur!" *The New York Times Magazine,* January 19, 1986.

Jamison, Kay Redfield. *Touched with Fire: Manic Depressive Illness and the Artistic Temperament.* New York: Free Press, 1993.

———. *An Unquiet Mind.* New York: Alfred A. Knopf, 1995.

Johnson, Denis. *The Incognito Lounge.* New York: Random House, 1982.

Johnson, Thomas H., ed. *The Letters of Emily Dickinson.* Cambridge, Mass.: Belknap Press of Harvard University Press, 1914.

Jones, Malcolm. "Mr. Wolfe Bites Back." *Newsweek,* January 4, 1999.

Kafka, Franz. *Letter to His Father,* trans. Ernst Kaiser and Eithne Wilkins. New York: Schocken Books, 1953.

Kaplan, Justin. *Walt Whitman: A Life.* New York: Simon & Schuster, 1980.

Klam, Matthew. "Some of My Best Friends Are Rich." *The New York Times Magazine,* June 7, 1998.

Konigsberg, Eric. "Making Book." *New York,* February 10, 1997.

Korda, Michael. *Another Life.* New York: Random House, 1999.

———. "The King of the Deal." *The New Yorker,* March 29, 1993.

———. "Wasn't She Great?" *The New Yorker,* August 14, 1995.

Koteliansky, S. S., and Philip Tomlinson, eds. and trans. *The Life and Letters of Anton Tchekhov.* New York: George H. Doran, n.d. (circa 1923).

Lamott, Anne. *Bird by Bird: Some Instructions on Writing and Life.* New York: Pantheon Books, 1994.

Lillelund, Niels. "Literature Lives: Interview with Gary Fisketjon." *Danish Literary Magazine,* Autumn 1998.

McCullough, David. "Interview." In *The Writing Life: National Book Award Authors.* New York: Random House, 1995.

MacFarquhar, Larissa. "The Cult of Joyce Maynard." *The New York Times Magazine,* September 6, 1998.

Mailer, Norman. *Advertisements for Myself.* New York: G. P. Putnam's Sons, 1959.

Malcolm, Janet. *The Journalist and the Murderer.* New York: Alfred A. Knopf, 1990.

Mandell, Judy. *Book Editors Talk to Writers.* New York: John Wiley & Sons, 1995.

Manus, Elizabeth. "Dale Peck: Now It's Time to Say Goodbye to Farrar." *The New York Observer,* July 13, 1998.

Max, D. T. "The Carver Chronicles." *The New York Times Magazine,* August 9, 1998.

Maynard, Joyce. *At Home in the World.* New York: Picador, 1998.

Middlebrook, Diane Wood. *Anne Sexton: A Biography.* Boston: Houghton Mifflin, 1991.

Miller, Alice. *Banished Knowledge: Facing Childhood Injuries,* trans. Leila Vennewitz. New York: Nan A. Talese/Doubleday, 1990.

———. *Prisoners of Childhood,* trans. Ruth Ward. New York: Basic Books, 1981.

Moore, Lorrie. *Self-Help.* New York: Alfred A. Knopf, 1985.

Nabokov, Vladimir. *Strong Opinions.* New York: McGraw-Hill, 1973.

Naylor, Gloria. "The Love of Books." In *The Writing Life: National Book Award Authors.* New York: Random House, 1995.

Neruda, Pablo. *Twenty Love Poems and a Song of Despair,* trans. W. S. Merwin. New York: Penguin, 1969.

Neubauer, Alexander. *Conversations on Writing Fiction.* New York: HarperCollins, 1994.

Orwell, George. *A Collection of Essays.* San Diego, Calif.: Harcourt Brace, 1981.

Parker, Dorothy. *The Portable Dorothy Parker.* New York: Viking 1944. Reprint, Penguin, 1976.

Paumgarten, Nick. "The Baby Binkys." *The New York Observer,* April 22, 1996.

Percy, Walker. *The Moviegoer.* New York: Alfred A. Knopf, 1961.

Phillips, Larry W., ed. *Ernest Hemingway on Writing.* New York: Charles Scribner's Sons, 1984.

Plath, Sylvia. *The Collected Poems*, ed. Ted Hughes. New York: Harper & Row, 1960.

Plimpton, George. *Truman Capote*. New York: Nan A. Talese/Doubleday, 1997.

———, ed. *Writers at Work: The Paris Review Interviews*, 2nd series. New York: Viking Press, 1963.

———, ed. *Writers at Work: The Paris Review Interviews*, 5th series. New York: Viking Press, 1981.

Proulx, E. Annie. "The Book Tour." In *The Writing Life: National Book Award Authors*. New York: Random House, 1995.

Reginato, James. "Nobel House." *New York*, November 9, 1987.

Rhodes, Richard. *How to Write*. New York: William Morrow, 1995.

Rilke, Rainer Maria. *Letters on Cézanne*, trans. Joel Agee. New York: Fromm International, 1985.

———. *Letters to a Young Poet*, trans. M. D. Herter Norton. New York: W. W. Norton, 1934.

Roorbach, Bill. "Ping-Pong: The Secret to Getting Published, Long Withheld, Is Revealed." *Poets & Writers Magazine*, September/October 1998.

Roskill, Mark, ed. *The Letters of Vincent van Gogh*. New York: Atheneum, 1986.

Roth, Philip. *The Facts: A Novelist's Autobiography*. New York: Farrar, Straus & Giroux, 1988.

———. *Goodbye, Columbus*. Boston: Houghton Mifflin, 1959.

Ruas, Charles. *Conversations with American Writers*. New York: McGraw-Hill, 1984.

Rush, Norman. "Healthy Subversions." In *The Writing Life: National Book Award Authors*. New York: Random House, 1995.

Safire, William, and Leonard Safir. *Good Advice on Writing*. New York: Simon & Schuster, 1992.

Schiff, Stephen. "Big Poetry." *The New Yorker*, July 14, 1997.

Scribner, Charles, Jr. *In the Company of Writers*. New York: Charles Scribner's Sons, 1990.

Sewall, Richard. *The Life of Emily Dickinson*. New York: Farrar, Straus & Giroux, 1974.

Sexton, Anne. *The Complete Poems*. Boston: Houghton Mifflin, 1981.

Sexton, Linda Gray. *Searching for Mercy Street: My Journey Back to My Mother, Anne Sexton*. Boston: Little, Brown, 1994.

Sexton, Linda Gray, and Lois Ames. *Anne Sexton: A Self-Portrait in Letters.* Boston: Houghton Mifflin, 1977.

Shengold, Leonard. *Soul Murder: The Effects of Childhood Abuse and Deprivation.* New Haven: Yale University Press, 1989.

Shnayerson, Michael. "How Wily Is Andrew Wylie?" *Vanity Fair,* January 1988.

Smith, Dinitia. "A Book Award Dark Horse." *The New York Times,* November 24, 1998.

Solotaroff, Ted. "Writing in the Cold." In *A Few Good Voices in My Head: Occasional Pieces on Writing, Editing, and Reading My Contemporaries.* New York: Harper & Row, 1987.

Stevens, Wallace. *The Necessary Angel.* New York: Vintage Books, 1942.

Streitfeld, David. "Betrayal Between the Covers." *The Washington Post,* October 27, 1998.

Strunk, William, Jr., and E. B. White. *The Elements of Style.* 2nd ed. New York: Macmillan, 1972.

Styron, William. *Darkness Visible: A Memoir of Madness.* New York: Random House, 1990.

Theroux, Paul. "Memory and Invention." *The New York Times Book Review,* December 1998.

———. *Sir Vidia's Shadow: A Friendship Across Five Continents.* Boston: Houghton Mifflin, 1998.

Trollope, Anthony. *An Autobiography.* Edinburgh: William Blackwood and Sons, 1883. Reprint, Berkeley, Calif.: University of California Press, 1978.

Turnbull, Andrew, ed. *The Letters of F. Scott Fitzgerald.* New York: Charles Scribner's Sons, 1963.

Twain, Mark. *On Writing and Publishing.* New York: Book-of-the-Month Club, 1994.

Updike, John. "At War with My Skin." *The New Yorker,* September 2, 1985.

———. "Interview." *The Writing Life: National Book Award Authors.* New York: Random House, 1995.

———. *Of Prizes and Print.* New York: Alfred A. Knopf, 1998.

———. "On One's Own Oeuvre." In *Hugging the Shore.* New York: Alfred A. Knopf, 1983.

———. *Picked-Up Pieces.* New York: Alfred A. Knopf, 1966.

———. *Self-Consciousness.* New York: Alfred A. Knopf, 1989.

Waldron, Ann. *Eudora: A Writer's Life.* New York: Doubleday, 1998.

Weinraub, Bernard. "Separating Fact, Fiction and Film." *The New York Times*, January 2, 1998.

Welty, Eudora. *The Eye of the Story: Selected Essays and Reviews.* New York: Random House, 1978.

———. *One Writer's Beginnings.* Cambridge, Mass.: Harvard University Press, 1984.

Wharton, Edith. *A Backward Glance.* New York: Curtis Publishing, 1933. Reprint, Touchstone, 1998.

Whitman, Walt. *Complete Poetry and Collected Prose.* New York: Library of America, 1982.

Woodhouse, Barbara. *No Bad Dogs.* New York: Fireside, 1978.

Woolf, Virginia. *A Room of One's Own.* New York: Harcourt Brace, 1929.

ABOUT THE AUTHOR

Betsy Lerner received an MFA from Columbia University. She was a coeditor of Columbia's literary magazine and a founder of the now defunct underground magazine *Big Wednesday*. She has won a Thomas Wolfe Poetry Prize and an Academy of American Poets Poetry Prize and was named by American PEN as one of three emerging writers in 1987. She has also received a Simon & Schuster Fellowship and the Tony Godwin Fellowship for Editors. She worked in the editorial departments at Simon & Schuster, Ballantine, and Houghton Mifflin, and finally as executive editor at Doubleday before becoming an agent with the Gernert Company in New York City.